Historical Women on Television

ALSO BY KAREN A. ROMANKO
AND FROM MCFARLAND

*Women of Science Fiction and Fantasy Television:
An Encyclopedia of 400 Characters and 200 Shows,
1950–2016* (2019)

*Television's Female Spies and Crimefighters:
600 Characters and Shows,
1950s to the Present* (2016)

Historical Women on Television

Portrayals of 120 Notable Figures in Scripted Programs

KAREN A. ROMANKO

McFarland & Company, Inc., Publishers
Jefferson, North Carolina

Library of Congress Cataloging-in-Publication Data

Names: Romanko, Karen A., 1953– author
Title: Historical women on television : portrayals of 120 notable figures in scripted programs / Karen A. Romanko.
Description: Jefferson, North Carolina : McFarland & Company, Inc., Publishers, 2025. | Includes index.
Identifiers: LCCN 2025028403 | ISBN 9781476681443 paperback ∞ ISBN 9781476655970 ebook
Subjects: LCSH: Women on television | History on television | BISAC: PERFORMING ARTS / Television / History & Criticism | HISTORY / Women | LCGFT: Television criticism and reviews
Classification: LCC PN1992.8.W65 R65 2025 | DDC 791.45/6522—dc23/eng/20250626
LC record available at https://lccn.loc.gov/2025028403

ISBN (print) 978-1-4766-8144-3
ISBN (ebook) 978-1-4766-5597-0

© 2025 Karen A. Romanko. All rights reserved

No part of this book may be reproduced or transmitted in any form or by any means, electronic or mechanical, including photocopying or recording, or by any information storage and retrieval system, without permission in writing from the publisher.

Front cover images: *left to right* Amelia Mary Earhart, July 24, 1897–ca. July 2, 1937 (National Portrait Gallery, Smithsonian Institution; gift of George R. Rinhart, in memory of Joan Rinhart); 1976 press photo with the caption "look alikes" for Susan Clark, who depicts Earhart in *Amelia Earhart* (NBC). TV © Gino Santa Maria/Shutterstock.

Printed in the United States of America

McFarland & Company, Inc., Publishers
  Box 611, Jefferson, North Carolina 28640
    www.mcfarlandpub.com

For the TV series *Timeless*,
which helped to inspire this book
For the women who came before me,
those I knew and those I didn't
And for Bob. Always for Bob.

Table of Contents

Preface:
What's in This Book
1

Introduction:
Meeting Historical Women
on Television
5

**Historical Women
on Scripted Television,
A to Z**
13

Appendix A:
Historical Women
Hall of Fame—TV Programs
189

Appendix B:
Historical Women
Hall of Fame—Actresses
199

A Note on Sources
207

Index
211

vii

Preface: What's in This Book

Queen Victoria in *Bewitched*. Harriet Tubman in *Timeless*. Amelia Earhart in *Star Trek: Voyager*. Historical women appear regularly in televised period dramas and biopics, but sometimes they also turn up in the darndest places, transported to worlds future or past via space operas, sitcoms, and time-travel series.

This book covers 120 historical women on scripted television, emphasizing American figures, but also including women from other areas of the world and eras before the founding of the United States. Coverage is selective, balancing notable females of history with women who are not household names. Figures in the history of religion are not covered, but women who have secular historical significance in addition to religious, such as Joan of Arc, are included. Figures more mythological than historical are also excluded, as are living persons. Deceased figures of the last 100 years, such as Diana, Princess of Wales, and Anne Frank, may be excluded at the author's discretion. The 120 women who are included are a cross section of notable females represented on scripted television and serve as an introduction to a vast topic. They were chosen by the author over a five-year period of research and writing.

Historical Women on Television discusses one or more televised presentations for each figure selected. The programming comprises weekly series, TV movies, miniseries, specials, and streaming originals, all with a cut-off date of June 2019. Coverage is again selective, emphasizing live-action programs produced in the United States, but other English-language programs well promoted in the U.S., such as British series on PBS, are included. Presentations where historical figures make brief appearances are sometimes excluded to give fuller coverage to more significant programs in the entry.

Entries are listed alphabetically by the historical woman's name, last

1

name first, followed by the years of her birth and death, when known. Her occupation or claim to fame appears on the next line, and under that is a list of the actresses who have portrayed her, in the order they are mentioned within the entry. For the sake of consistency, this book uses the word "actress" to refer to female actors, à la the Emmy Award for Lead "Actress," the term still employed by the Academy of Television Arts and Sciences.

The text of the entry itself follows the list of actresses, featuring biographical details of the real woman's life and analysis of her fictional portrayals on television. Among those analyses, the occasional spoiler creeps in, so readers using the book as a viewer's guide should consider this a universal spoiler alert.

The beginning of a sample entry looks like this:

Zaharias, Babe Didrikson (1911–1956)

Athlete, Olympian
Portrayed by: Susan Clark, Emily Deschanel

One of the greatest athletes, male or female, of the 20th century, Babe Didrikson Zaharias won two gold medals in track and field at the 1932 Summer Olympics....

Compound names are handled as in the sample entry above, filed by the last surname. A woman is generally listed under her most well-known name, whether that is her birth name, her married name, or an alias. If she is known by more than one name, that is handled with a cross-reference, as in:

Didrikson, Babe

See: **Zaharias, Babe Didrikson (1911–1956)**

Historical women who were not chosen to receive their own entry, but who have televised depictions mentioned within another woman's entry, are listed with a cross-reference, which includes their dates of birth and death, such as:

Sullivan, Anne (1866–1936)

See (mentioned in): **Keller, Helen (1880–1968)**

Preface: What's in This Book

Historical Women on Television shines a light on the representation of women in history, using the special lens of their representation on the small screen. The inspiring, fascinating, and sometimes heartbreaking stories of these women come to life in the compendium's entries, which sort fact from televised fiction, but also serve as a starting point for further investigation by TV fans, history buffs, students, teachers, and scholars.

Introduction: Meeting Historical Women on Television

History. Names and dates that must be memorized, or so it seems in school. Where is the joy? Where is the life? What is the point?

The joy and the life and the point are lurking just below those memorized names and dates. They begin with the STORY, which emerges with ease, once those names and dates are used as keys to open the doors of the past. Scripted television provides its own keys, with movies and shows where history comes alive, sometimes in obvious ways, as in period dramas, and sometimes by more circuitous means, as with time-travel and fantasy series.

Time-travel shows, with their easy juxtaposition of past and present, their shiny objects that sweep through decades, if not centuries, of people and events, inspire viewers to learn more about the temporal destinations they depict. *Timeless* (2016–2018) conveys the joy of meeting historical figures, people who are like rock stars to the show's intrepid time travelers, especially history professor Lucy Preston (Abigail Spencer). Women such as actress and inventor Hedy Lamarr (Alyssa Sutherland), abolitionist Harriet Tubman (Christine Horn), mathematician Katherine Johnson (Nadine Ellis), physicist Marie Curie (Kim Bubbs), and lesser-known figures such as lawyer and investigator Grace Humiston (Sarah Sokolovic) and Shawnee Chief Nonhelema (Karina Lombard), all find their way into the plots of *Timeless*, reminding us that history is herstory too.

Voyagers! (1982–1983), a time-travel series aimed at the young (and young at heart), offers viewers a direct invitation to research its historical subjects. At the end of each episode, as the credits roll, young series star Meeno Peluce tells the audience how to learn more about the subject(s) of that week's show. "…take a voyage down to your public library.

It's all in books!" Despite the two male leads, Peluce and hunky Jon-Erik Hexum, and the show's boyish ethos, some notable historical women appear, including Cleopatra (Andrea Marcovicci), journalist Nellie Bly (Julia Duffy), Queen Victoria (Lurene Tuttle), and sharpshooter Annie Oakley (Diane Civita), who offers a feminist sentiment about competing with men. "You learn you got to be twice as good as a man just to be considered equal."

Yes, time-travel shows can be little historical encyclopedias, if you like your reference works without stodginess, and sometimes without accuracy. *Timeless*, for example, gives a rousing portrayal of the bravery and sacrifice displayed by early 20th-century suffragists in "Mrs. Sherlock Holmes"(2018), but kills off a major historical figure, Alice Paul (Erica Dasher), to advance its story about investigator Humiston. *Voyagers!* takes historical inaccuracy to laughable, albeit adorable, heights in "Cleo and the Babe" (1982), with an English-speaking Cleopatra (Andrea Marcovicci), who is accidentally transported from ancient Egypt to 1929 New York. (The broadness does not stop there.)

You can imagine, then, the historical liberties that might be taken in a show that mixes time travel with other elements of science fiction and fantasy. *Doctor Who* (1963–1989, 2005–), a series about a Time Lord who bounces across space and time, adds alien wasps and werewolves to the (secret) historical record, leaving author Agatha Christie (Fenella Woolgar) with a temporary case of amnesia in "The Unicorn and the Wasp" (2008) and Queen Victoria (Pauline Collins) with a dead(ly) lycanthrope in "Tooth and Claw" (2006). While fighting evil forces and preserving the timeline, the Doctor encounters other female historical luminaries, including Queen Elizabeth I (Joanna Page and Angela Pleasence) and African American activist Rosa Parks (Vinette Robinson).

Fantasy shows offer a different type of time travel—no machines required. *Bewitched* (1964–1972), a '60s sitcom, hits all the witchy hotspots with stops in 17th-century Salem and Plymouth, but also engages in a kind of reverse time travel by bringing historical figures to the present, such as ubiquitous Queen Victoria (Jane Connell) in "Aunt Clara's Victoria Victory" (1967). *Sabrina, the Teenage Witch* (1996–2003) follows in the magical footsteps of *Bewitched*, also conjuring unwanted historical guests, as in "Aging, Not so Gracefully" (1999), when physicist Marie Curie (Pamela Dillman) pops in from the past.

Other fantasy series feature immortals, those peculiar beings who are unable to die, barring specific injuries, such as stakings or beheadings. Immortals live for centuries, if they are lucky, giving them ample opportunity to cross paths with prominent historical figures along the way. In *Forever Knight* (1992–1996), 800-year-old vampire Nicholas Knight (Geraint

Wyn Davies) works as a homicide detective in Toronto, while flashbacks reveal his tortured past, including encounters with Empress (Czarina) Alexandra of Russia (Caroline Yeager) and French warrior Joan of Arc (Christina Cox).

Highlander: The Series (1992–1998) tells the story of Duncan MacLeod (Adrian Paul), a relative youngster at 400 years old, whose immortal associates inspired Mary Shelley (Tracy Keating) to write *Frankenstein* in "The Modern Prometheus" (1997). In *Sleepy Hollow* (2013–2017), Revolutionary War soldier Ichabod Crane (Tom Mison), while not a traditional immortal (if there is such a thing as a "traditional immortal"), is resurrected in present-day Sleepy Hollow to fight supernatural armies of evil, while historical women such as Abigail Adams (Michelle Trachtenberg), Mary Todd Lincoln (Karen Boles), and Sacagawea (Dayana Rincon) are shown to have waged similar battles in the past, according to Hollow mythology.

Science fiction and fantasy are not the only television genres to fictionalize the lives of notable women from history. Westerns also include historical women, but coverage is limited by the short timespan portrayed, generally 1865–1890, and by the male-centric ethos of the Old West, as mythologized in dime novels, Wild West shows, and magazine articles.

Calamity Jane, a.k.a. Martha Jane Cannary, was one woman of the era who managed to find her way onto TV screens throughout the decades. Beginning with classic westerns such as *Bonanza* (1959–1973), where she was played by Stefanie Powers, and continuing through modern interpretations, such as Robin Weigert's in *Deadwood* (2004–2006), Calamity Jane became the female face of the Old West.

Outlaw Belle Starr, although not the household name that Calamity was, quietly racked up even more appearances in TV westerns than Jane did. Starting in 1954 with an eponymous episode of *Stories of the Century*, starring Marie Windsor as Starr, Belle moved through shows like *Maverick* (1957–1962), *Overland Trail* (1960), *Dr. Quinn, Medicine Woman* (1993–1998), *The Pinkertons* (2014–2015), and more.

Lesser known women of the American frontier, including actress Dora Hand (Margaret Hayes), prospector Nellie Cashman (Randy Stuart), and prostitute Big Nose Kate (Carol Montgomery Stone and Collette Lyons), were featured as multi-episode characters in *The Life and Legend of Wyatt Earp* (1955–1961). These women and many more, including Union spy Pauline Cushman (Paula Raymond), dancer Isadora Duncan (Kathy Garver), and explorer Sacagawea (Angela Dorian), were profiled in the long-running western anthology series *Death Valley Days* (1952–1970), an ambitious, but largely forgotten series which deserves a second look despite its inconsistent viewpoints on women.

Historical women also find their way into adventures not set in the

Old West. In *The Young Indiana Jones Chronicles* (1992–1993), Henry "Indiana" Jones, Jr., travels the world as a boy (Corey Carrier) and a young man (Sean Patrick Flanery), meeting some famous and accomplished women on his journey to adulthood, including Princess Sophie of Hohenberg (Amalie Alstrup), social reformer Annie Besant (Dorothy Tutin), and famous spy Mata Hari (Domiziana Giordano), all brought to vivid life in this visually stunning series. *Jack of All Trades* (2000) aims its sights considerably lower, never allowing an opportunity for adolescent humor to pass, as its resident spies Jack Stiles (Bruce Campbell) and Emilia Rothschild (Angela Dotchin) thwart Napoleon's imperialistic designs on a South Pacific island, which is somehow a magnet for historical figures such as Catherine the Great (Danielle Cormack) and Sacagawea (Vanessa Rare).

Mysteries and police procedurals also set their stories in the past, where historical women pop up as witnesses, suspects, clients, and even detectives. In *Murdoch Mysteries* (2008–), a long-running Canadian series set in 1895 Toronto, Detective William Murdoch (Yannick Bisson) solves crimes, while running into the occasional historical figure, such as Annie Oakley (Sarah Strange), Elizabeth Arden (Kathryn Alexandre), and temperance leader Carrie Nation (Valerie Buhagiar). Another Canadian series, *Frankie Drake Mysteries* (2017–), borrows *Murdoch's* period mystery formula, but updates it to the 1920s, where a lady P.I. named Frankie Drake (Lauren Lee Smith) takes on clients in trouble, such as French designer Coco Chanel (Romane Portail). In *The Pinkertons*, Martha MacIsaac stars as Kate Warne, an operative for the Pinkerton agency and the first female detective in U.S. history, investigating crimes in Kansas City of the late 1860s.

Once in a while, a TV show is so unique it's a genre unto itself. *Drunk History* (2013–2019) is one such series. With a philosophy of preserving the past with alcohol, the series uses drunk narrators to describe important moments of history, while (presumably) sober performers take the parts of the historical figures mentioned to act out the stories. The actors, in costume and placed in believable settings, lip-sync the narrators' words, belches, and screams, sometimes to comic effect, but almost equally to annoying effect, depending upon one's tolerance levels.

As to the latter, the worst expletives are mock-deleted with beeps used frequently enough that you might fear losing your hearing, while people are sometimes so drunk that you wonder whether the show is more apt to encourage or discourage drinking. Every now and again, however, the series transcends its sophomoric premise and reaches moments of true emotion and depth. The stories mostly adhere to the known historical facts, but sometimes legends creep in, and anachronisms abound. Each episode contains three vignettes, running six to seven minutes each.

Introduction: Meeting Historical Women on Television   9

At 72 episodes, with three vignettes per episode, *Drunk History* covers lots of historical ground and features female historical figures prominently, while employing well-known actresses to portray them. Examples include Abigail Adams (Jayma Mays), Clara Barton (Mandy Moore), Agatha Christie (Kirsten Dunst), Ella Fitzgerald (Gabourey Sidibe), Joan of Arc (Vanessa Hudgens), Carrie Nation (Vanessa Bayer), Mary Shelley (Evan Rachel Wood), Babe Didrikson Zaharias (Emily Deschanel), and so many more. *Drunk History* pulls notable women from the pages of history books and brings them to life for a modern TV audience, who must view them through a shot glass.

Meeting of Minds (1977–1981) is another series in a genre by itself, thanks to the fertile imagination of Steve Allen, its creator and host. Originally aired on PBS, *Meeting of Minds* uses a *Tonight Show*–style format in which talk-show veteran Allen "interviews" guests from world history. It's an eclectic affair wherein guests, such as Egyptian Queen Cleopatra (Jayne Meadows), rub elbows with people from centuries far in the future, like political philosopher Thomas Paine (Joseph Sirola), or cultural differences are bridged, as when Chinese statesman Sun Yat-Sen (Keye Luke) pours tea for English poet Elizabeth Barrett Browning (Meadows again). One female historical figure appears in almost every episode, most often portrayed by Allen's wife Jayne Meadows, but sometimes other actresses participate, such as Salome Jens as Byzantine Empress Theodora and Beulah Quo as Chinese Empress Tz'u-hsi (Cixi). Allen wrote many of the scripts for this Emmy-winning series, using the actual words of the historical figures, whenever possible.

Moving beyond sf/fantasies, westerns, mysteries, et al., where the appearances of historical figures are infrequent or treated in unconventional ways, we finally arrive at a form traditionally associated with the stories of real people, the biographical movie, a.k.a. biopic. The list of TV biopics is long and decades-spanning, with stories of queens, athletes, stateswomen, entertainers, and more. These TV films and miniseries often feature the premier actresses of their time, some of whom go on to collect accolades for their outstanding lead performances. Emmy Award–winning portrayals in televised biographical films include Julie Harris as Queen Victoria in *Victoria Regina* (1961), Susan Clark as Olympic athlete Babe Didrikson Zaharias in *Babe* (1975), Ingrid Bergman as Israeli Prime Minister Golda Meir in *A Woman Called Golda* (1982), and Lynn Whitfield as world-renowned entertainer Josephine Baker in *The Josephine Baker Story* (1991).

Sometimes famous people have significance on their own and as part of a set, and when the set's story is compelling, it too receives the biopic treatment. Romantic couplings capture the public's imagination, whether they are first ladies and presidents, such as Eleanor and Franklin Roosevelt (Jane Alexander and Edward Herrmann) in *Eleanor and Franklin* (1976); writers and lovers like Dashiell Hammett and Lillian Hellman (Sam Shepard and Judy Davis) in *Dash and Lilly* (1999); or actors, married, unmarried, and remarried, such as Elizabeth Taylor and Richard Burton (Lindsay Lohan and Grant Bowler) in *Liz & Dick* (2012).

Families of exceptional accomplishment also hold fascination, like the Adams presidential dynasty with its two first ladies, Abigail and Louisa Catherine (Kathryn Walker and Pamela Payton-Wright), in *The Adams Chronicles* (1976) or the writing Brontë sisters, Charlotte (Finn Atkins), Emily (Chloe Pirrie), and Anne (Charlie Murphy) in *To Walk Invisible* (2016). Some women are related by one husband in an informal (and unfortunate) ex-wives club, such as the queens of England in *The Six Wives of Henry VIII* (1970), Catherine of Aragon (Annette Crosbie), Anne Boleyn (Dorothy Tutin), Catherine Howard (Angela Pleasence), et al.

Kinships can also be forged by circumstance, creating sisters in arms, like suffragists Alice Paul (Hilary Swank), Lucy Burns (Frances O'Connor), et al. in *Iron Jawed Angels* (2004), or sisters in bereavement, like Betty Shabazz and Coretta Scott King (Mary J. Blige and Angela Bassett) in *Betty and Coretta* (2013).

History, as written by humans, reflects not just the time it chronicles, but also the era of the person writing it. The same is true for historical presentations on scripted television, where the viewpoints and prejudices not only of writers, but also of producers, directors, actors, and network executives can affect how history is presented. What were the prevailing ideas about women's "place" at the time a program was produced?

Some presentations will reflect those ideas and some will try to counter them. The anthology series *Death Valley Days*, for example, displayed inconsistent views about women during its long run. Within the same year, 1964, the show featured a "put women in their place" episode, "The Wooing of Perilous Pauline," about brave Civil War spy Pauline Cushman (Paula Raymond), and an "accept women as they are" installment, "The Left Hand Is Damned," about nonconformist singer and actress Dora Hand (Phyllis Coates).

While bias is obvious, omission can be subtle, leaving unnoticed important questions, like why some women are not having their stories told. In 2018, the *New York Times* began a series of "Overlooked" obituaries. "Since 1851, obituaries in *The New York Times* have been dominated by white men. Now, we're adding the stories of other remarkable people." Like the obituaries in the *New York Times*, American and European history had been dominated by white men for centuries, often ignoring "the stories of other remarkable people."

Introduction: Meeting Historical Women on Television

As historians over the last few decades have worked to redress the balance, stories of women and people of color have become more prominent, providing new source material for televised presentations about historical figures. Recent series like *Timeless* have featured a diverse array of historical women, such as African American mathematician Katherine Johnson, Shawnee leader Nonhelema, and police investigator Grace Humiston. *Drunk History* cast its net even more widely, including stories about African American/Native American aviator Bessie Coleman (Samira Wiley), disabled spy Virginia Hall, and marriage equality pioneer Edie Windsor (Sugar Lyn Beard).

As television programs about historical women can inspire viewers to learn more about their subjects, so too can this book serve as inspiration for further research about the 120 notable women covered in the following pages. Many of these women fought not very long ago for the opportunities and rights women have today. We should know their names.

Historical Women on Scripted Television, A to Z

Adams, Abigail (1744–1818)

First Lady

Portrayed by: Kathryn Walker, Leora Dana, Laura Linney, Jayma Mays, Michelle Trachtenberg, Daisy Lewis

Abigail Adams was wife and advisor to the second president of the United States, John Adams, and mother of the sixth president, John Quincy Adams. While Abigail has historical importance as our second first lady (though that title wasn't used at the time), she also bequeathed to history a treasure trove of her correspondence, which documented the American Revolutionary War, the birth of the United States, and her husband's presidency.

Abigail Smith first met John Adams at her own home, when she was 15 years old. While John reported that he found the Smith sisters neither "fond, nor frank, nor candid," a different picture of the meeting emerges in *The Adams Chronicles* (Miniseries, 1976). While John (George Grizzard), then a young lawyer, lacks confidence, especially in front of women, Abigail (Kathryn Walker) doesn't hesitate to disagree with the visitor. When John speaks favorably of King George III, Abigail says, "Well, I would choose to wait before I would praise our new king." Her father, the Rev. William Smith (Addison Powell), notes that Abigail is subject to "these fits of opinion."

The Adams Chronicles continues the story of the political dynasty, with greatest emphasis on the long career of John Adams as revolutionary, diplomat, and statesman. Leora Dana takes over for Kathryn Walker as Abigail in "Chapter V: John Adams, Vice President." Dana reminds us that Abigail was not just a public person as the wife of a president, but also a flesh-and-blood woman who experienced disappointments and personal tragedies. When it becomes clear that John Adams has lost to Thomas Jefferson for a second term as president, Abigail tells her husband, "Well, I'm glad it's over, Mr. Adams. I'll be happy leaving this huge white barn. With my age and my infirmities, I'll be happier in Quincy." Abigail also knew the difficulties of being a mother during medically primitive times. When she learns of the death of her adult son Charles, she says, "I had never expected to see one of my children dead. Now I'll be laying my third baby to rest. It seems against nature." Abigail had earlier lost two daughters, Grace Susanna, aged one, in early 1770, and Elizabeth, who was stillborn in 1777.

Kathryn Walker won an Emmy Award for her portrayal of Abigail in *The Adams Chronicles*, which collected three other Emmys in categories from writing to videotape editing. The Adamses made not only American political history, but also TV history, with a second miniseries, *John Adams* (2008), which garnered 13 Emmy Awards, more than any other miniseries, including one for Laura Linney as Abigail Adams. Linney's Abigail shows what it is like for a woman to hold a family together during wartime, with the added burden of having the war right in your own backyard. Abigail must tend the farm and care for her children, while John

First Lady Abigail Adams (Leora Dana) and President John Adams (George Grizzard) in *The Adams Chronicles* **(PBS).**

(Paul Giamatti) is away, first in Philadelphia working with the Second Continental Congress, and later in Europe in search of foreign allies during the Revolutionary War. Abigail is dutiful and stoic as she waits, although she admits, "If I were a man, I would be in the field of action."

Abigail Adams (Jayma Mays) makes a cameo appearance in the *Drunk History* episode "Philadelphia" (2014), which focuses on the nastiness of the 1800 presidential election between John Adams (Joe Lo Truglio) and Thomas Jefferson (Jerry O'Connell). The first lady pops up again briefly in "Pittura Infamante," a 2015 episode of *Sleepy Hollow*, where flashbacks reveal that Abigail (Michelle Trachtenberg) was also an amateur sleuth, who tracked a supernatural murderer. (Anything is possible in the Hollow.) And, finally, Abigail (Daisy Lewis) turns up in *Sons of Liberty* (Miniseries, 2015), where the boys, as you might expect from the title, have all the fun, planning a revolution, when they are not drinking ale.

The 1,200 letters between John Adams and his wife reveal Abigail to be a woman of intelligence, literary knowledge and accomplishment, sound political judgment, and prescience. In March of 1776, as John prepared with his colleagues to write a statement of principles that would become the Declaration of Independence, Abigail had a few notes. "And, by the way, in the new code of laws which I suppose it will be necessary for you to make, I desire you would remember the ladies and be more generous and favorable to them than your ancestors. Do not put such unlimited power into the hands of the husbands."

Yes, "remember the ladies." And, remember Abigail Adams, an extraordinary woman of American history.

Adams, Louisa (1775–1852)

First Lady
Portrayed by: Pamela Payton-Wright

As the wife of John Quincy Adams, the sixth president of the United States, Louisa Adams became first lady at a time when the duties of her position were still evolving. That challenge would be enough for most people, but Louisa's father-in-law was John Adams, the second president of the United States, and having such a distinguished "in-law" made her role as president's wife even more complicated.

Louisa's health didn't make her public life any easier. By the time she arrived in the White House, she had suffered nine miscarriages, although she had eventually given birth to four children, and frequently experienced poor health throughout her entire life. While not as well-known as her mother-in-law, Abigail, or other first ladies, Louisa's sheer fortitude in dealing with all her trials, including indifference from a famously cold and dour husband, is worthy of modern attention.

Louisa once wrote to her son that the Adams men were "peculiarly harsh and severe in their relations with women." This aspect of her life is (politely) emphasized in *The Adams Chronicles* (Miniseries, 1976), with Pamela Payton-Wright as Louisa and William Daniels as John Quincy Adams. In Chapter 9, "John Quincy Adams, President," Louisa chides her husband for his self-absorption and inability to enjoy himself, as musicians outside celebrate his new presidency. When the topic of their son George comes up as Adams is writing to his father, she says, "Mr. Adams, I wish you could give as much specific attention to your own firstborn, as you do to your mother's." Louisa's put-down is rich, and she also lets her husband know that an acknowledgment to the musicians is in order, but Adams doesn't plan to change. He notes that some say he is a "gloomy misanthrope" and others "an unsocial savage," so knowing those defects, he doesn't have the pliability to reform his character.

In the end, the biography of Louisa Adams is less the tale of a famous lady and her many accomplishments and more the story of a woman living at the turn of the 19th century, with its primitive health care and lack of concern for a woman's agency, just played out on a large, public stage.

Alexandra (1872–1918)

Empress of Russia
Portrayed by: Gayle Hunnicutt, Caroline Yeager, Greta Scacchi

A boy with hemophilia. A "mad monk" with the seeming ability to ease the child's suffering. An empress devoted to her son and blinded to the debauchery of her "holy man." A revolution. A family executed. No, this isn't the most contrived melodrama ever—it is the true story of Empress Alexandra of Russia.

Born Princess Alix of Hesse and by Rhine, Alexandra, a granddaughter of Queen Victoria, married Emperor Nicholas II of Russia in 1894. Like her grandmother, Alexandra was a carrier of hemophilia, which she passed on to her son and the heir to the throne, Alexei. Since medical doctors were unable to help the young heir, Alexandra turned for help to a mystic, Grigori Rasputin, who seemed to bring the boy back from the brink of death. Alexandra would not hear a bad word about her "Man of God," although most of his "rituals" involved sex with young women.

The link to Rasputin did little for Alexandra's reputation with the Russian people at a time when autocratic rule was falling out of favor. World War I exacerbated the tension between the Romanov rulers and their people, with food shortages, inflation, and strikes bringing the situation to a full boil. Eventually Nicholas II abdicated his throne, but the fate of the royal family was sealed after the Bolshevik Revolution of November 1917. Eight months later, Alexandra, Nicholas, and all their children were shot to death by Bolshevik security forces in the basement of the house where they were being confined.

The story of Nicholas and Alexandra is told in generous detail in *Fall of Eagles*, a 13-part BBC miniseries originally aired in 1974. *Fall of Eagles* dramatizes the end of the ruling families of Germany, Austria-Hungary and Russia, with coverage of the Romanovs in episodes such as "The Last Tsar," "Dearest Nicky," and "Tell the King the Sky Is Falling." Nicholas (Charles Kay) and Alexandra (Gayle Hunnicutt) are portrayed as a loving couple, but are totally out of their depth as 20th-century rulers who can't leave behind their 19th-century mindsets. When Nicholas goes to the front lines to take personal command of the army in 1915, he leaves Alexandra in charge in Petrograd (St. Petersburg). She complains, "…away from me he is so vulnerable and he listens to everybody," as though a ruler with an open mind is a bad thing. The series shows that the effects of both despotism and World War I led to the demise of the three ruling dynasties, each of which used an eagle in their heraldry, the "fall of eagles."

Forever Knight views the Alexandra/Rasputin story through a dark fantasy lens in "Strings" (1995). Caroline Yeager stars as the empress, whose story is told in flashback as a counterpoint to a contemporary story of mind control and murder, which vampire detective Nicholas Knight (Geraint Wyn Davies) is out to solve. Nick knew the Romanov family in the past, and tried to help them when Alexandra fell under the evil sway of Rasputin (Sam Malkin). Nick recognizes that Rasputin is a fellow vampire, and that the monk is the cause of the young heir's disease. Alexandra hears only Rasputin's words, however, so eventually Nick must kill the monk, but it is already too late to save the royal family. Alexandra had sensed it earlier. "The world is no longer the world I knew. I fear for our survival."

Greta Scacchi won an Emmy Award for her portrayal of Empress Alexandra in *Rasputin: Dark Servant of Destiny*, a 1996 HBO TV movie. Unlike *Fall of Eagles*, which focused on larger currents of history, *Rasputin: Dark Servant of Destiny* is a smaller story, delving into the personal relationships amongst Alexandra, Nicholas (Ian McKellen), Rasputin (Alan Rickman) and young Alexei (Freddie Finley). Against a backdrop of amazing opulence, *Rasputin* makes us see how the mystic was able to tame Alexei's devastating illness, whether through hypnosis or plain old dumb luck, drawing the gratitude and loyalty of Alexandra. When she says to Rasputin "the future of Russia is in your hands," we know she is right, but not in the way that she thinks. While this personal story may be light on historical context, it brings the principals to life and makes them relatable, allowing us to understand at last how this strange monk came to be the downfall of a family and an empire.

Anthony, Susan B. (1820–1906)
Suffragist
Portrayed by: Jayne Meadows

A giant in the American women's suffrage movement, Susan B. Anthony initially devoted herself to the social reform issues of temperance and the abolition of slavery, but after the Civil War, women's right to vote became her consuming passion. Working with Elizabeth Cady Stanton, she founded a weekly newspaper called *The Revolution* in 1868, which focused primarily on women's rights. Anthony soon began giving lectures on women's suffrage, eventually averaging 75 to 100 speeches per year. In 1872, she was arrested for voting in a United States presidential election, and was convicted by Justice Ward Hunt, who had written his guilty verdict before the trial had even begun.

When asked if she had anything to say, Ms. Anthony had a few choice words to offer Hunt, who had just been confirmed as an associate justice of the United States Supreme Court. "...you have trampled under foot every vital principle of our government. My natural rights, my civil rights, my political rights, my judicial rights, are all alike ignored." Even with those basic rights ignored, Susan B. Anthony used her voice to stand up to a Supreme Court Justice. Anthony was fined $100, which she never paid.

Jayne Meadows portrays Anthony in "Susan B. Anthony, Socrates, Sir Francis Bacon, Emiliano Zapata" (parts one and two), a 1978 episode of *Meeting of Minds*. Meadows's Anthony is also no shrinking violet, taking on the antiquated beliefs of all the men present, including host Steve Allen, in this "talk show" for historical figures. While noting that married women of her time could not own property, sign a contract, or make a legal claim to their children, she says, "Male ignorance was part of the problem, Mr. Allen." When Francis Bacon (James Booth) says that Susan sounds very angry, and asks if she were ever married, she replies, "Oh, not that old chestnut.... If you are implying that I was a man hater, and how many times we heard that assertion, and from women as well as men, no sir, no sir, no.... I had more than one proposal of marriage, strange as it may seem. But I had decided to devote my life to social reform and I made the choice not to marry."

When Emiliano Zapata tells her that women are not experts in the field of violence, she says, "Women have had generations of experience with violence, and almost always as its victims. In almost every case, our abusers and murderers have been men. How many hundreds of thousands of us were killed in Europe during the 300-year slaughter of women supposed to be witches. No one will ever know." The role of Susan B. Anthony is a perfect fit for Ms. Meadows in *Meeting of Minds*.

Susan B. Anthony did not live to see passage of the 19th amendment (1920), which gave women the right to vote, but the amendment was commonly known as the Susan B. Anthony Amendment, honoring her work for women's suffrage. Still, she saw many improvements for women during her own lifetime, and some due to her own efforts. In an 1889 address, she said, "Now, after 40 years of agitation, the idea is beginning to prevail that women were created for themselves, for their own happiness, and for the welfare of the world."

Arden, Elizabeth (ca. 1884–1966)

Businesswoman
Portrayed by: Kathryn Alexandre

In "Operation: Murder," a 2018 episode of *Murdoch Mysteries*, we meet a young woman named Florence Nightingale Graham (Kathryn Alexandre), a Toronto nursing student who becomes a witness in a hospital homicide. Although Graham tells Constable George Crabtree (Jonny Harris) that she is destined to become a nurse like her namesake, Florence Nightingale, destiny has other plans for her. Graham's interest in burn treatments at the hospital has led her to experiment with "concoctions" that might also serve as beauty creams. "Every woman has the right to feel beautiful," she tells Crabtree.

As the constable helps her sell the creams, Graham decides she doesn't want her name associated with them, as "Florence Nightingale" would evoke images of hospitals and illness. Crabtree suggests the name, "Elizabeth," while Graham contributes the name "Arden" for their mutual favorite poem, "Enoch Arden" by Alfred Tennyson. At that moment "Elizabeth Arden" is born, and Graham leaves behind her disappointed suitor for a position as a bookkeeper at a cosmetics company in New York.

The historical record doesn't report a Toronto cop in the story of Elizabeth Arden, but some of the preceding is true, especially Graham's nursing school stay and experimentation with burn creams and salves. Once in New York, Graham became an assistant to a beauty specialist, Eleanor Adair, and opened a beauty salon on Fifth Avenue in 1910 with a partner, Elizabeth Hubbard. When that partnership collapsed in 1914, Graham opened a beauty salon of her own, using the name "Elizabeth Arden."

In addition to her technical acumen, Arden was a marketing whiz, convincing the public that makeup was respectable and not merely coloring for painted ladies, an effort aided by the growing use of makeup in the movie industry. With her early success, the company she founded grew, eventually manufacturing more than 300 cosmetic products and establishing 100 beauty salons around the world.

The French government awarded Arden the Légion d'Honneur (Legion of Honor), its highest order of merit, in 1962.

Aspinwall, Nan (1880–1964)

Horsewoman, Sharpshooter
Portrayed by: Penny Edwards

Born in New York City, Nan Aspinwall spent most of her early life in Nebraska, but in her mid-20s, she became the "Montana Girl," an expert horsewoman, sharpshooter, and roper. She performed with her husband Frank Gable for the combined Buffalo Bill's Wild West and Pawnee Bill's Great Far East show. Nan's career as a "Wild West" star would eventually lead her to the adventure of a lifetime.

Death Valley Days chronicles her astounding feat in "Two Gun Nan" (1958), starring Penny Edwards as the title character. While performing with her husband Frank Gable (Buzz Henry) in Buffalo Bill's Wild West show, Nan hatches a plan to ride on horseback from coast to coast ALONE. Frank wants to accompany her, but Nan knows what an accomplishment this would be to do on her own, especially as a female. Ever the horsewoman, she says to her husband, "Stop yanking, darling, and give me my head." While some historical accounts say that Nan undertook the dangerous journey on a bet from Buffalo Bill, the Bill depicted here (William O'Neal) asks to be left out of the affair entirely.

Aspinwall chooses her own horse for the trip, a mare named Lady Ellen. Nan soon departs from San Francisco with a letter from Mayor McCarthy (Harry Woods) addressed to the mayor of New York City. The journey is indeed arduous, and Nan collapses at one point, but is helped by some cowboys on the trail. In one town, all doors are closed to her, with no one willing to provide food or lodging. Nan gets angry, and shoots at doors and windows, as she rides out of town. This scene reflects the real-life experience of Nan Aspinwall, who said, "Talk about Western chivalry! There's no such thing. Why, in one place I felt so bad that I rode through the town shooting off my revolver just for the deviltry." After 180 days, Nan arrives in New York City, presenting her letter to the mayor's representative. *The New York Times* describes her arrival in an article published on July 9, 1911: "A travel-stained woman attired in a red shirt and a divided skirt and seated on a bay horse drew a crowd to City Hall Park yesterday afternoon."

While showing overall adherence to the historical record up to that point, *Death Valley Days* throws in a gratuitous scene where Nan is robbed at gunpoint in her hotel room, and later tells her husband on the phone that she needs his protection in the city. This from a woman who traveled 4,500 miles across the country with the company only of a horse. But then the series makes up for its sexism by presenting the real Nan Aspinwall, still beautiful at 78 years old, in a coda to the story. When asked by the show's host, The Old Ranger (Stanley Andrews), why she lives in obscurity, she tells him it is by choice. "In our day, the crowds chased Frank and me just as they do poor Elvis Presley nowadays."

Nan Aspinwall's desire to live in peace may have assisted in pushing her epic tale into the shadows, but it emerges into the bright light here.

Austen, Jane (1775–1817)

Author
Portrayed by: Olivia Williams

Viewers are familiar with Jane Austen through the adaptations of her novels, including *Pride and Prejudice* (1995), a six-part BBC series that made Colin Firth famous, *Emma*, a 1996 theatrical film starring Gwyneth Paltrow, and many more. Austen herself wasn't famous in her lifetime, writing her novels anonymously, like many female authors of the time, who couldn't appear ambitious lest they tarnish their femininity. The role of women in middle-class English life at the end of the 18th century is a major theme in her novels, which explore the question of marrying for love or money at a time when women were dependent on men for economic security.

Austen confronted the "love or money" question in her own life, as dramatized in *Miss Austen Regrets*, a 2007 TV movie starring Olivia Williams as the novelist. The story opens in 1802, when Jane hastily accepts a marriage proposal from wealthy Harris Bigg (Samuel Roukin), but promptly changes her mind, telling herself, "Dear God let me never regret this day." The scene flashes forward 12 years, where Jane must counsel her niece Fanny (Imogen Poots) on a romantic prospect, one Mr. John Plumptre (Tom Hiddleston). Jane tells Fanny, "If we could only see into the future, and know in advance if our choices will turn out to be wise." Jane gives conflicting advice to Fanny, at one point saying, "Do anything but marry without affection," but later telling her, "Single women have a dreadful propensity for being poor."

At the same time, according to Jane's brother, Edward Austen Knight (Pip Torrens), Jane shouldn't be thinking about money at all, family financial troubles notwithstanding. When she wonders whether she should find a new publisher and ask for more money, Edward says, "Dear lord, I do wish you wouldn't think of it as writing for money." Against a backdrop of lush, green landscapes, Jane frolics and flirts, but never escapes her conundrum. When Jane's sister Cassandra (Greta Scacchi) chides her for tormenting a painfully shy minister with her flirting, she says that Jane is like a cat with a mouse, an apt comparison. Williams's Austen is smart, playful, a bit of a wise guy, and a total breath of fresh air, simultaneously natural in the 18th century and timeless. She almost single-handedly eradicates the stereotype of the stuffy, 18th-century writer.

Baker, Josephine (1906–1975)
Singer, Dancer, Spy
Portrayed by: Tiffany Daniels, Lynn Whitfield

In "The Lost Generation," a 2017 episode of *Timeless*, historian Lucy Preston (Abigail Spencer) tries to give one of her fellow time travelers a crash course on Josephine Baker (Tiffany Daniels). As they arrive at Baker's show in Roaring 20s Paris, Lucy says, "Think Beyoncé, 1927." It's a reasonable frame of reference that will bring 21st century, non-historical types up to speed, and Lucy goes on to describe Baker as the most famous performer in the country. But there's really no one comparable to Josephine Baker, who went on to perform the exquisite balancing act of being a famous person with a capital "F," while at the same time fading into the background as that most inconspicuous of persons, a spy.

Josephine Baker, born Freda Josephine McDonald in St. Louis, Missouri, grew up in poverty, dropping out of school and marrying at the age of 13. She made money as a street performer, and after divorcing, remarrying, and divorcing again, found success as a dancer in the chorus lines of all-black Broadway productions, such as *Shuffle Along*. In 1925, she moved to Paris, eventually achieving star billing at the Folies-Bergère. While there, she created a stir with her "Danse Sauvage" and especially her costume, which consisted only of a beaded necklace and a G-string ornamented with artificial bananas. Ernest Hemingway called her, "the most sensational woman anybody ever saw. Or ever will."

Lynn Whitfield won an Emmy award for her portrayal of the Jazz Age superstar in *The Josephine Baker Story* (TV movie, 1991). It's hard to rise above a glorified outline when dramatizing a complex life in 130 minutes, so some important stories are rushed here. Baker's work for the French Resistance receives a quick montage and a 15-second scene, where the Nazis invade her château without explanation. In real life, Josephine Baker was a hero, carrying information about German military strategies and troop movements on her sheet music, written in invisible ink. Yes, invisible ink. Because of her celebrity, Baker was able to socialize with German, Italian, and Japanese officials at embassies and nightclubs, where she kept her ears open for information. She jotted down notes in the bathroom and pinned them to her underwear, notes containing secrets that would make their way to top officials in England.

For her bravery and service to her adopted country of France, Josephine Baker received many honors, the highest of which came on November 30, 2021, when she entered the Panthéon in Paris, France's resting place for its national heroes. She became the first black woman to receive the honor, and, in so doing, spoke for inclusion in death, as she always had in life.

Ball, Lucille (1911–1989)
Actress, TV Producer, Entrepreneur
Portrayed by: Gypsi DeYoung, Suzanne LaRusch, Frances Fisher, Madeline Zima, Rachel York

Once known as "Queen of the B's" for her many roles in B movies, Lucille Ball moved up to "A" productions in a new medium, television, with her show *I Love Lucy* (1951–1957). Ball's fearlessness and hard work created her own brand of comedy magic, showcasing her unique ability to keep her character, Lucy Ricardo, real amidst her outrageous and hilarious weekly stunts. But Lucy wasn't just a superstar. She was also an innovator. She insisted that her real-life husband, Desi Arnaz, be cast as her TV spouse over the network's objections that America would not accept a heavily-accented Cuban as her partner.

When real-life Lucy became pregnant, so did Lucy Ricardo, and her/their on-screen pregnancy was the first time a visibly pregnant women had been seen on television. Knowing that Lucy worked best in front of an audience, Desi Arnaz brought fans into the studio to watch filming of the episodes, setting the template for future situation comedies by using three cameras, and distinct, connected sets. Filming on 35mm film rather than kinescopes helped to preserve the footage, allowing *I Love Lucy* to survive in syndication to this day.

Fictional Lucy had a couple of bit parts in programs with widely disparate themes. In *The Scarlett O'Hara War*, a 1980 TV movie about the search for an actress to play the lead in *Gone with the Wind* (1939), Gypsi DeYoung portrays Ball, who was one of many actresses, including Tallulah Bankhead (Carrie Nye), Carole Lombard (Sharon Gless), and Joan Crawford (Barrie Youngfellow) to try out for the role of Scarlett. Lucy (Suzanne LaRusch) also has a cameo in "Stalker," a 1997 episode of *Timecop*, where Marilyn Monroe (Susan Griffiths) asks Lucy about having kids, while a time traveling cop pursues a stalker on a 1956 studio lot.

Lucy becomes the title character in two television movies, both of which cover similar territory, her life until her divorce from Desi in 1960. In *Lucy & Desi: Before the Laughter* (1991), Frances Fisher portrays Ball in a story which follows Lucy's life from meeting Desi in 1940 to the end of their marriage. Their first encounter in a studio commissary doesn't go well. Lucy overhears some conversation from Desi (Maurice Benard) in his less than perfect English. "Lucille Ball is Queen of B movies. I don't do picture with her. Ruin my career." She sets out to change his mind, alternating between flirting and put-downs, a combination which piques his romantic interest, mission accomplished.

They end up working together on the film *Too Many Girls* (1940), which Lucy says should be the title of a film about Desi's life, since he is already known for his many relationships with women. Lucy does fall prey to his charm, but the problem of Desi and his "too many girls" will plague her throughout their marriage. In fact, it's one of the reasons that Lucy wants Desi with her on *I Love Lucy*. An on-set admirer of Desi receives the warning, "Just remember, Lucy's doing this show to keep him anchored in home port." Frances Fisher looks enough like Lucy that you sometimes think she is Lucy, but Benard's Desi falls too easily into caricature and misses the force of nature that was Desi.

Lucy (2003) begins its story 15 years earlier, in 1925, when teenaged Lucy (Madeline Zima) has early acting success, but must deal with the trauma of family bankruptcy after a negligence lawsuit. She says, "Is it always gonna be like this? Just when things are going good, something comes along and ruins everything." Suddenly the scene shifts to 1931 New York City, and it's goodbye, Madeline, hello, Rachel York, as older Lucy. After a failed dance audition, Lucy lands work as a Carnegie Model, and later becomes the Chesterfield Girl in cigarette ads.

Hollywood calls, and Lucy has some small success, allowing her to move her mother and family to California, where she has a Scarlett O'Hara "I'll never be hungry again" moment. Lucy says, "This family is gonna walk in the front door, fat and sassy, and sit at table number one. I lay claim to this town." From there, she moves toward the inevitable courtship and marriage to Desi Arnaz (Danny Pino). Claim the town she does, with her hit show *I Love Lucy*, although Hollywood Boulevard is paved with more than a few of Lucy's broken dreams. The final scenes are sad, where Lucy and Desi tell the kids about the divorce and later have a bittersweet last kiss in front of a studio audience. The epilogue tells us that Lucy and Desi built the first television empire with their Desilu Studios, and remained friends for the rest of their lives. York looks less like Lucy than Fisher did, but has more of her voice and physicality. She and Pino have an easy chemistry, which makes them convincing as the famous couple.

Of course, Lucille Ball led an accomplished life after her marriage to

Desi Arnaz. She had two successful sitcoms, *The Lucy Show* (1962–1968) and *Here's Lucy* (1968–1974), the latter co-starring her real-life children, Lucie and Desi Jr. She bought out her ex-husband's share of Desilu Productions, becoming the company's president and the first woman to head a major studio in Hollywood. She won two Emmy Awards for her portrayal of Lucille Carmichael in *The Lucy Show*, equaling the two Emmys she had received for *I Love Lucy*. The list goes on.

In 1989, Lucille Ball was posthumously awarded the Presidential Medal of Freedom by George H.W. Bush. Her citation begins, "A gifted comedienne known and loved by generations of audiences around the world, Lucille Ball left a lasting impression on American entertainment."

Bankhead, Tallulah (1902–1968)

See (mentioned in): **Lombard, Carole (1908–1942)**

Barceló, Maria Gertrudis (ca. 1800–1852)

Businesswoman
Portrayed by: Katy Jurado

Maria Gertrudis Barceló, often called "La Tules," was a casino owner and businesswoman who built a small fortune in the American Southwest. Married at the age of 23, Barceló was a woman ahead of her time, retaining her maiden name, property, and the right to sign contracts, all practices contrary to the customs of her era. In 1835, she opened an opulent hotel and casino in Santa Fe, where she was not only owner/operator, but also a dealer of monte, renowned for her skill and winnings at the table. International events would intrude on Barceló's small corner of the world in the next decade, after the United States declared war on Mexico, and an American civilian government established itself in Santa Fe in 1846.

Death Valley Days picks up the story from there in "La Tules" (1962), mostly following the historical record, murky though it may be. The biggest deviation comes in giving Barceló (Katy Jurado) a grown son named Miguel (John Mauldin), while the real Miguel had died in infancy. Miguel joins a conspiracy to oust the Americans from Santa Fe, while La Tules supports the new government, saying that any good gambler knows when the cards are against him. The U.S. Army, in the person of Colonel Price (Robert McQueeney), asks Barceló for a loan at interest, and she agrees, as long as he will escort her to an upcoming ball. Entrée to the upper echelons of Santa Fe society is one thing she has been denied as a Mexican.

Historical Barceló exposed a conspiracy against the Americans, according to some accounts, and Jurado's La Tules follows suit, informing

Four faces of Katy Jurado as Maria Gertrudis Barceló in "La Tules" (*Death Valley Days*).

the Army of the cabal's insurrection plans. Somehow everyone managed to live happily ever after, including fictional, conspiratorial Miguel, according to series host and narrator "The Old Ranger" (Stanley Andrews). The episode frames all of Barceló's actions in terms of her gambling prowess, with her making wagers on outcomes small and momentous, and always winning.

American descriptions of La Tules in travel writings and newspaper serials of the time were inconsistent, but tended to be unflattering due to their xenophobia and sexism. Sometimes she was referred to as the "Queen of Sin," who was either a raven-haired beauty or a toothless crone. Clearly Americans of that time and place had trouble dealing with a strong woman from a culture different from theirs, who played life by her own rules and usually won.

Barton, Clara (1821–1912)

Nurse, Humanitarian
Portrayed by: Mandy Moore, Patricia Donahue

Clarissa Harlowe Barton, more commonly known as Clara Barton, was a pioneering American nurse, who, with no formal training, provided medical services to soldiers during the American Civil War. She solicited supplies, distributed them, even passing through battle lines, applied field dressings, served food to the wounded, and even searched for missing soldiers.

Drunk History shines a spotlight on Barton's dramatic battlefield experiences in a sanguinary installment of the series, "Heroines" (2018). Mandy Moore portrays Barton as a valiant potty mouth who swoops in with wagon loads of medical supplies just as Dr. James Dunn (Alexander Skarsgard), a Union Army surgeon, is despairing due to a lack of antiseptic and bandages at the battle of Antietam. Barton finds herself smack in the middle of the action, when a bullet pierces her sleeve, killing the soldier she is assisting. Dunn deems her "the angel of the battlefield," a name that fictional Barton resists with a bit of temper. She is more polite, however, when President Abraham Lincoln asks her to head the Office of Missing Soldiers, replying "I super will."

In need of a rest after her numerous labors, Barton traveled to Europe in 1869, but armed conflict caught up with her in the form of the Franco-Prussian War. Barton answered the call to service again, distributing relief supplies to war victims, preparing military hospitals, and furthering the goals of the International Red Cross. The TV series *Voyagers!* finds Barton during this period in "The Travels of Marco ... and Friends" (1982). Time travelers Jeffrey Jones (Meeno Peluce) and Phineas Bogg (Jon-Erik Hexum) drop (literally) onto a French battlefield in 1870, where Barton (Patricia Donahue) is tending to a wounded soldier. Barton has been moving injured men from a burning hospital wagon to a trench until the shelling stops. When Clara is overcome with smoke during the operation, young Jeffrey, who comes from the 20th century, uses mouth-to-mouth resuscitation to revive her. History is set back on course, so Clara can go on to establish the American Red Cross, something the real Clara Barton did in 1881, becoming the organization's first president.

In the annals of history, generals are towering figures, heroes who win wars and save countries. But Dr. James Dunn, Barton's Antietam colleague, had a different perspective after working with Clara: "In my feeble estimation, General McClellan, with all his laurels, sinks into insignificance beside the true heroine of the age, the angel of the battlefield."

Besant, Annie (1847–1933)

Social Reformer, Author
Portrayed by: Dorothy Tutin

Annie Besant had a remarkable and restless mind, too restless, it turned out, for her to stay married to an Anglican vicar for long. After separating from Frank Besant, Annie began writing a column for the newspaper of the National Secular Society and gave lectures across England on reform topics of the day, including women's rights, birth control, and workers' rights. Besant's intellectual journey led her through socialism to theosophy, a philosophy which combined teachings of Eastern and Western religions, including mystic traditions. She joined the Theosophical Society, ultimately becoming its president in 1907, and much of her focus shifted to India, where she established the Central Hindu College based on theosophical principles.

The Young Indiana Jones Chronicles picks up Annie's story from there in "Benares, January 1910" (1993). Dorothy Tutin portrays Besant, who hosts a reception at the Theosophical Society to introduce a 14-year-old boy named Jiddu Krishnamurti (Hemanth Rao), thought to be the new "World Teacher," someone who will bring enlightenment to the world. This didactic episode uses the relationship between young Indiana Jones (Corey Carrier) and Krishnamurti as a vehicle to explain some of the tenets of theosophy, as the boys tour the churches and temples of Benares. Equally important are the meetings between Besant and Helen Seymour (Margaret Tyzack), Indy's tutor, which contrast their viewpoints on religion, faith, and morality, while each woman comes to view the other as "highly intelligent, dignified, and independent."

In the real world, Annie Besant continued her relationship with Krishnamurti, becoming his legal guardian and surrogate mother. The two remained close, even after Krishnamurti had renounced theosophy and his World Teacher role.

Annie Besant left behind a prodigious record of achievement. She was the author of over 300 books and pamphlets, the founder of Banaras Hindu University, the president of the Indian National Congress, and a champion of human freedom.

Big Nose Kate (ca. 1850–1940)

Frontier Prostitute

Portrayed by: Grace Lee Whitney, Carol Stone, Collette Lyons, Sheena Marshe, Chantel Riley

Big Nose Kate continues to confound library catalogers with the many names she wore throughout her life. Was she Kate Fisher, convent school student? Or Katie Elder, Dodge City prostitute? Was she Kate Holliday, troublemaking wife of Tombstone's Doc Holliday? Or Mary Katherine Horony Cummings, wife of George Cummings, an Irish blacksmith? Surprisingly enough, it's probably all of the above.

Orphaned at the age of 14, Mary Katherine Horony later fled foster care and began her journey into Western lore. Like many women without means of her era, she accepted work as a prostitute, eventually arriving at a Fort Griffin, Texas, saloon during the fall of 1877, where she met Doc Holliday. *Death Valley Days* imagines what might have happened during the couple's Fort Griffin days in "The Quiet and the Fury" (1964). Doc (Skip Homeier) has been in town for about a week, and Kate (Grace Lee Whitney), here with the last name Fisher, has already fallen in love with him. Townspeople are out to lynch Doc after he shoots a man in self-defense during a poker game, and Kate is determined to save this man who isn't about to run away. She takes matters into her own hands and disguises herself as a man, entering the saloon to learn the mob's plans. As the vigilantes depart to find Doc, Kate sets a fire to distract them. She then helps to rescue Doc from a sheriff's deputy, and finally convinces her love to leave town. Not much real history here, but a definite breath of fresh air for 60s TV, as the independent actions of a woman are allowed to save the day, and in a western, no less.

Death Valley Days shows the couple leaving for Dodge City, Kansas, as the story ends. The real Kate and Doc did travel to Dodge City, where they registered at a boarding house as Dr. and Mrs. John H. Holliday. Perhaps they had married at some point, although no documentary evidence of their union exists. *The Life and Legend of Wyatt Earp* (1955–1961) picks up the story from there, but in sanitized tellings. Kate, portrayed at various times by Carol Stone (10 episodes) and Collette Lyons (4 episodes), is much concerned with Doc's health during the series, as his habits of drinking and smoking exacerbate his consumption (tuberculosis). While in real life, the two sometimes fought violently, here they are portrayed as a loving couple, although each spouse can be intolerant of the other's foibles.

In "The Reformation of Doc Holliday" (1958), Kate (Lyons) threatens to leave Doc (Myron Healey), because he isn't following doctor's orders. Wyatt Earp (Hugh O'Brian) convinces Doc to reform so Kate will stay, but Doc turns out to be more of a handful sober than drunk. Realizing that Doc is miserable and causing different kinds of trouble for her, Earp, and the citizens of Dodge City, Kate hands him a drink. She says, "I was wrong. You're hard to take with it or without it." She then offers him a cigar too. We've learned a lot about addiction and codependency since this episode was made.

Historical Kate, Doc, and Earp eventually made their way to Tombstone in the Arizona Territory for an appointment with destiny known as the Gunfight at the O.K. Corral. *Doctor Who* finds the trio there in a four-part serial called "The Gunfighters" (1966). The First Doctor (William Hartnell), a Time Lord, is in need of dental care, and seeks the services of Doc Holliday (Anthony Jacobs) in Tombstone, embroiling his time-traveling companions in the events surrounding the most famous shootout in the Old West. Kate Fisher (Sheena Marshe) is on hand as Doc's lady, who is, as always, concerned about Doc's welfare. This Kate is less the proper lady and more the saloon girl than in the earlier depictions, with a low-cut dress, an exaggerated sashay, and regional twang. "I'm plumb wore out worrying about you, Doc." Everything about this serial is broad, not helped by bad American accents from British actors.

Kate (Chantel Riley) has miraculously survived to the present day, albeit as a vampire, in the supernatural western *Wynonna Earp* (2016–). Although she wasn't immortal, as in *Wynonna Earp*, the real Kate Holliday, Big Nose Kate, Mary Katherine Cummings, whatever you want to call her, lived until the age of 90 or so, startling longevity for a woman trying to eke out an existence in the aptly named Wild West. As she had been throughout her life, Kate, just Kate, was the ultimate survivor.

Bisland, Elizabeth (1861–1929)
    See (mentioned in): **Bly, Nellie (1864–1922)**

Black, Shirley Temple
    See: **Temple, Shirley (1928–2014)**

Bly, Nellie (1864–1922)
Journalist
Portrayed by: Laura Dern, Ellie Kemper, Linda Purl, Christina Ricci, Julia Duffy

Born Elizabeth Cochran, Nellie Bly took her pen name from a Stephen Foster song and turned it into a synonym for crack female reporting. At a time when female reporters were consigned to "women's pages," writing about fashion or society, Bly made her mark with an exposé about conditions at a women's asylum on Blackwell's Island in New York. The pioneer investigative journalist had gone undercover as a patient at the asylum for Joseph Pulitzer's *New York World*, later collecting her reports into a book, *Ten Days in a Madhouse* (1887).

Nellie Bly achieved even greater fame for her trip around the world, challenging the record of Jules Verne's fictional character Phileas Fogg from *Around the World in Eighty Days* (1872). Bly departed New York on November 14, 1889, traveling by steamship, and used trains, horses, and any conveyance necessary to complete her trip around the globe in just 72 days. Nellie Bly had made most of the trip alone, filing brief reports by telegraph. Once again her experiences led to a book, *Around the World in Seventy-Two Days* (1890).

Drunk History used its inimitable slurred style and two different actresses to portray Bly. In "New York City" (2014), Laura Dern is eager reporter Nellie, who agrees to be committed to an asylum not only to uncover its inhumane treatment of patients, but also to show that she should be taken seriously because women are "really cool." In "Journalism" (2015), Ellie Kemper is Bly, racing around the world to beat Fogg's fictional record, and unaware that *Cosmopolitan* has sent out its own female reporter, Elizabeth Bisland (Natasha Leggero), to give Nellie a run for her money. Bly ultimately won the race by four days, but Bisland still beat the fictional record, and both women "transformed travel writing."

Portrait of Nellie Bly, ca. 1890, by H.J. Myers, photographer (Library of Congress).

Other programs about Nellie Bly used the same model, depicting one or the other of these brave, but disparate achievements. In *The Adventures of Nellie Bly* (TV movie, 1981) Linda Purl portrays Bly, emphasizing her undercover assignments for the *World*, including work as a chorus girl and even a streetwalker, which culminated in her harrowing "madhouse" stay. The Blackwell's Island story was also the focus of *Escaping the Madhouse: The Nellie Bly Story* (TV movie, 2019), with Christina Ricci as Nellie, in an overwrought telling only loosely based on Bly's undercover work at the asylum.

Voyagers! used Bly's circumnavigation of the globe as an opportunity to place her in London for a "Ripping" tale in "Jack's Back" (1983), wherein Bly (Julia Duffy) interrupts her voyage to trap Jack the Ripper.

Duffy wears a deerstalker cap and floor-length plaid coat, in imitation of Bly's actual look (except for Duffy's blond curls) upon her New York departure. Time-travel hijinks ensue, and Nellie learns about the importance of accuracy in reporting before resuming her voyage in the newly restored timeline.

Nellie Bly had begun her writing career by responding to an article in the *Pittsburgh Dispatch* entitled "What Girls Are Good For." With little formal schooling, she went on to become a famous journalist who showed that "girls are good for" much more than the article's author ever imagined.

Boleyn, Anne (ca. 1507–1536)
Queen of England
Portrayed by: Dorothy Tutin, Natalie Dormer, Jodhi May, Helena Bonham Carter, Claire Foy

Anne Boleyn was the second of King Henry VIII's six wives, crowned queen of England in 1533. Her marriage to Henry was short, but certainly not sweet. The union began in controversy, as Henry sought an annulment for his first marriage to Catherine of Aragon, a development which eventually led the Church of England to break from the Roman Catholic Church. In the same year, Boleyn gave birth to a daughter, who would become the future queen of England, Elizabeth I. Hopes for a male heir to succeed Henry were dashed, when Anne had a miscarriage and later a stillborn male child.

As one does when a marriage doesn't turn out as planned, Henry had his second wife committed to the Tower of London on charges, most likely fabricated, of adultery and incest, and she was tried, convicted, and beheaded. And Henry, Supreme Head of the Church of England, married wife number three, Jane Seymour, less than two weeks later.

Dorothy Tutin portrays the ill-fated queen in "Anne Boleyn," the second episode of the award-winning miniseries *The Six Wives of Henry VIII* (1970). All is happiness at first between Anne and Henry (Keith Michell), as they enjoy a flirtatious, loving relationship, and the birth of their daughter brings much joy. But signs of strain begin to show, as Anne suspects Henry of infidelity, and he grows tired of waiting for her to bear a son. Anne isn't shy in confronting the king about his indiscretions, and her brother George (Jonathan Newth) urges her to be cautious.

The closeness between brother and sister will soon spur rumors of incest, as promoted by George's jealous wife Lady Rochford (Sheila Burrell). The marriage of the king and the now pregnant queen hangs by a slender thread, the birth of a healthy son. Anne dares to tell philandering

Henry, "You're not fit to be the father of my son." Henry replies, "All you have to do is give me a son, and I will love you as is fitting." When Henry screams, "You killed my son!" after their son is stillborn, Anne's fate is sealed. The scene is harrowing as Tutin and Michell dig deep to reach the emotional truth of the tragedy.

While *The Six Wives of Henry VIII* was a BBC production which reached American shores later via the CBS television network, *The Tudors* (2007–2010) was an American production, albeit with British and Canadian co-producers, for the Showtime premium cable channel. The lavishly produced series focuses on the reign of King Henry VIII (Jonathan Rhys Meyers) with the Boleyn years covered in seasons one and two. Natalie Dormer portrays Anne in a riveting performance, her face both amazingly expressive and intriguingly beautiful. Her portrayal of Boleyn's last days is a tour de force, as shown in a scene where Anne is imprisoned in the Tower of London, and Sir William Kingston (George Irving) arrives to tell her that the executioner has been delayed, postponing her beheading. Is this good news? How does one behave upon receiving such news? Kingston is trying to be considerate, but Boleyn begins to laugh, especially when he assures her there will be no pain for her during the execution. She tells him, "And in any case, I have only a little neck," laughing even more. The absurdity of the situation is written all over her face, and one ends up feeling almost more sorry for Kingston in his misguided hope that he has brought some comfort to the queen.

Except for *The Tudors*, fictional portrayals of Anne Boleyn remained the province of UK productions. Jodhi May portrayed Anne in the 2003 British TV movie *The Other Boleyn Girl*, which centers on Mary Boleyn (Natascha McElhone), her sister Anne, and the complicated love affairs of both women, including their competition for the affections of Henry VIII (Jared Harris). Helena Bonham Carter was Anne to Ray Winstone's Henry in the two-part TV movie *Henry VIII* (2003), which won an International Emmy Award for Best TV Movie or Miniseries. Claire Foy played Anne in *Wolf Hall* (2015), a six-episode series which focuses on the rise to power of Thomas Cromwell (Mark Rylance) within the court of Henry VIII (Damian Lewis).

On May 6, 1536, Anne wrote to husband Henry from her imprisonment in the Tower of London. She said, "Try me, good king, but let me have a lawful trial, and let not my sworn enemies sit as my accusers and judges; yea let me receive an open trial, for my truth shall fear no open flame...." These words make it clear that Anne Boleyn already knew what fate was in store for her.

Borden, Lizzie (1860–1927)
Murder Suspect
Portrayed by: Carmen Mathews, Elizabeth Montgomery, Christina Ricci

It's inspiring when women become famous for feats of courage, intellectual accomplishments, or athletic achievements, but sometimes they become famous for crimes they commit (or may have committed). Lizzie Borden is one of the most famous women to fall into the murder suspect category. Borden was tried for the murders of her stepmother and father in June of 1893. A popular folk rhyme described the charges against her, with some exaggeration:

> Lizzie Borden took an axe
> and gave her mother forty whacks.
> When she saw what she had done,
> she gave her father forty-one.

While the axe was actually a hatchet, and the whacks were fewer than 20, the killings were grisly, and Lizzie quickly rose to the top of the suspect list. She was arrested in Fall River, Massachusetts, on August 11, 1892, one week after the murders, and spent nine months in a small jail cell awaiting trial. She was never to return to prison, however, as a jury of 12 men acquitted her of both crimes. Lizzie Borden remains the lead suspect in the case until this day and is the subject of continued study, speculation, and fascination.

Television took an early interest in Borden's story with "The Older Sister," a 1956 episode of *Alfred Hitchcock Presents*. Carmen Mathews is suitably creepy as Lizzie, while Joan Lorring is the essence of demure sweetness as her older sister Emma. Looks can be deceiving, however, as we learn that Lizzie, now approaching the one-year anniversary of the murders, has been covering for Emma, who found her "wicked" stepmother's restrictions intolerable. Unfortunately Dad had been corrupted by his wife's wickedness, according to Emma, and also had to go. Emma finally turns on her younger sister as well, but Lizzie is saved by the reappearance of a persistent, inquiring reporter (Polly Rowles). Eerie theremin music pushes this overwrought production over the top, but the program is noteworthy for its all-female cast, with six speaking parts, and not a man in sight, except for Alfred Hitchcock, who introduces and concludes the program.

The Legend of Lizzie Borden (TV movie, 1975) revisits the story, and is "based largely on fact," at least according to the film's opening frames. The action begins on August 4, 1892, just after the murders have been discovered. Lizzie Borden (Elizabeth Montgomery) greets a guest at her door with the words, "...do come in. Someone has killed Father." Her continued detachment will prove problematic, as suspicions grow about Lizzie's role in the brutal murders. The film follows the case from inquest through trial, using flashbacks to bring the Borden household to life, even while two of its members will perish. The most significant flashback occurs when Lizzie faces the jury foreman to hear the verdict.

The film moves into the speculative realm at that point, as Borden

Elizabeth Montgomery as Lizzie Borden (right) with Katherine Helmond as her sister Emma in *The Legend of the Lizzie Borden* (Paramount Television).

replays the murders in her head. She sees herself taking off all her clothes before committing the unspeakable acts, washing the blood from her bare body afterwards, and then dressing again in the same clothing. One factor in favor of acquittal was that there was no blood on Lizzie's garments when she was seen shortly after the murders were committed, and the movie offers this daring, especially for 1975 TV, explanation of how Lizzie might have managed that.

The trailer for *Lizzie Borden Took an Ax* (TV movie, 2014) clearly announces its intentions with the tagline, "It's time to bury the hatchet." We've moved from Montgomery's restrained portrayal of Lizzie to Christina Ricci's hatchet-wielding, slasher-movie Lizzie, who tortures her sister Emma (Clea DuVall) by whispering details of the crime into her ear and kissing her cheek. Lifetime network did well enough with this movie to order a limited series, *The Lizzie Borden Chronicles* (2015), which picks up Lizzie's story four months after her acquittal for the infamous murders.

With Ricci and DuVall reprising their roles, the series ventures further into mayhem, as the bodies pile up, and history escapes out the window. Pinkerton Detective Charlie Siringo (Cole Hauser) arrives in 1893 Fall River to take a closer look at Lizzie's case. He'll end up dead at the hands of one of the Borden sisters, while the real Charlie died in 1928 on the other side of the country in Altadena, California.

Historical Lizzie Borden lived a quiet life in Fall River after the acquittal, except for an 1897 accusation of shoplifting in Providence, Rhode Island, not exactly fodder for TV movie scripts. When she died at the age of 66, she left substantial sums of money to the Fall River Animal Rescue League, as well as to numerous friends and family members.

Brontë, Anne (1820–1849)

See (mentioned in): **Brontë, Emily (1818–1848)**

Brontë, Charlotte (1816–1855)

Author
Portrayed by: Finn Atkins

Charlotte Brontë was, in many ways, a woman of her time and place, 19th-century England. She worked as a governess when family debts needed paying, cared for her father when his eyesight began to fail, and married, probably not for love, after rejecting several proposals. In her writing, however, Brontë was revolutionary, not only in the themes she tackled in her novels, but also in her approach to getting her words out into the world. Charlotte and her sisters, Emily and Anne, published a volume of poems at their own expense, writing under the gender-neutral names Currer, Ellis and Acton Bell respectively. Although their poetry book received little notice, the women soldiered on, and in 1847, Charlotte placed her novel *Jane Eyre: An Autobiography* with Smith, Elder, and Company. *Jane Eyre* was a success right out of the gate, and attained literary classic status, as the decades passed.

The novel follows its eponymous heroine from childhood through adulthood, weaving a story of Gothic mystery and romance, while touching upon topics of class, religion, and feminism. It considers the latter in emotional and spiritual terms rather than political or social ones, but equality is definitely on Brontë's mind. Her protagonist, Jane, says to her brooding love, Rochester: "…Do you think, because I am poor, obscure, plain, and little, I am soulless and heartless? You think wrong—I have as much soul as you—and full as much heart.…"

Finn Atkins portrays Charlotte in the 2016 TV movie *To Walk Invisible*. The film focuses on the three Brontë sisters, who push to become published authors, while dealing with their infirm father, the Rev. Patrick Brontë (Jonathan Pryce), their alcoholic and troublemaking brother Branwell (Adam Nagaitis), and a correspondingly tumultuous home life. Charlotte, the eldest sister, is as sunless as the bleak, grey streets of the town. She's not much interested in writing anymore, although it was once a childhood passion for the siblings, because there's no prospect of publication. A conversation with Branwell sparks her interest in publishing, but she laments the lack of opportunities for women, while speaking to Emily (Chloe Pirrie). Charlotte says, "Why is it that a woman's lot is so very different to a man's? I've never felt inferior.… You or I could do almost anything we set our minds to.…"

So set her mind, she does, to publishing a volume of poetry from the Brontë sisters, but not before riding out a major storm of resistance from Emily. The poetry book sells only two copies, so the sisters turn their attention to writing novels, keeping their aspirations secret from both their father and brother. By the end of the film, Charlotte has achieved success with *Jane Eyre*, while Branwell has died, probably from tuberculosis, aggravated by delirium tremens, alcoholism, and other addictions.

A postscript notes the deaths of Emily and Anne from tuberculosis within eight months of Branwell's passing, but finds transcendence in the lives that now pass through the Brontë Parsonage Museum, dedicated to the literary legacy of the sisters. The film ends with the note that "Charlotte went on to publish *Shirley* and *Villette*, and was hugely celebrated in her own lifetime."

Brontë, Emily (1818–1848)
Author
Portrayed by: Chloe Pirrie

Emily Brontë produced only one novel during her lifetime, *Wuthering Heights* (1847), which didn't see much critical success at the time, but went on to acclaim as one of the finest novels ever written in the English language. We know less about Emily's life than we do about her sister Charlotte's, as Emily, ever reserved, left behind little correspondence, while Charlotte was an avid letter writer. From the various scraps of information that have survived, Emily emerges as a homebody, who loved nature and walking on the moors near the family home in Haworth, England. She had few friends, and there are hints she had a hot temper. These tidbits have led to modern speculation about agoraphobia, Asperger's syndrome, and other medical conditions as explanations for Emily's behavior.

So who was Emily Brontë? *To Walk Invisible* tries to fill in some of the gaps, bringing Emily to life in a riveting performance by Chloe Pirrie. As sister Charlotte (Finn Atkins) turns ambitious, wanting the three Brontë sisters to join forces in publishing a poetry volume, Emily says no, not wanting her work to be, "rubbished and ridiculed." Charlotte searches Emily's room for her sister's poems, finds them, and is more convinced than ever the sisters should work together. Emily discovers Charlotte's invasion of her privacy, and here the telefilm leans into the angry Emily theory. Emily lunges at Charlotte, saying, "You stay out of my room, and you don't speak to me. You don't speak to me generally and you don't speak to me specifically about your misguided, tedious, grubby little publishing plans." During this exchange, Emily strikes Charlotte on the forehead with her palm, not once, but twice, a show of restrained violence, but violence nonetheless.

Third Brontë sister Anne (Charlie Murphy) smooths things over with Emily, explaining Charlotte's plan to publish a poetry volume first, using that as a springboard to novels for all of them. Emily lights up at the idea of a novel, describing to Anne a local tale she's heard, a tale of "anger so rich." That story will serve as inspiration for Emily's novel *Wuthering Heights*, a work of passion, hatred, and revenge, set on the West Yorkshire moors.

Alas, Emily did not live to see the book's success. When *Wuthering Heights* appeared in December 1847, many of the early reviews were, shall we say, not glowing. *The Examiner*, for example, found some elements to praise in its January 1848 review, but also said that the novel "...is wild, confused, disjointed, and improbable...." *Douglas Jerrold's Weekly Newspaper* described an unhappy reading experience around the same time, saying, "...the reader is shocked, disgusted, almost sickened by details of cruelty, inhumanity, and the most diabolical hate and vengeance...."

Later analysts would be more kind, but Emily succumbed to the family curse of tuberculosis in December of that year, and never saw the contemporary success that her sister Charlotte had achieved. Emily's novel did not end up as a historical footnote, however, attaining the status of literary classic in its own right and through frequent adaptation into film and television productions.

Brown, Margaret "Molly" (1867–1932)

Philanthropist, RMS Titanic *Survivor*
Portrayed by: Cloris Leachman, Fionnula Flanagan, Marilu Henner, Linda Kash

Margaret Brown, called "Maggie" by her friends, became "The Unsinkable Molly Brown" in death, a woman who, almost by sheer force of will, refused to go down when RMS *Titanic* sank in 1912. The legend of Molly was always bigger than the real Maggie, but the legend had some basis in fact. After the *Titanic* hit an iceberg in the North Atlantic Ocean, Maggie Brown helped others to board lifeboats, took an oar to row in her own boat, and used her fluency in several languages to assist survivors.

In "The Unsinkable Molly Brown," a 1957 episode of the anthology series *Telephone Time*, Mrs. Brown, here correctly called Maggie (Cloris Leachman), returns to her stateroom after the crash, putting on bloomers under her elegant gown and filling them with jewelry. She straps a flask to her leg, which will come in handy later in the lifeboat, when a passenger is in need of some liquid courage. Maggie boards the boat wearing her fur coat, which she quickly hands to a young girl for warmth. When panic sets in among the passengers, a woman screams, "We're going to die!" Maggie yells, "Nobody's going to die. Now get hold of them oars and pull!"

Mrs. Brown moves from unflappable Maggie to larger-than-life Molly in "Voyagers! of the Titanic," a 1983 episode of *Voyagers!* As portrayed by Fionnula Flanagan, Molly is a pipe-smoking rule-breaker, and her iconoclasm will come in handy when she encounters two time travelers on a mission that has nothing to do with rescuing the *Titanic*. Molly must help Jeffrey Jones (Meeno Peluce) and Phineas Bogg (Jon-Erik Hexum) save the *Mona Lisa* from going down on the *Titanic* to put history, which tends to meander, back on course.

Cloris Leachman surfaces again (so to speak) as Molly Brown in *S.O.S. Titanic*, an ambitious 1979 TV movie which attempts to capture the onboard ship experience and its aftermath from the viewpoint of a plethora of first-, second-, and third-class passengers. Marilu Henner portrays

Molly in *Titanic*, a star-studded 1996 miniseries, where she gets to say things like, "Here's to a rip-roarin' maiden voyage for us and the *Titanic*," things that lead you to believe her character is a darn tootin' caricature. Linda Kash's Molly Brown gets swamped by a tsunami of fictional characters in *Titanic*, a four-part miniseries from 2012, which features multiple romances and myriad class conflicts.

Historical Maggie Brown's contributions didn't end after her lifeboat was rescued by RMS *Carpathia*. She organized a Survivors' Committee among the first-class passengers, raising $10,000 (over $250,000 today) for survivors in need by the time the ship had reached New York. In later life, Maggie worked with the American Committee for Devastated France after World War I, promoted the rights of workers and women, and advocated for children in the areas of education, literacy, and juvenile justice. In 1932, Brown received the French Légion d'Honneur (Legion of Honor), its highest order of merit, for her actions during and after the sinking of the *Titanic*, and her activist and philanthropic efforts during the years thereafter.

Browning, Elizabeth Barrett (1806–1861)
Poet
Portrayed by: Katharine Cornell, Jane Lapotaire, Jayne Meadows

Elizabeth Barrett Browning has two claims to fame, an illustrious career as a Victorian poet and membership in a power couple forged by forbidden romance. Not surprisingly, popular culture has focused on the latter.

Born in County Durham, England, Elizabeth wrote poetry from an early age, but suffered from poor health, leaving her homebound for much of her life. She devoted her time to literary pursuits, and in 1844, her collection *Poems* appeared, receiving an enthusiastic reception, especially from fellow poet Robert Browning. Mr. Browning wrote Elizabeth a fan letter, which concluded, "I do, as I say, love these books with all my heart—and I love you too." A correspondence developed between the two, conducted in secret, lest the relationship rile her domineering father. The couple married in secret as well, moving to Italy, where Elizabeth regained some of her health and eventually gave birth to a son. Edward, her strict, disapproving father, disinherited Elizabeth, and, in fact, each of his children who married.

The juicier aspects of the family story received greater attention after the appearance of *The Barretts of Wimpole Street*, a 1930 play by Rudolf Besier. First staged in England, the play made its way to Broadway, and later was adapted into two theatrical films. Television took note as well with a 1956 adaptation for *Producers' Showcase*, an anthology series that was telecast live, but preserved in kinescopes. Katharine Cornell reprised her Broadway role as Elizabeth, who is described as a "40-year-old invalid" as the story opens in 1845. Elizabeth's father, Edward (Henry Daniell), emphasizes "her precarious state of health," and thinks he is the best judge of what is good or bad for her, although she is a grown woman. Edward is obsessed with Elizabeth, although she is one of his many children, saying, "You are everything in the world to me, you know that."

Edward's control issues notwithstanding, Robert Browning (Anthony Quayle) manages to arrange a meeting with Elizabeth in her room by being, in his own words, "tiresomely insistent," and their courtship begins. Daniell's Edward, who could win the "creepiest television dad" award, is none too pleased, and once Elizabeth escapes to Italy, he wants to kill her dog. (Not to worry, as the brave poet has taken her beloved canine with her.) The program ends with Elizabeth's voice-over narration of her famous "Sonnet 43," which begins, "How do I love thee? Let me count the ways." Historical Elizabeth had written the sonnet during her secret courtship with Robert, and later released it in the collection *Sonnets from the Portuguese* (1850).

Television visited *The Barretts of Wimpole Street* again in 1982, with a movie from the BBC. Jane Lapotaire stars as Elizabeth, a virtual prisoner in her own room, who finds some release in poetry, visits from her siblings, and the love of her dog Flush. Joss Ackland is her father Edward, the jailer in this family prison, while Jeremy Brett, sporting a wispy, mustache-less beard, portrays Browning, who shows Elizabeth that love can be her route of escape.

In "Aristotle, Niccolo Machiavelli, Elizabeth Barrett Browning, Sun Yat-Sen" (parts one and two, 1979), an episode of *Meeting of Minds*, host Steve Allen introduces Elizabeth (Jayne Meadows) by noting that her personal life has tended to overshadow her poetry. The discussion that follows doesn't help to redress the balance, emphasizing Elizabeth's personal life over her literary contributions. When asked about her relationship with her father, Elizabeth notes that she was "papa's favorite," describing how her mother used her as an intermediary to get things she wanted. After more description of the intense father-daughter relationship, Aristotle (Bernard Behrens) comments, with obvious discomfort, "Your father's love seems very ... unnatural."

There is also concern over Elisabeth's use of opium, prescribed by her doctors, which she says lowered her pulse, allowing her to sleep. She observes that using the drug never got in the way of her writing, but the rest of the panel, all men, are concerned about addiction. At the end of part one, Elizabeth, weeping, flees the room, lamenting that her father went to his death never having forgiven her. The men are paternalistic and almost as creepy as Edward, making this an ironic outing of *Meeting of Minds*.

In addition to having a difficult father and a famous husband, Elizabeth Barrett Browning produced a body of work that influenced many well-known writers of her day, including Edgar Allan Poe and Emily Dickinson. Her verse-novel *Aurora Leigh* (1856), a semi-autobiographical story about a female poet, helped to mold suffragist Susan B. Anthony's thoughts on women's roles in society. In the 20th century, the women's movement and feminist scholarship both rediscovered the strong and independent woman Barrett Browning had created in *Aurora Leigh*.

Elizabeth Barrett Browning was undoubtedly influenced by the two most important men in her life, but, in her own story, Elizabeth is the lead.

Burns, Lucy (1879–1966)

Suffragist
Portrayed by: Frances O'Connor

Lucy Burns was a suffragist whose talent for political organizing and dedication to activism helped to secure the right to vote for women in the United States. Burns graduated from Vassar College in 1902, moving on to graduate work in linguistics at various schools, including Oxford University. While in England for her studies, she became interested in the women's suffrage movement, working with Emmeline Pankhurst and enduring several arrests. During her stay, she also made the acquaintance of Alice Paul, who would become her partner in fighting for national women's suffrage in the United States. When Burns returned to America in 1912, she and Paul joined forces to change the U.S. Constitution and the course of women's history.

The TV movie *Iron Jawed Angels* (2004) begins at this juncture, as Lucy (Frances O'Connor) and Alice Paul (Hilary Swank) meet with representatives of the National American Woman Suffrage Association (NAWSA) to push for a constitutional amendment to give women the vote. The organization's leaders, especially Carrie Chapman Catt (Anjelica Huston), are concerned that the younger women will use the more radical tactics of the British suffragists, but Paul assures Catt that they will cause no trouble. Paul is portrayed as practical and deliberate here, while Burns is more the agitator and hothead.

When Catt later accuses Paul of possible financial improprieties in the running of NAWSA's Congressional committee, it is Burns who says they should leave NAWSA, while Paul says she doesn't want to fight with other women. But Paul later reconsiders and they do leave, forming their own organization, the National Woman's Party. Soon women from the

NWP are picketing the White House as "silent sentinels" for women's suffrage.

The biggest inflection point comes when the United States enters World War I, and Lucy and Alice disagree about whether they should continue the daily White House demonstrations, as the picketing might be viewed as unpatriotic. Lucy wants to continue, and the women finally agree that Burns will lead the line each day, while Paul will stay out of it to keep her safe, as the organization's leader. Onlookers soon become enraged by the picketing, which they view as a treasonous act, and the women are arrested for obstructing traffic. Lucy is a most uncooperative prisoner, and the guards handcuff her hands above her head. Further events, including the imprisonment of Alice Paul, lead to hunger strikes and force-feeding. Word gets out to the newspapers about the harrowing treatment of the women in prison, public sentiment begins to turn, and President Woodrow Wilson (Bob Gunton) finally gives his support to the suffrage amendment.

The last part of the film feels rushed; the more than two-and-a half-year period it took to pass and ratify the 19th amendment is collapsed into a single scene. While the movie sometimes plays fast and loose with historical fact, especially in the use of invented and composite characters, *Iron Jawed Angels* is truly inspirational in depicting the brave self-sacrifice of Burns, Paul, and the women who joined them in the fight for the vote.

The real Lucy Burns was worn out by the long battle for women's suffrage, retiring from political life after passage of the 19th amendment. She said, "I think we have done all this for women, and we have sacrificed everything we possessed for them, and now let them fight for it now." Her accomplishments and sacrifices are commemorated in The Lucy Burns Museum, which resides on the site of the former Occoquan Workhouse in Lorton, Virginia, where Burns and other suffragists were confined in 1917.

Byron, Ada
See: **Lovelace, Ada (1815–1852)**

Calamity Jane (ca. 1852–1903)
Frontierswoman
Portrayed by: Dody Heath, Norma Crane, Stefanie Powers, Fay Spain, Carol Burnett, Jane Alexander, Anjelica Huston, Robin Weigert

For such a well-known woman, Calamity Jane remains a mystery, the details of her life obscured by her own fanciful tales and the legends that followed. Generally accepted facts about "Calamity" include her birth name, Martha Jane Cannary, and the death of both her parents by the time she was 12 years old. From that point on, Jane was forced into an itinerant life, taking any work to survive, including prostitution. Sometimes she did "men's work," such as bullwhacking, and adopted male clothing, which she wore throughout her life. Accounts differ as to how she gained her nickname, but most place her as "Calamity Jane" in Deadwood, South Dakota, by 1876. In that lawless town, she met or didn't meet Wild Bill Hickok, and they did or didn't have an affair, but their names became linked, increasing her star status as Western tales grew in popularity.

With the facts of Jane's life so muddled, fictional representations filled

Calamity Jane during the 1880s, by C.E. Finn (Cowan's Auctions).

in the blanks as they saw fit. Western series wove her legend into the fabric of their storylines, placing Calamity in the paths of their regular characters, however far afield that may have taken her. In "Calamity," a 1959 episode of *Colt .45*, a tough, but sensitive Jane (Dody Heath) helps government agent Christopher Colt (Wayde Preston) transport smallpox vaccine through dangerous territory to quarantined Deadwood. *Have Gun—Will Travel* finds Calamity, here Martha Jane Conroy (Norma Crane), in need of help from Paladin (Richard Boone), when a business dispute leads her to alcohol and depression in "The Cure" (1961). *Bonanza* inserts Doc Holliday (Christopher Dark) of Tombstone fame into a broad story about a love triangle between Doc, Little Joe (Michael Landon), and "Cal" (Stefanie Powers) in "Calamity Over the Comstock" (1963).

Jane's own story is finally center stage in the *Death Valley Days* episode "A Calamity Called Jane" (1966). Fay Spain stars as Calamity in a tale focused on questions of what it means to be a "lady." A petite, blond Jane meets Wild Bill Hickok (Rhodes Reason) in Custer, South Dakota, but Bill isn't wild about adding her to his show. Bill says to Charlie Utter (Ed Peck), "She's dirty, cusses like a man, drinks like a fish, picks fights. She's trouble, Charlie." Later, after Calamity has whooped it up too much on the group's entry into Deadwood, Bill calls her a mockery to her own sex.

Jane replies, "You think just 'cause you wear pants that you're superior. I found that out when I was a little girl in Missouri and I made my mind up that I was just as good as anything in pants." Then, despite Bill's unvarnished assessment of her, Calamity proceeds to fall in love with him and buy a dress. Bill isn't receptive to the change, and things go downhill from there. The episode gives us some food for thought, but the overall judgment seems to be that Calamity is damaged because she doesn't fit society's image of a lady, not a surprising viewpoint for an episode produced in the mid–60s.

Calamity, the stereotype, is at the center of another '60s production, *Calamity Jane* (TV special, 1963). Carol Burnett stars as the Western legend in this musical comedy which takes Jane to Chicago in search of a famous actress to entertain at the Golden Garter saloon in Deadwood. A love quadrangle ensues, and Calamity receives the requisite makeover, going from buckskin-clad boor to dress-wearing lady. At the end, only Jane and Wild Bill Hickok (Art Lund) are left, both conveniently realizing at the same time that the ones they love each are other. They sing, "Secret Love."

When the heyday of TV westerns passed, Jane disappeared from the small screen for almost 20 years, and didn't reappear until the '80s, popping up on television once a decade thereafter. In *Calamity Jane*, a 1984 TV movie, Jane Alexander portrays the title character in a tale highlighting

Carol Burnett stars in the musical special *Calamity Jane* (CBS).

her romance with Hickock (Frederic Forrest), their secret marriage, and a subsequent daughter (Talia Balsam, Sara Gilbert), all parts of Calamity's legend that are disputed by historians. *Buffalo Girls* (Miniseries, 1995), based on a novel by Larry McMurtry, celebrates three women of the Old West, especially Calamity Jane (Anjelica Huston), and what Jane calls "the last of the Wild West times ... them last few days of wildness."

Deadwood (2004–2006) features Calamity, here known as Jane Canary (Robin Weigert), throughout its three seasons, portraying her as a foul-mouthed (not surprising for this series) drunk, who becomes romantically involved not with Wild Bill, but with Joanie Stubbs (Kim Dickens), a bordello madam. While "rough around the edges" would be an understatement for *Deadwood's* Jane, she is capable of great compassion, assisting Doc Cochran (Brad Dourif) in tending the sick and injured, and nursing a man back to health who has been left to die of smallpox in the woods.

It's a long way from *Colt .45's* sweet and scrubbed Calamity to *Deadwood's* coarse and abrasive Jane in 2004. While that says a lot about television in the intervening years, it also speaks volumes about the elusiveness of the real Martha Jane Cannary. She could and can be whatever you imagine her to be, as long as she's wearing those buckskins.

Cannary, Martha Jane
See: **Calamity Jane (ca. 1852–1903)**

Cashman, Nellie (ca. 1844–1925)
Gold Prospector, Businesswoman, Philanthropist
Portrayed by: Randy Stuart, Grace Lee Whitney

Nellie Cashman was a woman of contradictions, driven throughout her life by the search for gold, yet possessing a spirit of generosity which earned her the title "Angel of Tombstone." (And "Angel of the Cassiar." And "Saint of the Sourdoughs.") Cashman's prospecting adventures led her to Arizona, Mexico, the Canadian Yukon, and Alaska, among others, but she still managed to care for five orphaned nieces and nephews. She also led an expedition to rescue stranded miners in British Columbia, and helped to establish hospitals, churches, and schools throughout the West.

Randy Stuart portrayed Cashman in 12 episodes of *The Life and Legend of Wyatt Earp* (1955–1961) during the show's fifth season. In "Tombstone" (1959), Cashman works as a peacemaker between warring factions of miners and cowboys, just as Wyatt Earp (Hugh O'Brian) arrives to shake things up in Tombstone. Although fictional Cashman is a romantic interest for Earp, elements of the real Cashman's amazing life are still present, such as her work as a nurse and her ownership of the Cashman Hotel. (Where did she find the time?)

Grace Lee Whitney was a decidedly glam Nellie Cashman (including frontier false eyelashes) in the *Death Valley Days* episode "The Angel of Tombstone" (1969). Cashman's signature gold fever is present when she journeys to Baja, California, in search of her big score, but her charitable impulses are also on display when she realizes the work of a Catholic mission will be jeopardized if she stakes a claim.

The United States Postal Service featured the real Nellie Cashman on a commemorative stamp as part of its Legends of the West series in 1994, emphasizing her roles as peacemaker and businesswoman. But you can't tell Nellie's story without mentioning the GOLD.

Catherine of Aragon (1485–1536)
Queen of England
Portrayed by: Annette Crosbie, Maria Doyle Kennedy, Charlotte Hope, Assumpta Serna, Joanne Whalley

Catherine of Aragon was the first of King Henry VIII's six wives, crowned queen of England in 1509. She was an accomplished and popular queen, serving as regent in 1513, when Henry was on a military campaign in France. As the Scots invaded England later that year, Catherine rode in full armor, while pregnant, to address the troops about courage and patriotism. She ultimately gave birth to six children, but only one, a female, survived infancy, later becoming Queen Mary I. King Henry, however, wanted a male heir to secure an orderly succession to the throne, and had his eye on Anne Boleyn anyway, so he sought an annulment from Catherine.

The Six Wives of Henry VIII tells us what happens next in "Catherine of Aragon" (1970), starring Annette Crosbie as Catherine and Keith Michell as Henry. The king visits Catherine in her chamber, where she is delighted to receive a visit from her husband. He casually picks up a Bible and cites a text from Leviticus that implies, according to "learned and pious men," that because Catherine was once married to Henry's brother, their current marriage is unlawful in the sight of God. Them's the breaks. They need to separate. She will have to find another place to live. Catherine starts to wail.

In later court proceedings before a papal legate to determine the legitimacy of the marriage, Catherine says to Henry, "My Lord, I beg of you to spare me this court, but, if you will not, I appeal my case to God." The queen turns her back on Henry, walking away, and will not return when summoned. She appears on a balcony and hears shouts of "Long live the Queen." Neither the love Catherine's subjects have for her nor the love Catherine has for her husband mean anything to Henry, of course. He has their marriage annulled, after breaking with the Church of Rome, and marries Anne Boleyn (Dorothy Tutin). Annette Crosbie won the 1971 BAFTA TV Award for her stunning portrayal of Catherine in an impressive field of contenders that included Glenda Jackson, Gemma Jones, and Dorothy Tutin. Maria Doyle Kennedy

Annette Crosbie as Catherine of Aragon in *The Six Wives of Henry VIII* **(PBS).**

also received accolades for her portrayal of Catherine, an IFTA (Irish Film and Television Award) and a Gemini Award for her supporting role in *The Tudors* (2007–2010). Her Catherine says to Henry (Jonathan Rhys Meyers) in front of the Legatine Court, "By me you have had many children, although it has pleased God to call them from this world...." The real Catherine went a bit further. "This 20 years or more I have been your true wife and by me ye have had divers children, although it hath pleased God to call them from this world, which hath been no default in me...." Kennedy's Catherine is more convincingly Spanish than Crosbie's, and more glamorous, perhaps too much so, but both actresses effectively convey the anguish of a woman who loved her husband and did everything asked of her only to be discarded on a trumped up charge.

Catherine of Aragon receives her own series in *The Spanish Princess* (2019–), based on the novel *The Constant Princess* (2005) by Philippa Gregory. Charlotte Hope portrays Catherine, a young beauty with red hair, while Ruairi O'Connor is Henry, called Harry. Hope's Catherine is a woman who's not going to let anyone or anything stand in the way of her ambition or what she perceives to be her destiny. She says, "I came here to forge an alliance with England, and that is what I'll do." And, "I came here to marry the future king of England, and that is what I'll do."

This Catherine has a modern edge for a modern TV audience, which values strong women and soapy plots above historical accuracy. Reviews in Spain were particularly critical on the historical accuracy front. The newspaper *20 Minutos,* for example, said on June 12, 2019, "...let us point out that there are special cases: series that, rather than disrespecting history, knock it down with a kick in the face and then tap-dance on its spine. Judging by some reactions, *The Spanish Princess* is one of them."

Catherine of Aragon also appears as a character in *Henry VIII* (TV movie, 2003), with Assumpta Serna as the queen and Ray Winstone in the title role. Joanne Whalley portrays Catherine in *Wolf Hall* (2015), a six-episode series about the rise to power of Thomas Cromwell (Mark Rylance) within the court of Henry VIII (Damian Lewis). As Henry's advisor, Thomas Cromwell was instrumental in engineering the annulment of the king's marriage to Catherine. While no fan of that union from a strategic perspective, the real Cromwell nonetheless said of Queen Catherine, "If not for her sex, she could have defied all the heroes of History."

Catherine the Great (1729–1796)
Empress of Russia
Portrayed by: Julia Ormond, Catherine Zeta-Jones, Jayne Meadows, Danielle Cormack

Born Princess Sophie of Anhalt-Zerbst, Catherine the Great rose from noble, though modest, German origins to become Empress of Russia, reigning for 34 years. Although her engagement to Grand Duke Peter, heir to the Russian throne, sounds like the start of a fairy tale, her royal marriage was anything but a warm-and-fuzzy princess story. The couple's magical union in 1745 quickly became a nightmare, as Peter was fit to be neither spouse nor emperor. Catherine handled the former problem by taking lovers, and the latter by taking the throne. The born ruler of the two, Catherine saw her opportunity years later and took it, staging a coup to depose Peter while the Emperor was on holiday in 1762.

Catherine's story up to her takeover is dramatized in the miniseries *Young Catherine* (1991), starring Julia Ormond in the title role. The teleplay begins in 1744, as Elizabeth, empress of Russia (Vanessa Redgrave), seeks a bride for her nephew and heir, Peter (Reece Dinsdale). The future Empress Catherine II starts out as naive teenager Sophie, but after her arrival in Russia, and especially her marriage to Peter, Catherine begins to learn the rules of the game at court, deciding she will be no one's pawn, not even Elizabeth's. Eventually this resolve will lead Catherine, in military uniform and tricorn hat, to address infantry troops, whose support she needs to overthrow her husband. On the back of a white horse, she proclaims, "Today I appeal to you to cast him out, route out this evil, and restore the true Russia." Young Sophie had wanted to marry for love, and how far reality had come from her glass-slipper dreams.

Catherine the Great (TV movie, 1995) starts the story a bit later, with the marriage of Catherine (Catherine Zeta-Jones) to Peter (Hannes Jaenicke) in 1745. There's no chance to celebrate the lavish nuptials, however, as the viewer is whisked seven years into the future, to the news that the marriage remains unconsummated. Empress Elizabeth (Jeanne Moreau) arranges for a handsome young man, Saltykov (Craig McLachlan), to seduce Catherine, in hopes of ensuring an heir to the throne. In real life, Catherine left hints in her memoirs that the heir, who later became Emperor Paul I, was indeed Saltykov's son.

The movie follows Catherine's story through Pugachev's Rebellion of 1774, a major uprising of Cossacks and peasants. Her decision to have Pugachev (John Rhys-Davies) executed alienates her trusted adviser and lover Potemkin (Paul McGann), who proclaims, "...I think we're both damned." In a coda years later, she says his words broke her heart, but neither of them was much for moping or sighing. "Well, I won every war I fought, I added immense territories to the empire, I reformed laws and institutions, I carried Russia into the modern age. I think I earned the title Catherine the Great." A handy summary of Catherine's legacy, delivered after another abrupt shift in the narrative's timeline.

Other depictions of Catherine the Great moved beyond the biopic to less traditional forms. In "Catherine the Great, Oliver Cromwell, Daniel O'Connell" (parts one and two, 1981), an episode of *Meeting of Minds*, the empress (Jayne Meadows) discusses her devotion to her adopted country and her personal life in a talk-show format where ideas and intellect are prized above all else.

Going from the sublime to the ridiculous, "A Horse of a Different Color" (2000), an installment of *Jack of All Trades*, finds Catherine (Danielle Cormack) on an island in the South Pacific, where much puerile humor is derived from her too-close relationship with her steed. The jokes in this outing allude to a myth about the empress and how she died, which won't be repeated here.

Catherine the Great ruled her adopted country for over 30 years, longer than any other female in Russian history, but her reign was full of complexity and contradiction. She had planned to emancipate the serfs, who were legally bound to the land and considered the property of their owners, but she abandoned the idea after taking power, realizing Russia's nobles would rebel. She spent two years drafting a statement of legal principles, called The Instruction, filled with Enlightenment ideals, which was to serve as a guide for a modern Russian legal code, but her Legislative Commission of 1767 was a bust. As Zeta-Jones's fictional Catherine boasted, however, the empress did lead Russia out of the past and into the contemporary political and cultural life of Europe. She championed the arts, purchasing several hundred paintings, mainly Flemish and Dutch, which became the foundation of the Hermitage Museum in Saint Petersburg.

Catherine the Great was a modern woman in many ways, but she still believed in the antiquated concept of the monarchy's absolute power.

Catt, Carrie Chapman (1859–1947)

Suffragist
Portrayed by: Anjelica Huston

Carrie Chapman Catt didn't fool around when it came to fighting for women's rights. In 1890, when she married George W. Catt, she asked for and received four months each year to work for women's suffrage per a prenuptial contract signed by her husband. After initially working with the Iowa Woman Suffrage Association, she became an active member of the National American Woman Suffrage Association (NAWSA), eventually succeeding Susan B. Anthony as the organization's president in 1900. Catt grew to be a shrewd tactician, embracing the goal of an eventual amendment to the U.S. Constitution, while continuing to work in individual states for women's full suffrage, and even for primary suffrage in more conservative Southern states.

The fight for the 19th amendment to the U.S. Constitution is chronicled in *Iron Jawed Angels*, a television movie from 2004. Anjelica Huston stars as Carrie Chapman Catt, but the focus of the movie is the contributions and sacrifices made by suffragists Alice Paul (Hilary Swank) and Lucy Burns (Frances O'Connor). Catt, who in real life was no fan of the militant actions taken by Paul and Burns, is more adversary than sister-in-arms here. Everyone makes nice at first, as Catt meets with Alice and Lucy, but she cautions that the two younger women must avoid the radical tactics used by the British suffragists if they wish to work with NAWSA.

The shaky alliance works for a while, as Catt appoints Paul and Burns to NAWSA's Congressional Committee, but falls apart after Catt alleges that the funds raised by Alice and Lucy for the committee are being handled improperly. Carrie Chapman Catt fades from the film at this point, as the story shifts to the protests and hunger strikes by Paul and Burns, although Catt resurfaces towards the end during the pro-suffrage speech made by President Woodrow Wilson (Bob Gunton) to Congress. As Alice Paul enters the chamber to hear Wilson's speech, Carrie Chapman Catt stands, so all the women can move down one chair to give Alice Paul a seat. Huston is a striking presence in black, tall, imperious, and forbidding. Although her portrayal sometimes veers into caricature, she won a Golden Globe award for her supporting performance.

After the Wilson speech, the last part of the film glosses over the hard work and the two and a half years it took to pass and ratify the 19th amendment, as though the battle was mostly won after Wilson gave his speech. The real Carrie Chapman Catt was there every step of the way during those two and a half years, lobbying endlessly in Congress and leading the battle for ratification in the states after that. When the final showdown took place in Tennessee, Catt was there during the long, hot summer of 1920, fighting for every vote with her troops, while "a nefarious lobby" tapped their telephones and attacked their "private and public lives." The amendment passed the Tennessee House by one vote, and the 19th Amendment to the U.S. Constitution was adopted on August 26, 1920, enfranchising 27 million women. The fate of 27 million women was decided by one vote.

The words of Carrie Chapman Catt have resonance to this day. "Roll up your sleeves, set your mind to making history, and wage such a fight for liberty that the whole world will respect our sex."

Cattle Kate (1861–1889)
Pioneer, Rancher
Portrayed by: Jean Parker

Born in Ontario, Canada, Ellen Watson became Cattle Kate in death, a rustler who met her end at the hands of cattle barons in Wyoming. It's an ugly story of lynching, made uglier by the fact that Ellen, or Ella, as she was known, was not named Kate, was no rustler, and was simply an independent woman who set out to make a living in a man's world.

After leaving and later divorcing an abusive husband, Ella moved from Nebraska to Colorado to Wyoming, landing in Rawlins, where she worked as a cook and waitress. There she met James "Jim" Averell, who would become her partner in homesteading, with their small cattle ranches sitting side by side. Their land and its access to water was coveted by a wealthy cattleman, Albert John Bothwell, who accused Watson of cattle rustling and rounded up a mob of like-minded ranchers.

Ella and Jim were hanged without a legal proceeding of any kind. To cover for this unspeakable act, newspapers friendly to the cattlemen printed reports of Ella's allegedly lurid crimes, conflating her with a hard-drinking woman named Kate Maxwell. Thus, "Cattle Kate" was born from the lynching of Ella Watson, less a phoenix rising from the ashes and more a vulture feeding on the bones of Ella's good name.

Stories of the Century changes lots of facts about Ella, especially the most important one, her innocence of criminal wrongdoing. In "Cattle Kate" (1954), Jean Parker portrays the title character as a rough and ruthless cattle rustler, one always a bit disheveled, even when not on the trail, no doubt a comment on her questionable character. Her "partner in crime," Jim Averell (James Seay), on the other hand, is well-dressed and more cultured, described as a leading citizen of the town. Kate is the ringleader of the gang, telling Jim, "I'll keep stealing from these big outfits 'til I break 'em."

In the course of one of her operations, Kate orders an investigator killed, which puts railroad detective Matt Clark (Jim Davis) on the case. Matt infiltrates the gang as a trail boss, and Kate kisses him, again indicating she's a bad girl, since she is already in a relationship with Jim. After a big shootout, Kate and Jim are jailed, but a mob drags them out for a lynching. Hero Matt arrives too late to stop the vigilantes, noting as he leaves town, "All they that live by the sword shall perish by the sword."

Ella Watson's family worked to restore her reputation over the years, and historians took notice. The story of thievin' Cattle Kate, loose woman and villain, who got what she deserved, has given way to the story of Ella Watson, a kind woman who was murdered because she dared to own land and stand up to important men.

Chanel, Coco (1883–1971)
Fashion Designer
Portrayed by: Romane Portail, Shirley MacLaine, Barbora Bobulová

Born Gabrielle Bonheur Chanel in Saumur, France, Coco Chanel grew up in poverty, but rose to international prominence as a fashion designer, known for her innovations that freed women from the burdens of 19th-century clothing. Chanel emphasized both style and comfort, saying, "luxury must be comfortable, otherwise it is not luxury." Where others saw silhouettes requiring traditional corsets and petticoats as the way to attract wealthy customers, Chanel charted a new course, designing casual looks with jersey fabric that led to a thriving fashion house within 10 years. Her later signature innovations include the famed "little black dress," the Chanel suit, costume jewelry, and even a foray into fragrances with her wildly successful Chanel No. 5.

Her life was not without controversy. Chanel had affairs with many men, usually wealthy and powerful ones, including the Duke of Westminster, Hugh Richard Arthur Grosvenor, and possibly even the Prince of Wales, Edward VIII. Her liaison during World War II with Baron Hans Gunther von Dincklage, a German diplomat, led to accusations that she had collaborated with the Nazis. She was arrested after Paris was liberated, but was never charged, giving rise to speculation that her old friend Winston Churchill had intervened on her behalf.

Chanel's scripted television appearances show her smoking cigarettes and spouting aphorisms almost to the point of caricature. The designer visits 1920s Toronto in the aptly titled "Dressed to Kill," a 2018 episode of *Frankie Drake Mysteries*. Romane Portail portrays Chanel, who appears to be the target of a killer, and seeks out the help of iconoclastic detective Frankie Drake (Lauren Lee Smith). The two women seem to be cut from the same cloth, as evidenced by Chanel's snappy line, "If there is one thing I have learned over the years, Miss Drake, it's that I can always trust a woman in pants."

Portail's tyrannical, fussy, and haughty Chanel sleeps with both of her male business partners, and jealousy turns out to be the crux of the case. Afterwards Chanel concludes, "I never again want to weigh more heavily on a man than a bird," a close approximation of words uttered by the real Coco. This episode, ostensibly about mystery-solving, does a good job of placing Chanel at the center of the action, highlighting her personality, methods, and the historical context of her revolutionary changes to women's fashion.

A fuller view of Chanel's life, but one still emphasizing cigarettes and maxims, emerges in *Coco Chanel*, a 2008 TV movie, with Shirley

MacLaine and Barbora Bobulová as old and young Coco respectively. The film begins with MacLaine's Coco, who is mounting a comeback in 1954, and she squeezes off Chanelisms in rapid fire, such as, "To be irreplaceable you have to be different." It then flashes back to Bobulová's Gabrielle, an innocent learning to work as a seamstress, and concentrates on Coco's years as a young designer, framed by her love triangle with Etienne Balsan (Sagamore Stevenin) and Boy Capel (Olivier Sitruk). MacLaine's Coco, although well-hyped in the promos for this Lifetime movie, isn't around much, leaving the viewer with two pictures of Coco with no connecting frames.

But that fractured view of Chanel's life might not have bothered the woman herself. After all, she once said, "My life didn't please me, so I created my life."

That's Chanel. Creator of fashions, maxims, and Coco.

Child, Julia (1912–2004)

Chef, Author, TV Personality
Portrayed by: Dan Aykroyd, John Candy, Michaela Watkins

Julia Child was larger than life, abetted by her 6'2" frame, but also by her distinctive warble of a voice, and her enthusiastic, accessible, and sometimes just-a-little-goofy TV presence on *The French Chef* (1963–1973) and later TV series. It's natural the medium that made her famous would find one or two elements to parody in her persona, and *Saturday Night Live* came up with a doozy of a sketch in "The French Chef," part of its 1978 episode "Eric Idle/Kate Bush." Dan Aykroyd is pitch-perfect (and adorable) as Julia in this cooking-show-gone-horribly-wrong that finds Child injured in the kitchen while deboning a chicken. Despite her mortal wound, Julia keeps talking until the bitter end, when she reminds us one more time to "save the liver" of the chicken. Apparently Ms. Child, a very good sport, found this sketch so enjoyable that she showed it to friends at parties, but be advised that there's LOTS of blood here.

A parody with a little less meat, so to speak, appears on "Battle of the PBS Stars," a 1982 episode of *SCTV Network*. Here John Candy portrays Child, bearing an eerie facial resemblance to the French chef under some good makeup. Julia battles Mister Rogers (Martin Short) in the boxing ring, and after a few ups and downs, she loses when Rogers clonks her over the head with his puppet King Friday. The best Julia moment comes when she's in her corner taking water from a turkey baster and spitting it into a baking pan. Not exactly high humor, but at least it makes the connection to her cooking.

Drunk History gives more historical perspective, if not time, to

Child's story in "Food" (2016). Michaela Watkins is Julia, who goes to work for the OSS (Office of Strategic Services), predecessor to the CIA, during World War II. The episode reveals one of the most fascinating tidbits of Julia's early life, when her first "cooking job" involved making repellent to keep sharks away from OSS explosives. In narrator Lyric Lewis's humorous telling, Child's main ingredient is a jar of "against blood."

In 1944, Julia is posted to Sri Lanka (then Ceylon), where she meets her future husband, Paul Child, also an OSS employee. Julie is portrayed as always eating out of cans, while Paul introduces her to more sophisticated cuisine. Eventually the couple moves to Paris, and Julia graduates from the Cordon Bleu cooking school. The rest of her life is glossed over in this lackluster outing, with too much credit given to Paul for making Julia who she later became.

Julia Child received many awards throughout her lifetime, including a Peabody Award (1964), three Emmy Awards, and the National Book Award (1980). In 2003, President George W. Bush conferred upon her the Presidential Medal of Freedom, the highest civilian award in the United States: "Before Julia Child came along, no one imagined it could be so interesting to watch a meal being prepared. The reason, of course, is Julia, herself—her friendly way, her engaging conversation and her eagerness to teach. American cuisine and American culture have been enriched for decades by the unmistakable voice and the presence of Julia Child."

Christie, Agatha (1890–1976)

Author

Portrayed by: Olivia Williams, Bonnie Wright, Anna Massey, Fenella Woolgar, Kirsten Dunst, Ruth Bradley

Agatha Christie is the best-selling novelist of all time. Her 66 detective novels, especially those featuring her beloved albeit idiosyncratic sleuths Hercule Poirot and Miss Jane Marple, have made her famous the world over. Myriad film and television productions have adapted her works, such as *And Then There Were None* and *Murder on the Orient Express*, making her name synonymous with the word "mystery" even to those who have never read her books.

Televised depictions of her life have tended to focus on a real-life mystery, Christie's strange disappearance in 1926. The author had argued with her husband, Archibald Christie, who had asked for a divorce to marry a woman named Nancy Neele. The British police mounted a highly publicized nationwide search, and even authors Sir Arthur Conan Doyle and Dorothy L. Sayers became involved in the frenzy. Christie surfaced 10 days later at a hotel in Harrogate, Yorkshire, registered under the name Mrs.

Neele (the name of her husband's lover). She never spoke publicly about the incident at the time or in later years.

Drunk History sticks broadly (with a capital B) to the known facts of Christie's disappearance in "Drunk Mystery" (2018), with Kirsten Dunst as Agatha. After her husband's callous request for a divorce, the author, who may or may not be suffering from a nervous breakdown, turns up at the spa hotel in Harrogate. Once she's found, policemen and a chambermaid voice competing theories about her disappearance, echoing actual public conjecture at the time, that the disappearance was a publicity stunt, or a revenge ploy against her husband, or a misadventure induced by amnesia after a car crash.

Agatha and the Truth of Murder, a British TV movie also produced in 2018, goes further afield than *Drunk History* (hard to believe), into the realm of alternate history, in fact, to explain Christie's infamous disappearance. Ruth Bradley portrays Christie in this telling, whose disappearance occurs during her investigation into the murder of Florence Nightingale Shore (Stacha Hicks), the goddaughter of Florence Nightingale.

Moving from far afield to out of this world was the explanation offered in the *Doctor Who* episode "The Unicorn and the Wasp" (2008). Here Agatha (Fenella Woolgar) drops out of sight due to exposure to an alien wasp called a Vespiform, an encounter which leaves her with a temporary case of amnesia. The doctor (David Tennant) drops Christie off at the Harrogate hotel, and, with that circumstance for an explanation, it's little wonder that she never spoke of the incident again.

A more substantial portrait of Christie had emerged in the earlier production *Agatha Christie: A Life in Pictures* (TV movie, 2004), although the touchstone was still the '26 disappearance. Olivia Williams portrays Christie in the days after the incident, undergoing psychiatric care (and possible hypnosis) to fill in the gaps of her memory. But the film also offers a second vantage point via an older Christie (Anna Massey), who looks back on her life when she is interviewed in 1962 on the 10th anniversary of her long-running play *The Mousetrap*. Bonnie Wright fills out the portrait as young Agatha, who is seen in hazy flashbacks.

Whether or not Christie's disappearance was intentional, it seems fitting that she left us a mystery that evokes speculation to this day.

Cixi (1835–1908)
Empress Dowager of China
Portrayed by: Beulah Quo

Empress Dowager Cixi (alternately Romanized Tz'u-hsi) was one of the most powerful women in the history of China, controlling the government for 47 years, from 1861 until her death in 1908. Rising from a low-ranking concubine of the Xianfeng Emperor, she gave birth to his only son, Zaichun, in 1856, becoming Empress Dowager and Regent after the emperor's death in 1861. It wasn't an easy ascent to the top, as power struggles had ensued after the emperor's death, but Cixi went to work, ousting a group of regents appointed by Xianfeng. She ultimately assumed the regency herself, which she shared with Empress Dowager Ci'an, a higher ranking consort. Cixi's ruling troubles weren't over, however, because her son, the Tongzhi Emperor, died in 1875, but she hatched a successful plan to install her nephew as emperor and retained the regency.

Beulah Quo stars as Empress Dowager Tz'u-hsi (Cixi) in *Meeting of Minds*, a "talk show" for historical figures, hosted by Steve Allen. In "Frederick Douglass, Tz'u-hsi, Cesare Beccaria, Marquis de Sade" (parts one and two, 1978), Tz'u-hsi takes Allen to school repeatedly, as he misunderstands much about her history and culture. When Allen talks about her low status as a concubine, she explains that such women were upper class in Chinese society, and more like American debutantes. When she notes that the emperor had not wanted her to ascend to the imperial throne because of her gender, Allen says, "how terrible." She retorts, "Don't talk like an idiot. In your country at that time, women couldn't even vote. Even today is there any likelihood that you would elect a woman president?"

Tz'u-hsi is also combative with famous abolitionist Frederick Douglass (Roscoe Lee Browne), questioning his right to contradict her. Douglass politely, but forcefully, explains, "Here I have every such right, for it is merely a matter of speaking the truth, which can be addressed as properly to the highly placed as the low." It would be hard to call this entry "a meeting of minds," but culture clashes can be revelatory too.

The reign of Empress Dowager Cixi was long, and its history through troubled times for an evolving China was intricate. Assessments of Cixi have evolved too, depending upon the shifting winds of culture, politics, and society. Was she a corrupt despot or a conscientious ruler? A "she dragon" or a powerful woman maligned for being a powerful woman? Or was she all of the above?

Cleopatra (ca. 69 BCE–30 BCE)

Queen of Egypt
Portrayed by: Elizabeth Thompson, Andrea Marcovicci, Danielle Nicholas, Gina Torres, Josephine Davis, Jayne Meadows, Janet Suzman, Jane Lapotaire, Lynn Redgrave, Leonor Varela, Ann Morgan Guilbert

Like Queen Victoria of England, Cleopatra VII of Egypt is a go-to historical figure for TV creatives. Cleo can slide into comedies, dramas, and fantasies at the drop of a hat, not bad for a woman born over 2000 years ago. With her trademark heavy eyeliner, braided wigs, and killer jewelry, Cleopatra is iconic—imagine her reach, if she were alive and tweeting today.

There was much more to the real Cleopatra than her looks, of course, but some televised presentations preferred to stick with superficial Cleo. In "Samantha's Caesar Salad," a 1969 episode of *Bewitched*, Elizabeth Thompson portrays a scantily clad Cleo, who pops into the 1960s to lure Caesar (Jay Robinson) back to the past, when an inept magical spell traps him in the present. Cleopatra (Andrea Marcovicci) goes time-traveling again in *Voyagers!* ("Cleo and the Babe," 1982), this time to 1929 New York, where she suddenly speaks English and works with Lucky Luciano to kidnap Babe Ruth. (Don't ask.) Cleo (Danielle Nicholas) drops by briefly in another fantasy series, *Relic Hunter*, during a flashback about her lost necklace and the reincarnation of one of her handmaidens in "Out of the Past" (2001).

The queen's two appearances in yet another fantasy series, *Xena: Warrior Princess*, highlight the controversial topic of Cleopatra's race. Both scholars and fans have debated the subject, with some proposing that Cleopatra was of African ancestry. In "The King of Assassins," a 1997 tale of the attempted murder of Cleopatra (Gina Torres), the Egyptian queen is indeed black. In the later episode "Antony & Cleopatra" (2000), a white actress, Josephine Davis, portrays the queen, whose assassination is successful this time. Series hero Xena (Lucy Lawless) impersonates Cleopatra, and it is Xena as Cleo who has the love affair with Marc Antony. (Historians, take note of the deception.) While these depictions leave the race issue unresolved, the scholarly consensus is that Cleopatra had no African blood and was predominantly Macedonian Greek, as a descendant of Ptolemy I Soter, the founder of the dynasty that ruled Egypt for 275 years.

Leaving the realm of fantasy behind (sort of), Cleopatra (Jayne Meadows) becomes more the woman of substance in *Meeting of Minds*, an innovative PBS series hosted by Steve Allen, who "interviews" historical figures in a talk-show format. In "Queen Cleopatra, Theodore Roosevelt, Thomas Aquinas, Thomas Paine" (parts one and two, 1977), we learn about the real woman behind the makeup. Some of the presentation is didactic, as Cleopatra describes her history and role in Egyptian life at the time. "I was treated not only as a queen, but literally as a goddess."

She shrugs off her marriage to her brother, saying, "husband, brother, whatever," a confirmation that sibling marriage was nothing unusual for the Ptolemies. The queen speaks of her relationships with Julius Caesar and Mark Antony, saying she shared the dream of a world empire with Caesar and "wept for hours" at the loss of Antony. Meadows is impressive as she reels off fact after fact, and riveting as she shares the final tragedies of Cleopatra's life.

The story of Cleopatra is one of power won, lost, won and lost again, as political alliances brought lovers who came and went, sometimes into the great beyond. Her relationship with Roman general and politician Mark Antony, later her spouse, ultimately led to the end of Ptolemaic rule in Egypt and both their suicides. Comprising so much history and tragedy, Cleopatra's romantic/political entanglements have received lots of dramatic attention, not the least of which from the bard himself in *Antony and Cleopatra* (1607). Not surprisingly, televised versions of Shakespeare's play emerged in the modern era, including the Royal Shakespeare Company's 1974 production, with Janet Suzman as the queen of "infinite variety," and the BBC's 1981 entry, starring Jane Lapotaire as Cleopatra. A 1984 version was surprisingly obscure, given the star-wattage of its cast, with Lynn Redgrave and Timothy Dalton as the ill-fated lovers, and *Star Trek* alums Nichelle Nichols and Walter Koenig in supporting roles.

The sheer sweep of Cleopatra's story (not to mention the lure of sweeps period) made the miniseries format a natural choice for *Cleopatra*, a May 1999 adaptation of Margaret George's novel *The Memoirs of Cleopatra* (1997). Leonor Varela stars as the title character in the two-part series, with Timothy Dalton again in Cleo's thrall, this time as Julius

Thomas Paine (Joseph Sirola) and Cleopatra (Jayne Meadows) sit down for a chat on *Meeting of Minds* (PBS).

Caesar, while Billy Zane takes the Antony role. The story begins as Cleopatra is fighting with her siblings, no petty squabble, as nothing less than the throne of Egypt is at stake. Cleo enlists the help of Caesar, and their alliance leads to a temporary victory for Cleopatra, a son for both of them, and Roman entanglement in Egyptian affairs, from which much tragedy will ensue. A lavish production, with lots of different acting styles—not necessarily a good thing.

There are more televised Cleopatras, seemingly one for every taste. The queen even makes an appearance in suburban New Rochelle via a play-within-a-play on *The Dick Van Dyke Show*. In "Somebody Has to Play Cleopatra" (1962), Ann Morgan Guilbert is a hoot as housewife Millie Helper, who rehearses the part of Cleopatra by channeling Mae West. (Or is it Wallace Beery?) When she says, "Mark Antony Pray Tell, how are things in Rome," director Rob Petrie (Dick Van Dyke) has to explain that "Pray Tell" is not part of his name.

Yes, "infinite variety."

Cleveland, Frances (1864-1947)

First Lady
Portrayed by: Alia Shawkat

Frances Cleveland was a woman of firsts, a first lady of the United States, to be sure, as the wife of President Grover Cleveland (1886-89, 1893-97), but also the youngest first lady in the nation's history at just 21 years of age, and the only wife of a president to marry and give birth in the White House. President Cleveland believed that "a woman should not bother her head about political parties and public questions." Frances, known as "Frank," stayed out of his business, but found some public business of her own, especially when it came to supporting women's causes. She hosted receptions on Saturday mornings for working-class women, who were unable to visit the White House during the week.

She was a strong believer in higher education for women, accepting a position on the board of trustees for her alma mater, Wells College, and helping to found the University Women's Club. Frances also supported The Washington Home for Friendless Colored Girls, helping to raise funds for the purchase of an orphanage. Despite Mrs. Cleveland's many efforts to promote the interests of women during her lifetime, she did not think women should have the vote, a belief she held strongly enough to accept the vice presidency of the New Jersey Association Opposed to Woman's Suffrage in 1913.

Alia Shawkat portrays Frances Cleveland in the *Drunk History* episode "First Ladies" (2014). The vignette describes, with some embellishment, the president's courtship of Frances and her rivalry with her mother, Emma Folsom (Paget Brewster), for Grover's affections. Fictional Emma, in a jealous snit, ships Frances off to Europe to get her out of the way, while historical Emma actually accompanied her daughter to the continent so the first-lady-to-be could learn about aristocratic customs and protocol.

When Frances returns from her year abroad, the nation becomes enthralled with the young woman who marries the president in the White House. Narrator Molly McAleer explains how Frances then becomes an "it girl," whose image appears, without her permission, on all manner of products, from cleansers to pillboxes, and in similarly varied advertisements. The first lady chooses to ignore this exploitation, focusing instead on work that elevates her fellow women.

Not done with her firsts, Frances Cleveland lived longer than any other first lady after leaving that position, another 51 years. Widowed at the age of 44 when her 71-year-old husband died, Cleveland married archaeologist Thomas Jex Preston in 1913, becoming the first presidential widow to remarry.

Frances Cleveland was indeed a woman of firsts.

Coleman, Bessie (1892–1926)

Aviator
Portrayed by: Samira Wiley

Drunk History saluted Bessie Coleman in its 2019 episode "Trailblazers," and the title was apt. Some women are trailblazers to their core, and Bessie Coleman was one of them, breaking barriers for African Americans, Native Americans, and women during the early 1920s. Coleman, sometimes called "Queen Bess," was the first African-American woman and first Native American to hold a pilot's license. When her attempts to become an aviator had stalled in the United States due to racial and gender discrimination, Bessie departed America for flight school in France. On June 15, 1921, she became the first American woman to obtain an international pilot's license.

Drunk History tells us what happened next, as Bessie (Samira Wiley) returns to the United States, but finds opportunities as a commercial pilot closed to her. It's back to France again, this time for training as a stunt pilot, and Bessie excels, even as the dangers of the occupation become abundantly clear. Coleman finally finds work at home, performing "barnstorming" tricks at airshows, where she gains immense popularity. Queen Bess insists that her performances be open to blacks as well as whites, as she isn't much for those who like to drink "haterade," in the parlance of narrator Lyric Lewis.

Alas, Bessie's aviation skills were ultimately no match for a faulty aircraft, and she died during a training exercise. Lewis says, "She died doing what she loved. She died doing what she believed in." But Lewis notes that Coleman's story didn't end there, as Queen Bess went on to inspire black aviators for decades, including Mae Jemison (Aasha Davis), the first African American woman in space, who brings a photo of Bessie with her onto the space shuttle in 1992. And, since this is *Drunk History*, the photo talks back to her, with Coleman offering some sassy advice for the astronaut.

The real Mae Jemison, an inspiration in her own right, gets the final word. "...I point to Bessie Coleman and say here is a woman, a being, who exemplifies and serves as a model for all humanity, the very definition of strength, dignity, courage, integrity, and beauty."

Colvin, Claudette (1939–)

See (mentioned in): **Parks, Rosa (1913–2005)**

Coolbrith, Ina (1841–1928)

Poet, Librarian
Portrayed by: June Lockhart

Known as the "Sweet Singer of California," Ina Coolbrith became California's first poet laureate, but she contributed more than just poetry to the cultural world of the late 18th century. Her literary salons in San Francisco brought together authors and publishers, helping to promote new talent, especially poet Cincinnatus Hiner Miller, who became Joaquin Miller, right down to his mountain-man makeover, at Coolbrith's suggestion.

Since writing poetry is rarely a lucrative career, and with increasing obligations to shelter and support relatives, Coolbrith accepted the position of librarian for the Oakland Library Association, which later became the Oakland Free Library. While the long hours of work diminished her poetry output, Coolbrith managed to extend her cultural impact into the next generation, mentoring a young Jack London, who later called Coolbrith his "literary mother."

At the library, Coolbrith supervised the reading of another young patron, Isadora Duncan, and that relationship is the inspiration for the *Death Valley Days* episode "The Magic Locket" (1965). June Lockhart portrays poet and librarian Coolbrith, who takes a scruffy, but brilliant 12-year-old girl named "Dorita" (Kathy Garver) under her wing, bringing her to the ballet and later introducing her at a literary salon. Woman and girl discuss literature and dance, even disagreeing about the place of discipline in art. A framing device reveals that Dorita, once the poor child who sold mittens and dance lessons, went on to become famed dancer Isadora Duncan. Coolbrith takes no credit for Duncan's or London's or Miller's genius, saying she just opened "a few doors that perhaps they might not have had time to notice otherwise."

The episode, while a little saccharine for current tastes, meets other modern standards, such as passing the Bechdel test, surprising for an episode of a '60s western series. While not Coolbrith's complete story, it is a fitting introduction to her life.

Crabtree, Lotta (1847–1924)
Actress
Portrayed by: Sharon Baird, Gloria Jean, Yvonne De Carlo, Sally Kellerman

Lotta Crabtree, known as "The Nation's Darling" during the 19th century, gives her name to a 1954 episode of *Death Valley Days*, which tells her life story in less than 30 minutes, several song and dance numbers included. In this (mostly) accurate account, Lotta (Sharon Baird) and her mother, Mary Ann (Kay Stewart), arrive in California from New York, as the teleplay begins. Lotta, a precocious and talented child, learns how to dance under the tutelage of singer and actress Lola Montez (Yvonne Cross). Soon little Lotta is performing at taverns and mining camps, where she is showered with gold coins, which her mother later sweeps up from the stage.

As Lotta, now portrayed by Gloria Jean, grows to young womanhood, mother Mary Ann guards her "like a dragon," in the words of narrator "The Old Ranger" (Stanley Andrews), leaving Lotta few opportunities for romance. At Mary Ann's behest, Lotta leaves the mining camps for San Francisco and later New York, taking the East Coast by storm, with her winning performances in plays. Eventually the actress, who remains unmarried, amasses a fortune, which she gives to charitable causes. Her bronze fountain, donated to the city of San Francisco, still survives today, The Old Ranger tells us, one of the few monuments to survive the 1906 earthquake.

Lotta makes two appearances in the long-running series *Bonanza*, neither of which are much concerned with historical accuracy. In "A Rose for Lotta" (1959), Yvonne De Carlo, looking breathtakingly beautiful, portrays Crabtree, who involves herself in a scheme with mining honchos to hold "Little Joe" Cartwright (Michael Landon) for ransom in return for timber rights. In "A Return Engagement" (1970), Lotta, now blonde and portrayed by Sally Kellerman, returns to Virginia City, where she had once appeared as a child, the adult Lotta of the 1959 episode thereby erased.

Here the story involves jealousy, murder, and gold stashed in Lotta's trunk. Mary Ann Crabtree, a constant presence in historical Lotta's life as mother and manager, doesn't appear in either installment, watchful guardians unwelcome in freewheeling plots.

"La Petite Lotta" retired at the height of her success in 1891, reputedly the richest actress in America and certainly one of the most beloved. When she died in 1924, she left an estate of $4 million (over $60 million with inflation today) in a charitable trust for disabled World War I veterans, "destitute thespians," animals, and agricultural college graduates from a school that became the University of Massachusetts at Amherst. In death, as in life, where she had enjoyed the occasional good cigar, Lotta Crabtree was an American original.

Crawford, Joan (ca. 1904–1977)

See (mentioned in): **Ball, Lucille (1911–1989)**

Curie, Marie (1867–1934)

Physicist, Chemist
Portrayed by: Kate Trotter, Kim Bubbs, Edie McClurg, Pamela Dillman, Klára Issová, Jane Lapotaire

It's hard to overestimate the importance of the life and work of Marie Curie, born Maria Salomea Skłodowska in Poland, then part of the Russian Empire. Curie was a pioneer, not only in science, but also in medicine and education, her accomplishments all the more remarkable because of the impediments she faced for simply being female during the era. She fought to receive an education equal to her intellect at a time when women were barred from pursuing higher education, eventually enrolling in an underground educational institution, the Flying University, in Warsaw. Later moving to Paris, "Marie" studied physics, chemistry, and mathematics at the University of Paris, accepting an offer of laboratory space from Pierre Curie, who would become her husband in 1895.

The two became partners in love and life, but it was their professional pairing that changed the world, beginning with the discovery of polonium, named by Marie in honor of her native land, and radium in 1898. Their research, based on Marie's original idea, earned them the Nobel Prize for Physics in 1903, shared with Henri Becquerel, who had discovered a new phenomenon which Marie had named "radioactivity." After her husband's death in 1906, Curie went on to win a second Nobel Prize in 1911, this time for Chemistry, and on her own.

For all her time spent in a laboratory, Marie Curie never forgot the outside world. During World War I, she used her knowledge and resources to develop mobile radiography units or "petites Curies," which surgeons used near the front lines to assess battlefield injuries. Curie's war-time contributions are the focus of two programs, broadcast 20 years apart, and with different audiences in mind, but each with a reverence for the formidable pathfinder. *Marie Curie: More Than Meets the Eye* (1997) tells the story of two young sisters (Natalie Vansier and Colleen Rennison) in World War I Paris, who believe that Marie Curie (Kate Trotter) is a German spy, but learn their mistake when one witnesses Curie on the battlefield with her x-ray invention.

Timeless finds Curie (Kim Bubbs) on the World War I frontlines again in "The War to End All Wars" (2018), a story about mothers and daughters, in which historian Lucy Preston (Abigail Spencer) and her mother Carol (Susanna Thompson) battle over conflicting time travel outcomes. The Preston women pull Marie Curie and her daughter Irene (Melissa Farman) away from the battlefield and into a quieter, but more momentous war, where the fate of history literally hangs in the balance.

It turns out that fictional Marie had an affinity for time-traveling adventures, reverent or otherwise. In *A.J.'s Time Travelers*, a noisy and frenetic children's fantasy series, young time-traveler A.J. Malloy (John Patrick White) visits Marie Curie (Edie McClurg) in 1905 Paris, and learns an important lesson about working mothers in "Marie Curie" (1995). A few years later, Madame Curie (Pamela Dillman) turns the tables, doing the time-traveling herself in "Aging, Not so Gracefully," a 1999 episode of *Sabrina, the Teenage Witch*. In this silly, but cute outing of the fantasy sitcom, Curie comes through a magic clock, arriving in modern-day Massachusetts after a breakup with husband Pierre (Alastair Duncan). Marie, who was attracted to Pierre because "he had a laboratory and no debts," is clumsy and obsessed with work, but witches Hilda and Zelda Spellman (Caroline Rhea and Beth Broderick) work to rekindle the lost chemistry between the famous scientists.

Marie is a part of someone else's story once again, this time Albert Einstein's, in "Einstein," chapters Four and Five, of *Genius* (2017). In these two episodes, Curie (Klára Issová) and young Einstein (Johnny Flynn) are depicted as friends who both faced discrimination and skepticism within the scientific community.

Curie has received the star treatment on scripted television only once, in the five-part miniseries *Marie Curie* (1977), produced by the BBC and shown in the United States on public television. Jane Lapotaire stars as Marie in this complex portrait, based on the biography by Robert Reid, which begins in 1886 when "Maria" works as a governess in Poland, and ends with her death in 1934. Nigel Hawthorne co-stars as Pierre Curie in the production, which won the BAFTA TV award for Best Drama Series/Serial in 1978.

Marie Curie was a woman of firsts—the first woman to win a Nobel Prize, the first person to win two Nobel Prizes, and the first woman to become a professor at the University of Paris. Despite her profound accomplishments, Madame Curie sought no fortune and never allowed fame to distract her from the advancement of science. Albert Einstein once said, "Marie Curie is, of all celebrated beings, the only one whom fame has not corrupted."

Like her discoveries, Marie Curie was elemental.

Cushman, Pauline (1833–1893)

Actress, Union Spy
Portrayed by: Phyllis Thaxter, Paula Raymond

Born in New Orleans and raised in Michigan, Harriet Wood changed her name to Pauline Cushman when she embarked upon an acting career. Her professional path would take a strange turn when she became a spy for the Union during the American Civil War. Cushman used her position and acting skills to court Southern sympathizers and rebel military men, eventually spying for the Army of the Cumberland in Nashville. While carrying Confederate battle plans in her boots, Cushman was captured and sentenced to death by hanging. A sudden illness delayed her execution, leaving Cushman very much alive when the Union Army invaded Shelbyville, scattering her Confederate captors. For her service and sacrifice, President Lincoln accorded her the honorary rank of Major, whereupon "Miss Major Cushman," dressed in a military uniform, toured the United States, giving lectures about her clandestine operations.

Cushman moved west to re-establish her acting career after interest in her wartime exploits waned. The TV western *Rawhide* finds her en route to Denver in "The Blue Spy" (1961), when Cushman (Phyllis Thaxter) encounters some cattle drovers who are delighted to have an actress in their midst, one willing to perform impromptu plays and readings in their campfire theater. The feelings of these mostly southern boys change, however, when they learn Cushman's identity as a former Union spy, and some of the men decide they should leave her behind to die on the range, while others, especially trail boss Gil Favor (Eric Fleming), disagree. A battle of wills ensues, revealing the price Cushman has paid for her war work, which was always more than just an exhilarating spy story.

Death Valley Days went in the opposite direction from serious consideration, finding questionable humor in Cushman's later love life. "The Wooing of Perilous Pauline" (1964) purports to tell the story of Cushman's courtship with her third husband, Jere Fryer, in Casa Grande, Arizona Territory, but takes an over-the-top "Taming of the Shrew" approach to her independent lifestyle. Here Cushman (Paula Raymond) runs a saloon and uses a bullwhip when men step out of line. She breaks a bowl over the head of Fryer (Ray Danton), when he first asks for a dinner date. Entranced by her beauty, if not her manners, Fryer makes a bet to marry Cushman within a week, and succeeds in winning her heart by insulting her, dropping her on the ground, and starving her into submission on the trail. The teleplay ends when Cushman learns of the bet after she's married, and cracks her handy bullwhip as newlywed Mr. Fryer flees their wedding reception.

Ms. Cushman deserves a better TV epitaph.

Pauline Cushman in uniform, 1865 (Library of Congress).

Dandridge, Dorothy (1922–1965)

Actress, Singer
Portrayed by: Halle Berry

Dorothy Dandridge was no stranger to firsts. She became the first black woman to be featured on a cover of *Life* magazine. She was the first black woman to be nominated for an Academy Award for best actress. Her road to that heady period of fame had its starting point during her childhood, when Dorothy and her sister Vivian had appeared as The Wonder Children, a song-and-dance act which toured the southern United States.

Dorothy embarked upon a solo film career in 1940, receiving her first credit in *Four Shall Die*. She also appeared in "soundies," precursors of music videos which were shown on video jukeboxes called "Panorams." Her first starring role came in *Bright Road* (1953), after which she won the title role in *Carmen Jones* (1954), her Oscar-nominated performance.

Introducing Dorothy Dandridge (TV movie,1999) catalogs the star's professional successes, while not shrinking away from her personal sorrows. Halle Berry stars as Dandridge, who must endure unspeakable abuse from her mother's live-in lover, "Auntie" (LaTanya Richardson), because Dorothy has returned home late from a date with Harold Nicholas (Obba Babatunde). Dandridge later seeks happiness in marriage to Harold, but tragedy follows when their only child, Lynn (Alexis Carrington), experiences serious developmental problems, which leave her unable to speak or even recognize her mother.

While Dorothy continues to bear the scars of her personal misfortunes, including a subsequent divorce from Harold, her career appears to flourish, but some doors still remained closed to a black woman. In a must-watch sequence set at a Las Vegas hotel where Dandridge is appearing, she is warned not to use the swimming pool because it would have to be drained if a black person set foot in it. After visiting her room, she returns in a bathing suit to dip her toe in the water. She later sees that her act of defiance has led to unexpected consequences, as three black workers must scrub the entire drained pool.

Based on the biography *Dorothy Dandridge* by Earl Mills, the film garnered a bevy of awards, including an Emmy, a Golden Globe, and an NAACP Image Award for Halle Berry's luminous performance. The movie concludes with Dorothy's death from a prescription drug overdose at the age of 42, leaving open the question of whether the overdose was accidental or intentional. The historical evidence about her demise is also ambiguous, but the picture of her life is clearer. Dorothy once said, "If it is possible for a human being to be like a haunted house, maybe that would be me."

de' Medici, Catherine (1519–1589)

Queen of France
Portrayed by: Joan Young, Megan Follows

Catherine de' Medici was a towering figure in the history of 16th-century Europe. Born in Italy to a prominent family, Catherine married Henry, heir to the French throne, when she was 14 years old, a marriage arranged by her uncle Pope Clement VII. While she became queen in 1547 upon her husband's accession to the crown as Henry II, her real power emerged after Henry's death, when she was named Regent for her

10-year-old son King Charles IX in 1560. Catherine's biggest challenge arose from conflicts between Catholics and Huguenots (Protestants), leading to the French Wars of Religion, which lasted beyond her lifetime. A particular blight on her record is the Massacre of Saint Bartholomew's Day, when thousands of Huguenots were slaughtered, although historians have disagreed as to whether Catherine authorized the massacre.

A 16th-century religious civil war might seem like an unlikely subject for a science fiction show, but it is just that in "The Massacre of St Bartholomew's Eve," a 1966 episode of *Doctor Who*. In this four-part serial, time traveler Doctor Who (William Hartnell) arrives in 1572 France, where he and his companion Steven (Peter Purves) become embroiled in the events leading up to the St. Bartholomew's Day massacre. Steven becomes associated with the Huguenots, a dangerous connection at that time, especially when Queen Mother Catherine (Joan Young) and the Marshall of France, Tavannes (André Morell), hatch a plot to assassinate a Huguenot leader. In a grand coincidence, Catherine's conspiracy involves the Abbot of Amboise (Hartnell in a dual role), who just happens to be a doppelgänger for Doctor Who. When her plan fails, Catherine does indeed authorize the massacre of the Huguenots within the city, shocking even the ruthless Tavannes, who says, "At dawn tomorrow this city will weep tears of blood."

Reign finds Catherine (Megan Follows) in pre-massacre times, while her husband Henry II (Alan van Sprang) is alive, at least at the start. The show's protagonist is Mary, Queen of Scots (Adelaide Kane), who marries Catherine's son, Crown Prince Francis (Toby Regbo), but Catherine is ever present, especially as Mary's mother-in-law in the first two seasons before Francis dies. Catherine has lots of choice observations for her daughter-in-law, saying things like, "Mary, sweet Mary, I don't *attempt* to do anything. I do it." And, "I don't carry poison everywhere. I might accidentally kill myself." (Practical advice.) If you like your history with heavy doses of camp and light doses of facts, then *Reign* delivers a Catherine de Medici for your tastes.

Deno, Lottie (1844–1934)

Gambler
Portrayed by: Lisa Gaye

Born Carlotta Thompkins in 1844 Kentucky, Lottie Deno gained fame as a gambler in Texas, eventually settling in Fort Griffin. Lottie Deno wasn't Carlotta's only alias, but she liked it best, allegedly shortening it from "Lotta Dinero," as in lots of money, and she used it for most of her life. Deno was an expert card player, reportedly besting renowned gambler Doc Holliday.

Lottie is said to have inspired the character of Miss Kitty Russell (Amanda Blake), owner of Dodge City's Long Branch Saloon, on the long-running series *Gunsmoke* (1955–1975), but similarities between the two are few. More on the mark, but still highly fictionalized, is "Lottie's Legacy," a 1968 episode of *Death Valley Days*. Lisa Gaye stars as Deno, who uses another of real-life Lottie's aliases, "Mystic Maude," as the story opens. Events quickly veer from the historical path, however, when Lottie's preacher beau, Peter Green (John Clarke), is introduced. Green, who is building a church in Willow Falls, believes his fiancée, Lottie, is a "schoolmarm" rather than a professional gambler. When Green travels to Fort Griffin, Lottie's lie is revealed, and he leaves town in a huff. Narrator Robert Taylor tells us that Lottie later gave Peter enough money to build his church, her "legacy" of the title, after which she was never heard from again.

Historical Lottie was definitely heard from again, and even helped build a church, St. Luke's Episcopal Church in Deming, New Mexico. At this point Lottie had married her on-again, off-again lover, Frank Thurmond, and settled down to a respectable life of bridge-playing with the society ladies of Deming.

Lottie was buried next to her husband. The monument reads, "Charlotte Thurmond," Lottie's need for aliases gone and her name etched in stone at last.

Dickinson, Emily (1830–1886)

Poet
Portrayed by: Katherine Helmond, Julie Harris

Emily Dickinson was one of the leading American poets of the 19th century. She led a reclusive life in Massachusetts, and only 10 of her almost 1800 poems were published during her lifetime, most without her permission. Although Dickinson's poetry was not available to the general public of the time, she sent many poems to friends during a lifetime of prolific correspondence.

Dickinson (Katherine Helmond) explains her feelings about publication in the *Meeting of Minds* episode "Emily Dickinson, Attila the Hun, Charles Darwin, Galileo" (parts one and two, 1977). When Charles Darwin (Murray Matheson) asks her why so few of her poems were published during her lifetime, the Belle of Amherst replies, "I did not write them for publication, Dr. Darwin. I wrote them to express my moods, my emotions, and to amuse those I loved." Had she no desire for fame? "I felt I had the right to live and die in obscurity, though I was aware that my view was a solitary one."

While Dickinson's home was her universe, there are hints she may have fallen in love, at least from afar. She appears to have experienced a romantic disappointment, and fictional Emily refuses to discuss it when *Meeting of Minds* host Steve Allen asks her about it. "I do not wish to discuss my personal life, Mr. Allen." She feels the only focus of the discussion should be her poetry, which she recites liberally throughout the broadcast. When Allen persists, Dickinson raises her voice above the volume of her usually breathless intonations, saying, "Now will you please ask me less personal questions." Emily isn't telling, and scholars have disagreed as to the identity of her love interest. Between 1858 and 1861, Dickinson wrote three letters to someone she calls "Master," begging him (or her) to "open your life wide, and take me in."

A different Emily Dickinson emerges in *The Belle of Amherst*, a one-woman play performed live and taped for broadcast by PBS in 1976. Julie Harris portrays the title character, who is lively, humorous, and bright, while offering observations on her life and those she has met. In so doing, she takes on the personas of 14 other people, a display of exuberance that is a far cry from the reticence of Helmond's Dickinson. Harris's performance is a tour de force, and she won a 1977 Tony Award for Best Actress in a Play.

While fame is elusive for most, it was obscurity that proved elusive for Emily Dickinson. In 1858, she began to make copies of her poems on quality stationery, sewing the sheets together into small booklets. She left no instructions for the disposition of these manuscripts after her death, so it's hard to know whether she desired or anticipated their publication. Emily's sister Lavinia thought Dickinson's poetry should be made public, and *Poems by Emily Dickinson* appeared in 1890. Her poetry, though, was atypical of her era, with its short lines, slant rhymes, and unconventional punctuation and capitalization, leaving her genius for later generations to appreciate.

> SUCCESS is counted sweetest
> By those who ne'er succeed.
> To comprehend a nectar
> Requires sorest need.

Didrikson, Babe
See: **Zaharias, Babe Didrikson (1911–1956)**

Douglas, Marjory Stoneman (1890–1998)
Author, Environmentalist
Portrayed by: Jayma Mays

In "National Parks," a 2019 episode of *Drunk History*, Tess Lynch narrates the story of Marjory Stoneman Douglas (Jayma Mays), the "mother of the Everglades." In this incongruous amalgam of deleted expletives, cartoon animals, and real emotion, Douglas works with Ernest Coe (Derek Waters) to establish the Florida Everglades as a national park beginning in the 1920s. Noting to Coe that "it's gonna be a long fought battle," the two work together over the decades, as Marjory researches and writes an influential book, *The Everglades: River of Grass*, published in 1947.

In later years, Douglas fights against the Nixon administration's plans to build an airport in the Everglades. A reflective Marjory notes her accomplishment at helping to establish the third largest national park in the country. After her death at 108, marked by a surprisingly touching tribute from an animated manatee, an ethereal Marjory speaks to the camera, saying, "Be a nuisance where it counts." Narrator Lynch, a bit misty-eyed, tells us that the students of Marjory Stoneman Douglas High School (site of a mass shooting in 2018) continue in Douglas's footsteps, turning their pain into action. "They are the pebble in the shoe."

The Everglades: River of Grass begins with the sentence, "There are no other Everglades in the world." Douglas's landmark book, which has never gone out of print, changed public perceptions of the Everglades, which had been viewed as dismal swamps rather than the vast and valuable ecosystem Douglas described in her book.

Bill Clinton awarded Marjory Stoneman Douglas with the Presidential Medal of Freedom, the country's highest civilian honor, in 1993, when Douglas was 103 years old. Clinton said, "And, Mrs. Douglas, the next time I hear someone mention the timeless wonders and powers of Mother Nature, I'll be thinking about you."

Duncan, Isadora (ca. 1877–1927)

Dancer
Portrayed by: Kathy Garver, Vivian Pickles

As the *Death Valley Days* episode "The Magic Locket" (1965) opens, a 12-year-old street urchin named "Dorita" (Kathy Garver), who sells mittens and dance lessons to other children, makes the acquaintance of Ina Coolbrith (June Lockhart), a cultured poet and librarian. Coolbrith becomes a friend and mentor to the girl, bringing Dorita to the ballet and introducing her at a literary salon. Even at her young age, Dorita expresses disdain for classical ballet, while communicating the rudiments of an artistic philosophy: "Dancing is art, and art should be formless and free like the wind." At the end of the episode, a framing device reveals that Dorita, Ms. Coolbrith's precocious protégée, went on to become world-renowned dancer Isadora Duncan, who never forgot Coolbrith's contribution to her development.

After the genteel poverty of her early years, as encapsulated in "The Magic Locket," Duncan took Europe by storm at the turn of the 20th century, dancing for patrons at private receptions, where she focused on natural movements rather than the strict forms of ballet. Soon she filled theaters and concert halls, where her free style of dance and skimpy Greek tunics captivated audiences, if not always professional critics. Duncan opened schools in Germany, Russia, and the United States to teach young women her philosophy of dance, while her love of freedom and iconoclasm also seeped into her private life, where she bore a daughter and son out of wedlock and embraced communism. Fate moved to add tragedy to Duncan's already dramatic life when both her children were drowned in a car accident in 1913. Her tragic relationship with automobiles continued and ultimately ended in 1927, when her flowing silk scarf became entangled in the wheels of a car in France, killing her.

Kathy Garver as young Isadora Duncan in "The Magic Locket" (*Death Valley Days*).

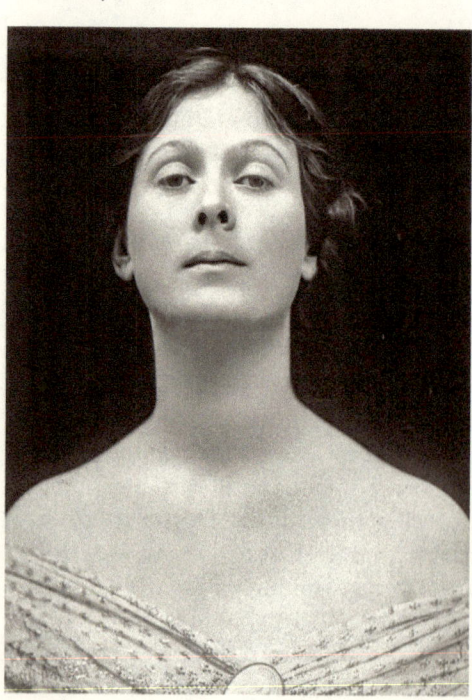

Portrait of Isadora Duncan, early 1900s (University of California).

Isadora Duncan, the Biggest Dancer in the World (TV movie, 1966), directed by Ken Russell for the BBC, views the outrageous life of Duncan (Vivian Pickles) through a 1960s pop prism. Sewell Stokes, who co-authored the script and had written a book on Duncan's last days, narrates the film, which races through her improbable life in a breathless 65 minutes. Duncan's obsession with the importance of art is on display in well-choreographed dance sequences, while her self-absorption and utter disdain for decorum are revealed in numerous shouting matches.

Called "the mother of dance" by some, Isadora Duncan's performances, innovations, and teaching helped to pave the way for the development and acceptance of modern dance. But she is also remembered for her tragic demise, giving her name to accidental strangulation by long scarf, a.k.a. "Isadora Duncan Syndrome." As Duncan's fame during her time was based on both her public and private lives, so her legacy reflects that dichotomy.

Earhart, Amelia (1897–?)

Aviator

Portrayed by: Sharon Lawrence, Susan Clark, Kim Diamond, Diane Keaton

Amelia Earhart was a celebrated aviator, a feminist icon, and an American original. The list of her aviation firsts is astounding, including not only records for female pilots, but records for ANY pilots. In 1932, five years after Charles Lindbergh's solo transatlantic flight, Earhart became the first woman to achieve the same feat, piloting a Lockheed Vega from Newfoundland to Northern Ireland. As a result of that historic event, Earhart became the first woman and the first civilian to receive the Distinguished Flying Cross for her "heroic courage and skill as a navigator, at the risk of her life." Unwilling to rest on her laurels, Earhart made history again in 1935, becoming the first aviator to fly solo from Hawaii to California, a distance longer than her storied transatlantic flight.

Alas, for all her records and accomplishments, Earhart is best known for the flight she did not complete, her attempted 1937 circumnavigation of the globe. Earhart, along with navigator Fred Noonan, departed Miami in a twin-engine Lockheed Electra on June 1, traveling 22,000 miles to reach New Guinea on June 29. They left for their next destination, Howland Island, on July 2, but encountered navigational problems and radioed that the plane was running out of fuel. After a final "questionable" transmission, Earhart, Noonan, and their plane disappeared over the Pacific Ocean. The United States Navy and Coast Guard undertook an extensive search for the pair until July 19, whereupon Earhart and Noonan were declared lost at sea.

The mystery of Earhart's disappearance generated many theories, including the claim that she had been captured or shot down by the Japanese. There wasn't much speculation about alien abduction, but the science fiction series *Star Trek: Voyager* went there in an episode entitled "The 37's" (1995). Sharon Lawrence portrays Earhart, who has been in cryo-stasis for 400 years, along with navigator Noonan (David Graf) and six others, all of whom have been whisked to a faraway planet by extraterrestrials. The crew of the starship *Voyager* discovers and defrosts (as it were) Earhart and the abductees from 1937. *Voyager's* commander, Captain Kathryn Janeway (Kate Mulgrew), recognizes Earhart immediately, later telling her, "Because of you, generations of women have become pilots."

It turns out that there is a human civilization on the planet, created by descendants of more Earth abductees, who had revolted against their alien captors and driven them away. Amelia and the 37s decide to stay with the humans on the planet rather than joining the crew on *Voyager*, which is about 75 years' travel from home. The enjoyable middle third of the episode, where Janeway expresses her respect and awe for Earhart, isn't enough to compensate for the final third, especially the poor decision to leave Earhart planet-bound. Earhart, as depicted here and in real life, was

A 1976 press photograph with the caption "look alikes" for Susan Clark (right) who depicts Amelia Earhart in *Amelia Earhart* (NBC).

an aviator, first, last, and always, and it's inconceivable that she would give up the opportunity to fly on a starship.

Two television biopics are less fanciful, keeping Ms. Earhart on terra firma, when she isn't flying, that is. *Amelia Earhart* (1976), stars Susan Clark as Earhart and covers her entire life, from farm girl, with Kim Diamond as young Amelia, to lost hero. Diane Keaton dons Earhart's signature leather jacket, to eerie effect given her physical resemblance to Earhart, in *Amelia Earhart: The Final Flight* (1994), which focuses on her life as an aviator until her disappearance. Both Clark and Keaton received Emmy Award nominations for their performances, while Keaton also picked up Golden Globe and Screen Actors Guild nominations.

Amelia Earhart was a woman of independence and courage, who inspired not only female aviators, but also other women who wished to break free from the traditional roles assigned to them. She kept her own name after marriage to George P. Putnam, and became an early supporter of the Equal Rights Amendment. Earhart also designed "active living" clothes, becoming a fashion icon with her pants and leather jackets, and wrote best-selling books about her flying experiences.

Secretary of State Hillary Clinton gave Earhart a fitting epitaph in 2012: "Her legacy resonates today for anyone, girls and boys, who dreams of the stars."

Elder, Kate
See: **Big Nose Kate (ca. 1850–1940)**

Elizabeth, Empress of Russia (1709–1762)
See (mentioned in): **Catherine the Great (1729–1796)**

Elizabeth I (1533–1603)
Queen of England
Portrayed by: Dorothy Black, Mildred Natwick, Judith Anderson, Glenda Jackson, Graham Chapman, Hattie Jacques, Miranda Richardson, Helen Mirren, Joanna Page, Angela Pleasence, Emma Thompson, et al.

Characters based on Elizabeth I have appeared in at least 50 different TV productions, making Elizabeth the queen of televised historical fiction as well as the most famous queen of England. It's not surprising, then, that she was present at the dawn of commercial television, portrayed by Dorothy Black in *The Dark Lady of the Sonnets*, a 1946 BBC production of the play by George Bernard Shaw. It took a few years, but Queen Elizabeth turned up on nascent American television as well, in *Mary of Scotland*, a

1951 entry in the *Pulitzer Prize Playhouse* anthology series, starring Mildred Natwick as the queen.

The life of Queen Elizabeth was not the focal point of those early productions, but Elizabeth gives her name and part of her story to *Elizabeth the Queen*, a 1968 production for the *Hallmark Hall of Fame*. Judith Anderson stars as the title character in this adaptation of Maxwell Anderson's play, which deals with her relationship with Robert Devereaux, Earl of Essex (Charlton Heston). The queen is eager for the attention of the younger man, Essex, but he has ambitions, which complicate their romance. History records that Essex attempted to raise a revolt against the queen in February 1601, leading to his execution for treason later the same month. As Shakespeare said, "The course of true love never did run smooth," and it was said of the real Elizabeth that "her delight is to sit in the dark, and sometimes with shedding tears to bewail Essex."

The gold standard in TV biographies of the queen is *Elizabeth R*, a six-part British miniseries from 1971. Glenda Jackson won two Best Actress Emmy Awards for her portrayal, double-dipping in the Drama Series and Movie/TV Special categories. The series begins in 1549, as battles for succession to the throne are waged by Elizabeth's half-brother, young Edward VI (Jason Kemp), and her half-sister Queen Mary I (Daphne Slater). Elizabeth herself ascends to the throne of England nine years later at the age of 25. Her Council advises her to marry quickly so she can produce an heir to the throne, but her personal feelings often clash with the needs of the country, especially when it comes to royal alliances and simmering religious disputes between Protestants and Catholics. The Earl of Sussex (John Shrapnel) tells her, "You must let the queen rule you in this, not the woman." Elizabeth's conflict between duty and desire is a continual theme throughout the miniseries.

As a counterpoint to this period pomp, British comedy series found humor in the life and depictions of Good Queen Bess. Graham Chapman portrayed a tall, and not unattractive, queen in a spoof of *Elizabeth R* called "Erizabeth L," a 1972 sketch from *Monty Python's Flying Circus*, where the queen's court attends her on motor-scooters and all the L's and R's in the script are swapped. Another title is corrupted in *Carry on Laughing*'s "Orgy and Bess" (1975), a riff on Gershwin's *Porgy and Bess*, wherein Elizabeth (Hattie Jacques) deals with the Spanish Armada and the romantic entanglements of Sir Francis Drake (Sidney James). Miranda Richardson had a continuing role as Elizabeth, called "Queenie," in the BBC comedy series *Blackadder II* (1986), and the subsequent specials *Blackadder's Christmas Carol* (1988) and *Blackadder: Back & Forth* (2000). Richardson's Queenie is immature, likes to yell, and gets her way by asking "Who's Queen?"

A 1972 press photograph of Glenda Jackson as Queen Elizabeth I in *Elizabeth R* (PBS).

Fun is fun, but much of Elizabeth's story, with its executions, war with Spain, and religious strife between Protestants and Catholics, is no laughing matter. Helen Mirren picked up an Emmy Award for her portrayal of the queen in the two-part drama *Elizabeth I* (2005). Politics complicate all of Elizabeth's relationships in this presentation, which covers the last 24 years of her reign. On the family end, her Catholic cousin, Mary, Queen of Scots (Barbara Flynn), may or may not be plotting Elizabeth's murder from a jail cell. As to romance, the "Virgin Queen's" quest for true love with men who work for her, but also crave power of their own, is an exercise in futility. The Earl of Leicester (Jeremy Irons) dies just when things are looking up both for England and his relationship with Elizabeth. Then his stepson, the Earl of Essex (Hugh Dancy), finds favor with Elizabeth, only later to find his head on the chopping block due to his own treachery.

If dramas or comedies are not your cup of Elizabethan tea, perhaps science fiction tales would be more to your liking. The first thing to know is that in the universe of *Doctor Who*, Queen Elizabeth did finally get married, not to one of her ministers, but to Doctor Who! In "The Day of the Doctor" (2013), the 50th anniversary special of the series, the Tenth Doctor (David Tennant) meets Elizabeth I (Joanna Page) during an attempted extraterrestrial invasion and marries her to foil the invaders' plans. (Very long story.) In "The Shakespeare Code" (2007), we find that the queen (Angela Pleasence) has ordered the execution of the Tenth Doctor, who is her sworn enemy. (It's complicated.) Tackling royal genealogies somehow seems less daunting than sorting through the time travel paradoxes of *Doctor Who*.

There are many more Elizabeths, such as the one portrayed by Emma Thompson in the *Upstart Crow* Christmas special "A Christmas Crow" (2017). Here an acting troupe plans a performance for the queen of "Eighth Night" by William Shakespeare (David Mitchell). Thompson is almost unrecognizable as "Liz," who bemoans the many problems she experienced as a youth, including being a "ginge" or redhead. While the comedy is broad here, Liz has a serious moment, one that brings us back to the theme that ran through Queen Elizabeth's entire life and the works about her. Upon reading one of Shakespeare's love poems, she says, "Such a love is not for me, for I am married to England, and though all the nation be my spouse, I am ever the loneliest person in the realm."

Fairfax, Sally (ca. 1730–1811)

See (mentioned in): **Washington, Martha (1731–1802)**

Fisher, Kate

See: **Big Nose Kate (ca. 1850–1940)**

Fitzgerald, Ella (1917–1996)
Singer
Portrayed by: Gabourey Sidibe

Called "The First Lady of Song," Ella Fitzgerald possessed an extraordinary voice, clear, flexible, and sweet. She first applied her talent to novelty songs, but later used her voice as a jazz instrument, gaining fame for her improvisational scat singing. After enduring a rough stretch in her teens and spending time in a reformatory, Ella literally escaped, eventually finding herself at the Apollo Theater's Amateur Night in 1934. The 17-year-old Ella had planned to dance, but she was intimidated by the talent of another act, and decided to sing instead. She won first prize, leading to a singing career that produced hit records and appearances with many big bands of the era, including Dizzy Gillespie's and the Benny Goodman Orchestra.

Although Fitzgerald was considered one of the leading jazz vocalists in the country by the mid-'50s, she still faced incidents of racial discrimination, including one that led to a successful lawsuit against Pan-American Airlines in 1954. In a now famous story, Marilyn Monroe convinced the owners of the Mocambo, a popular club in West Hollywood, to book Fitzgerald for an initial run, but it is not clear that their reluctance had been due to racial bias. Other African American singers, including Eartha Kitt and Herb Jeffries, had performed at the club, and theories have emerged about different types of bias, especially in regard to Ella's weight.

The only dramatic interest in Fitzgerald's life so far has been in the story of her relationship with Marilyn Monroe. In 2008, an American-British playwright, Bonnie Greer, adapted her own radio play, which became *Marilyn and Ella*, performed in Stratford and London theaters. *Drunk History*

Portrait of Ella Fitzgerald, ca. 1946, by William P. Gottlieb (Library of Congress).

takes an unsurprisingly broad, albeit touching, view of the same story in "Legends" (2016), with Gabourey Sidibe as Ella and Juno Temple as Marilyn. Narrator Tymberlee Hill summarizes the various theories about the Mocambo's objections to hiring Ella with, "She's too Black, she's too chubby, she's too ugly." When a voice teacher recommends Ella's album to Marilyn Monroe, the movie star listens to it 100 times, saying, "This is the most astonishing voice I've ever heard in my life."

Marilyn calls the Mocambo, and promises to take a front-row table every night, where she will be visible to photographers, if the club books Ella. On March 15, 1955, Ella sings at the Mocambo, and is a smash hit. After Marilyn's death, Ella says, "I owe Marilyn a great debt. After she personally called the managers of the Mocambo room and allowed me to play there, I was never, ever, ever, ever again in my life relegated to a small club. Marilyn was extraordinary and ahead of her time." These sentiments are a reasonable approximation of words Fitzgerald uttered in real life as a tribute to Monroe.

Ella Fitzgerald sold 40 million albums in a career that spanned five decades. She won hundreds of awards, including 13 Grammy awards, the Kennedy Center for the Performing Arts Medal of Honor Award, and the Presidential Medal of Freedom. The Marilyn anecdote is a moving story about how one woman used her privilege and fame to help another, but it constitutes only a few frames in the blockbuster movie that was Ella Fitzgerald's life.

Fitzgerald, Zelda (1900–1948)
Author, Artist
Portrayed by: Blythe Danner, Natasha Richardson, Christina Ricci

In her public persona, Zelda Fitzgerald was the avatar of the liberated 1920s flapper, wild and free, indulging in parties, booze, and rebellion. Privately, however, Zelda struggled with mental illness, complicating her tumultuous marriage to F. Scott Fitzgerald, author of *The Great Gatsby* (1925). Zelda wrote her own novel in 1932, *Save Me the Waltz*, while under care at a psychiatric clinic in Baltimore. The semi-autobiographical novel, about a southern belle named Alabama Beggs, who marries a Yankee artist named David Knight, was a failure at the time, both critically and commercially. Zelda then turned her attention to playwriting and later painting, but found success along neither avenue.

F. Scott Fitzgerald and "The Last of the Belles" (TV movie, 1974) stars Blythe Danner as Zelda and Richard Chamberlain as Scott in a story-within-a-story about the famous Jazz Age couple. After a return from Europe, as Zelda's mental health continues to deteriorate, Scott writes a short story called "The Last of the Belles." The title character of the story is Ailie Calhoun (Susan Sarandon), Zelda's alter ego, who meets Andy McKenna (David Huffman), who stands in for Scott as a soldier stationed in Alabama during World War I. At the end of the film, Zelda cuts to the heart of the relationship between the Fitzgeralds and the doppelgängers Scott created. "Seems like no matter who you start out writin' about, it always turns out to be about us. Poor Goofo. I reckon you think if you write the story often enough maybe some time, some way, it'll have a happy ending."

Zelda, a 1993 TV movie, starts happily enough, as a radiant Zelda Sayre (Natasha Richardson) meets Army Lieutenant Scott Fitzgerald (Timothy Hutton) at a party in 1918 Alabama. Sparks fly immediately, but Zelda has many suitors, and fledgling writer Scott may not be wealthy enough to satisfy either Zelda or her father (Spalding Gray). The chemistry between Zelda and Scott is obvious, but hints of trouble ahead are already evident, as Scott likes his flask almost as much as he likes Zelda, and she does cartwheels with her dress hiked up at proper society parties.

When Scott's first novel, *This Side of Paradise*, is published in 1920, his financial picture looks rosier, and Zelda agrees to marry him. As Zelda searches for creative outlets of her own, she takes up ballet, becoming obsessed with the dance, but she has started too late to achieve mastery. The disappointment affects her mental health, and she continues a slide that will lead her to a sanitarium and Scott to the conclusion that "my wife is never going to get well again."

Christina Ricci stars as Zelda and does double duty as executive producer on *Z: The Beginning of Everything* (2015–2017), an Amazon Studios series, which covers the early relationship of Zelda and Scott (David Hoflin) in 27-minute installments. The sympathy here is with Zelda, who is shown to make continual sacrifices for her husband's career, while putting aside her own interests and ambitions. In "Playing House" (2017), when the Fitzgeralds rent a lovely house in Westport, Connecticut, so Scott can focus on his writing, Zelda is barred from entering his study. She's lost, without even household responsibilities, as they have domestic help, and has too much time on her hands, with her husband tucked away in his office.

She later asks Scott, "What am I supposed to do?" When she finally barges into his sanctum, Zelda wakes him from a stupor, and says, "There are more empty bottles in here than you have pages." Scott has been using Zelda's diary as inspiration for his stories, calling her words "automatic writing." She grabs the diary from his desk, saying, "How dare you? These are not random. These are my thoughts and my dreams."

While the series got off to a promising start, with an authentic 1920s look, accentuated by David Hoflin's resemblance to F. Scott Fitzgerald, the 10-episode first season was not renewed. It would have been fascinating to see how the viewpoint introduced in those episodes played out as the Fitzgeralds encountered later and deeper struggles. But in the show's very first scene, we already had a glimpse of how the story would end. We see a burnt-out room from above, as a fireman tosses aside a feathered pink slipper. Ricci's Zelda says in voiceover, "Things are sweeter when they're lost." The real Zelda Fitzgerald died in a fire at Highland Hospital, Asheville, North Carolina, after years of recurrent hospitalization for mental illness.

Folger, Abiah
See: **Franklin, Abiah Folger (1667–1752)**

Franklin, Abiah Folger (1667–1752)
Mother of Benjamin Franklin
Portrayed by: Jennifer Holmes, Sofia Vassilieva

Abiah Folger Franklin is less notable for her accomplishments in life than she is for a juicy coincidence within her life. Abiah was the mother of Benjamin Franklin, a Founding Father of the United States, and the sister of Bethshua Folger Pope, one of the accusers during the Salem witch trials. What's a TV writer to do with those intriguing morsels? Why, take Abiah to Salem, of course, where you can endanger her pre–Ben life, so the entire history of the United States is at stake. Two shows did just that, *Voyagers!* and *Timeless*.

In "Agents of Satan" (1982), *Voyagers!* finds Abiah Folger (Jennifer Holmes) in 1692 Salem, while the real Abiah had already married Josiah Franklin, settling in 1689 Boston. The episode begins with great tension, as Abiah is chased through a misty swamp by a mob, with torches even. The superstitious townsfolk believe Abiah to be a witch, and just as she asks for heavenly help, her prayers appear to be answered when two people fall from the sky. The man and boy turn out to be garden-variety time travelers, Phineas Bogg (Jon-Erik Hexum) and Jeffrey Jones (Meeno Peluce), who must make certain that nothing happens to Abiah, lest history and our nation lose the accomplishments of Ben Franklin. All three are put on trial, naturally, but the boys have a few tricks up their sleeves, and Abiah will live, presumably to go on and birth Ben.

"The Salem Witch Hunt," a 2018 episode of *Timeless*, also places "Abby Franklin" in 1692 Salem. Alone again, Abby (Sofia Vassilieva) has traveled to the village from Boston to protest scheduled hangings of accused witches. Little does Mrs. Franklin know, however, that her name will be added to the execution roster due to the machinations of that evil, history-warping organization, Rittenhouse. Its aim, of course, is to make sure that Benjamin Franklin is never born, thereby throwing the birth of our nation into chaos. Abiah's troublemaking sister, here called Bathsheba (Emily Swallow), even makes an appearance, but the decidedly unsupernatural motive for her participation in the witch trials is a disputed property line, at least according to time-traveling historian Lucy Preston (Abigail Spencer).

As you can guess, Lucy and her intrepid team succeed in rescuing Abby, so all will be right with Ben and our history. While this episode clearly acknowledges Abiah's marriage to Josiah by this point, with the use of her married name, it does ignore the fact that the real Abiah was very pregnant at the time, and had stepchildren and a baby son at home. It's highly unlikely that such a woman would have gone off on a lone crusade under those conditions, but, then, "highly unlikely" is the stock in trade of the science fiction subgenre known as time travel.

Frémont, Jessie Benton (1824–1902)
Writer
Portrayed by: Lorna Thayer, Alice Krige

In "The Gentle Sword," a 1960 installment of *Death Valley Days*, series host "The Old Ranger" (Stanley Andrews) introduces us to the dramatic, yet simple story of John and Jessie Frémont (Roy Engel and Lorna Thayer). John C. Frémont, a famous American explorer and Army officer, is fighting for title to the Mariposa Grant in the wilds of the Sierra foothills, where gold has been discovered. "His strongest weapon is his wife Jessie," the Ranger tells us. As the story opens, the Merced Mining Company is trying to jump Frémont's claim, and he dashes to be with his men in the Pine Tree Mine, where they are holed up with explosives. A standoff ensues, and the threatening, yet somehow gentlemanly representatives for Merced up the ante by telling Jessie they will burn down the Frémont family house to lure her husband out of the mine. Jessie has 24 hours to leave with her three children, and after dithering, she finds her spine, confronting them later at the saloon. "You can kill us, all of us, but you can't kill right. You can't kill the law," she says. Jessie's bravery and tenacity end up winning the day in this tense episode with a fine performance by Thayer.

While this tale of good and evil has little nuance, The Frémonts don't fare much better in *Dream West*, a 1986 three-part adaptation of the novel by David Nevin. Starring that king of the miniseries Richard Chamberlain as John and Alice Krige as Jessie, it covers more ground over the course of its 300+ minutes, but offers broad characterizations and corny dialogue instead of substance. Krige portrays Jessie as a feisty southern belle (is there any other kind?), and gets to say things like, "Papa, slavery makes bad table talk!"

To its credit, though, *Dream West* is not just the tale of pathfinder John Charles and his daring expeditions to survey the American west. It's also the story of the loving partnership between John and Jessie, who took work as a writer to supplement her husband's sometimes small income and supported his ambitions, wherever they took him. "Charles is going to make a mark on our time," she tells a friend, "and I want to be with him when he does."

In reality, however, the legacies of John C. and Jessie Benton Frémont are anything but simple. While John was considered a military hero and indeed dubbed "the Pathfinder of the West," his explorations in California were bloodied by the genocide of Native American peoples. Jessie contributed not only moral support for his expeditions, but also helped to raise his stature by co-authoring his reports, using a romantic style that made them popular with the public. When John ran for president in 1856, Jessie was his closest adviser, sometimes equaling her husband in popularity, as evidenced by the slogan, "Frémont and Jessie too." When John went bankrupt, Jessie helped again, writing articles, memoirs, and stories for magazines, which were later collected in books, such as *Far-West Sketches* (1890).

Jessie Benton Frémont was so much more than the woman behind the man. A talented and ambitious woman, Jessie was her own kind of pathfinder, constantly inventing roles for herself at a time when options for wives were circumscribed.

Fuldheim, Dorothy (1893–1989)

Broadcast Journalist
Portrayed by: Mary Elizabeth Ellis

A true trailblazer, Dorothy Fuldheim was television's first female news anchor. While "firsts" are often the province of the young, Dorothy began her TV news career at the age of 54, signing on as the nightly newscaster at Cleveland's fledgling WEWS-TV station in 1947. Fuldheim's initial contract was for 13 weeks, but she remained with the news program for 37 years, working into her early 90s. With few precedents to follow, Dorothy was able to develop her own format, which included straight news, interviews, and commentary.

Mary Elizabeth Ellis portrays Fuldheim in the *Drunk History* episode "Cleveland" (2015). This inspirational outing begins in 1918, as Dorothy travels the world giving speeches on issues of the day. In 1932, she seeks an interview with Adolf Hitler, and he agrees, unaware that she is Jewish. She continues to interview "everyone in the world," in the words of narrator David Wain, as she begins her TV career in 1947. Her subjects include Richard Nixon, Martin Luther King, Jr., the Duke of Windsor, Wilt Chamberlain, and the Kennedys, all shown in a montage, as portrayed by *Drunk History*'s company of actors. Fuldheim runs into trouble in 1970, when she voices her opinion about the shooting of unarmed Kent State University students by the Ohio National Guard. She says, in a reasonably close approximation of what the real Fuldheim said, "This is murder ... why are we killing our own children?" Viewers are outraged, and Fuldheim offers to resign, but the station supports her.

When Fuldheim passed away at the age of 96, Barbara Walters, a groundbreaking broadcast journalist in her own right, said that Dorothy "defied the prejudice against women in general, because there was a lot of prejudice about women working. She defied the prejudice about women doing the news, because she did the news.... And she defied all the prejudices about aging. She did her job well, and she made us all very proud."

Gable, Nan
See: **Aspinwall, Nan (1880-1964)**

Garrud, Edith (1872-1971)
See (mentioned in): **Pankhurst, Emmeline (1858-1928)**

Graham, Florence Nightingale
See: **Arden, Elizabeth (ca. 1884-1966)**

Greenhow, Rose O'Neal (ca. 1815-1864)
Confederate Spy
Portrayed by: Madolyn Smith Osborne, Nina Foch

Rose O'Neal Greenhow was a Washington, D.C., socialite before and during the American Civil War, who had the ear of powerful men, including U.S. President James Buchanan. Although Greenhow was a pro-slavery Southerner, she opted to stay in Washington after the outbreak of the war, using her valuable connections to become a spy for the Confederacy. She successfully passed information about Union troop movements to the Southern command in 1861, but famed detective Allan Pinkerton, then head of the Secret Service, arrested her in August of that year.

Although there is no evidence that Greenhow and Pinkerton were anything but professional adversaries, Turner Network Television thought they spotted romance in this historic pas de deux, producing the TV movie *The Rose and the Jackal* (1990), starring Christopher Reeve as Pinkerton and Madolyn Smith Osborne as Greenhow. In the TNT retelling, already married Pinkerton can't resist the charms of southern belle Greenhow, and indiscretions, as well as further historical inaccuracies, ensue.

Greenhow's supposed seductive gifts had also been the subject of an earlier program, "The Rebellious Rose," an episode of *The Americans* (1961). Here Rose (Nina Foch) tempts an undercover but conflicted Confederate soldier, Corporal Jack Canfield (Richard Davalos), to commit murder for her.

Rose Greenhow's life was dramatic on its own, and needed no such embellishment. After a few months in prison, she was exiled to the Confederacy, and later served as its unofficial diplomat in Europe. There she wrote a book based on her prison diary, *My Imprisonment and the First Year of Abolition Rule at Washington* (1863), but drowned on her way home, while trying to run the Union blockade of Wilmington, North Carolina. She was weighed down by gold coins hidden on her person.

Yes, that's drama enough.

Haile, Margaret (?–?)

Politician, Suffragist
Portrayed by: Nicole Underhay

Margaret Haile was the first woman to run for provincial office in Ontario, placing her name on the ballot in 1902, when women were not allowed to vote or sit in the legislature. Haile, the Ontario Socialist League's candidate for North Toronto, was well aware she could not win the election, but hoped to raise awareness of the League's universal suffrage platform and the plight of women in general. She was daring enough to discuss the issue of prostitution, viewing it as a consequence of poor employment opportunities for women rather than a moral failing.

Murdoch Mysteries pays homage to Margaret Haile in seven episodes of its eighth season, culminating in "Election Day" (2015). Nicole Underhay portrays Haile, who works with series regular Dr. Julia Ogden (Helene Joy), a psychiatrist and pathologist, to promote women's suffrage. Although women are not allowed to vote, Margaret is running for provincial office in North Toronto, but she learns on election day that her name is not on the ballot. Margaret and Dr. Ogden want the election stopped, and join other women in blocking the entrance to the polling place, where they refuse to break ranks, even as some men try to push their way through the line.

Eventually Margaret's name appears on the ballot, and she is thrilled to learn later that she received 79 votes. This symbolic victory is a harbinger of better things to come, as represented by the appearance of young Agnes Macphail (Zoe Fraser), who asks Haile for her autograph. In real life, Macphail would go on to become the first woman in Canada to be elected to the House of Commons.

History records no references to Margaret Haile after the election, but her words give a hint that she would have continued her non-conformist ways. "The new woman believes in being herself right down to the end of life...."

Hall, Virginia (1906–1982)
Spy
Portrayed by: Alia Shawkat

Virginia Hall accomplished remarkable, almost unbelievable, feats of derring-do as a spy during World War II, but her name has risen to prominence only recently. Hall, a Baltimore native, worked with the United Kingdom's Special Operations Executive (SOE), forming large networks of resistance fighters in France. In one of her most daring exploits, she organized a prison break for 12 captured agents, all of whom escaped safely from the Mauzac prison, eventually returning to England. Hall seemed to have a "spidey sense" for danger, recognizing when people or situations were suspicious, and she engineered her own escape from France when the Germans were closing in. She fled Lyon, climbing over a pass in the Pyrenees mountains to reach Spain, and she did so on a prosthetic leg she called "Cuthbert." While that sounds like the stuff of over-the-top spy shows like *Mission: Impossible*, it's all true.

Drunk History does a straightforward retelling of Virginia Hall's World War II exploits in "Spies" (2015). Alia Shawkat is Hall, who goes to work for a "British spy gang" (incorrectly called the "Secret" Operations Executive), and supplies weapons and money to the French resistance, while ostensibly working as a journalist. After her hike over the snowy Pyrenees, Hall hooks up with American spies (the unnamed Office of Strategic Services), and changes her appearance to look like "Mrs. Doubtfire," delivering cheese as a kindly old lady, while actually blowing up bridges. In the slightly slurred words of narrator Claudia O'Doherty, Virginia Hall "didn't let anybody tell her what she could or couldn't do." While this vignette has the blessing of no expletives (and, hence, no bleeping), its depiction of its larger-than-life subject is surprisingly bland.

Hall received the Distinguished Service Cross from General William Joseph Donovan in a private ceremony, refusing a public presentation by

President Harry Truman. "The limping lady," as she was known during her undercover years, was the only civilian woman in World War II to be awarded the Distinguished Service Cross for extraordinary heroism.

Hand, Dora (1844–1878)
Dance Hall Singer, Actress
Portrayed by: Margaret Hayes, Phyllis Coates

Dodge City, Kansas, knew and loved two Dora Hands. By night she was a dance hall singer, sometimes known as Fannie Keenan, who entertained drunken cowboys at saloons in town, although she was rumored to have come from good stock in Boston. By day she was an angel of mercy, conservatively attired while singing in church or assisting the poor with money saved from her saloon wages.

Dora's dual fame turned to Old West legend when she was mistakenly shot to death by a Texan named James W. "Spike" Kenedy, who was out for revenge after a fight with Dodge City's mayor, James H. "Dog" Kelley. Her voice silenced at the age of 34, Hand received a grand funeral, during which Dodge City's saloons and stores were closed.

The last days of Dora Hand were depicted in two western series, both of which took some liberties with the facts. *The Life and Legend of Wyatt Earp*, which featured the character of Dora Hand (Margaret Hayes) in three episodes, including the aptly named "The Double Life of Dora Hand" (1956), saw the shooting as the culmination of a love triangle. In "So Long, Dora, So Long" (1956), a man named Bob Rellance (Joe Turkel), standing in for real-life Spike Kenedy, sets out to kill romantic rival Jim Kelley (Paul Brinegar), but accidentally shoots Dora at Kelley's home.

Death Valley Days put its own spin on Dora's tragic story in "The Left Hand Is Damned" (1964). In this telling, the bad blood between Mayor Jim Kelley (Stephen Roberts) and "Slim Kennedy" (Peter Haskell) comes as a result of a poker dispute at Kelley's gambling house. Kelley shoots Kennedy, and Dora Hand (Phyllis Coates), a dance hall singer with a tendency to "adopt stray cats and saddle tramps," takes the wounded cowboy to her own room for treatment, despite what her boss Kelley or anyone in town might think. Coates gives Dora real dimension as a woman who had lost her fiancé in a gun battle before their wedding and is now determined to stay single, living outside society's rules. The ending is the same, alas, as Kennedy mistakenly shoots Dora through the window of Kelley's house.

The Boot Hill Museum in Dodge City remembers Dora Hand as someone who "was in the wrong place at the wrong time," a familiar Old West story with the added flair that only the two Doras could provide.

Hart, Pearl (ca. 1871–?)

Outlaw
Portrayed by: Beverly Garland, Anne Francis

The details of Pearl Hart's life have been more successful at eluding capture than the "Lady Bandit" herself was, but sources agree on the one story that made her famous. On May 30, 1899, Pearl, dressed as a man, and an accomplice named Joe Boot held up a stagecoach in Arizona, taking over $400 from the passengers. While that may not sound like a lot of money (it's a bit better when you know that translates to $12,000 today), Pearl's historical significance lies not in the amount she collected, but in the fact that she was the only female stagecoach robber in Arizona's history, committing one of the last stagecoach robberies in the country.

Fictional accounts of historical lives tend to take liberties with the facts, especially when required to sculpt history to an already established narrative. In "Pearl Hart," a 1960 episode of *Tales of Wells Fargo*, Pearl's capture bears little resemblance to the historical record, sparse though it may be. Beverly Garland stars as Pearl, who is apprehended after she is coaxed into a shooting contest by Jim Hardie (Dale Robertson), a special agent for Wells Fargo. Since Robertson was the star of the show, Hardie had to be at the center of the action, capturing Pearl with a ruse, but the real story is more dramatic.

According to an account in *The New York Times* on June 6, 1899, Sheriff Truman of Pinal County was the real lawman who captured Pearl and her confederate, catching up with the outlaws while they were sleeping. "When they were awakened, the man seemed paralyzed with fright, but the woman, reaching for the guns, which had been removed, sprang to her feet and fought vigorously."

Death Valley Days adheres more closely to the historical record in "The Last Stagecoach Robbery" (1964). Anne Francis portrays Hart as sweet, demure, and more refined than one might expect of a stagecoach robber, mentioning a boarding-school background the real Pearl appears to have shared. When Pearl robs the passengers after learning the stagecoach has no strongbox, she gives each of them one dollar for their bed and supper, an act also attributed to the historical Pearl. The rest of the teleplay is more sanitized right down to Pearl's desire for clean guns because she hates oily ones. She tells Joe Boot (Jesse Pearson), here her beau, that she plans to give the stolen money back, having concocted the whole adventure to become the first woman ever to rob a stagecoach.

The episode was played for laughs, but the real Pearl probably wasn't laughing when she was sent to Yuma Territorial Prison, not for the stagecoach robbery, for which she was acquitted, but for interfering with the

U.S. Mail. She was pardoned after two years, but the event is shrouded in mystery, with later rumors surfacing about a possible pregnancy that would have embarrassed prison authorities. After her release, she may have toured with Buffalo Bill's Wild West Show or become a rancher's wife in Arizona.

The story of Pearl Hart is still waiting for its proper ending.

Hayden, Sophia (1868–1953)
Architect
Portrayed by: Katherine Cunningham

In the *Timeless* episode "The World's Columbian Exposition" (2017), Sophia Hayden (Katherine Cunningham) becomes trapped by a serial killer, H.H. Holmes (Joel Johnstone), in an airtight room along with several others, including time travelers Wyatt Logan (Matt Lanter) and Rufus Carlin (Malcolm Barrett). Sophia, an architect, uses her design expertise to save the group, when she discovers a brick that doesn't match the others in their prison, one which provides an opening whereby they can yell for help. We learn that Hayden designed the women's pavilion at the World's Columbian Exposition, and that she was the first woman to pursue the program in architecture at MIT.

As the Meat Loaf song goes, "Two Out of Three Ain't Bad." While Sophia Hayden was indeed the first female graduate in architecture at MIT and did in fact design the Woman's Building at the 1893 Chicago World's Fair (also called the Columbian Exposition), her meeting with history's first known serial killer was fictitious, although Holmes's "murder castle," located just a few miles from the exposition, is well-documented.

The real Sophia, however, did find a different kind of nemesis at the fair. Her design for an Italian Renaissance structure had won the competition for the Woman's Building, but disagreements with the Board of Lady Managers and especially its chair Bertha Palmer over changes to the design, led to Hayden's firing. Stories of these difficulties were taken as proof that women were unsuited to the fields of architecture and construction. For her trouble, Hayden received a fee three to ten times less than the going rate for male architects who had designed buildings at the exposition.

Alas, Hayden's star didn't burn brightly for long. Her building was demolished after the Exposition closed, and she went on to live a quiet life in Winthrop, Massachusetts. But Sophia Hayden's trailblazing achievements, including the design of an exquisite building when she was just 21 years of age, still speak loudly today.

Hellman, Lillian (1905–1984)
Playwright
Portrayed by: Judy Davis

Lillian Hellman has more claims to fame than any one person should be allowed. As a playwright, she penned such notable dramas as *The Children's Hour* (1934), *The Little Foxes* (1939), and *Watch on the Rhine* (1941), all exhibiting her trademark social conscience and left-wing political views. As a screenwriter, she received two Academy Award nominations, but she turned down a multi-year contract from Columbia Pictures, refusing to sign a required loyalty clause. As a memoirist, she wrote books chronicling her adventures with myriad acquaintances, but she was also accused of reporting falsehoods, especially in *Pentimento* (1973), a chapter of which formed the basis for the film *Julia* (1977).

As an activist, she supported anti–Nazi causes, but her "casual" membership in the Communist Party landed her before the House Un-American Activities Committee (HUAC) in 1952. In her personal life, she was romantically involved for decades with novelist and fellow activist Dashiell Hammett, author of *The Maltese Falcon*, although the literary supercouple never married.

The latter claim to fame is the basis for the TV movie *Dash and Lilly* (1999), starring Judy Davis as Hellman and Sam Shepard as Hammett. The film uses the HUAC hearings as a framing device, beginning in 1952, as Hellman is about to be called before the committee. She then flashes back to 1930, when she meets Hammett at a nightclub. Dash and Lilly appear to be made for each other, and they are, assuming the goal is a destructive, love/hate relationship. Drinking, philandering, and quarreling quickly ensue, spanning three decades, as the couple witnesses World War II and the rise of McCarthyism. Their left-wing politics land them in trouble, during a time when many Americans see "Reds" under every bed. While high principles are not always on display in regard to each other, both rise to the occasion when it comes to public loyalty to friends and acquaintances, once the government investigations begin.

Historical Hellman wrote a letter to HUAC, wherein she agreed to testify before the committee, but refused to "name names" of past associates, communist or otherwise. "I am not willing, now or in the future, to bring bad trouble to people who, in my past association with them, were completely innocent of any talk or any action that was disloyal or subversive…. I cannot and will not cut my conscience to fit this year's fashions…."

Holiday, Billie (1915–1959)

Jazz Singer
Portrayed by: Paula Jai Parker, Audra McDonald

Billie Holiday was the leading jazz singer of her time, an all too brief time, given her tragic death at the age of 44. Although she had no formal training, Holiday had uncanny musical instincts, an intensely dramatic style, and revolutionary improvisational skills, making her one of the age's unique voices. After a difficult childhood, which included truancy and time spent in a Catholic reform school, Holiday began singing in Harlem nightclubs. She made her recording debut at the age of 18 with Benny Goodman, and went on to record such signature songs as "Strange Fruit," "Billie's Blues," and "God Bless the Child."

Portrait of Billie Holiday, ca. 1947, by William P. Gottlieb (Library of Congress).

"Strange Fruit" is the centerpiece of "God Bless the Child," a 2000 episode of *Touched by an Angel*. Three angels are trying to help a troubled teen, Charnelle Bishop (Kenya Williams), who could be dead by midnight if she continues with her plan to buy drugs. Angel Monica (Roma Downey) introduces a resistant Charnelle to the music and story of Billie Holiday (Paula Jai Parker), who appears in flashbacks, revealing her struggles with substance abuse. Billie faces further hurdles, when Angel Andrew (John Dye) brings her "Strange Fruit," a song about the lynchings of black Americans, a song Holiday says, "no colored person would dare sing...."

With further angelic intervention from Tess (Della Reese), Holiday finds the courage to sing this important song, and eventually Charnelle does the right thing as well. The episode is mostly affecting, especially while depicting Holiday's internal struggles over performing the song. It also provides a clever supernatural solution to the disputed question of how the real Holiday came to record "Strange Fruit." Whatever the answer, Holiday's 1939 interpretation of the song is considered so historically and musically significant that it was included in the National Recording Registry in 2003.

Holiday is center stage in *Lady Day at Emerson's Bar & Grill*, a Broadway production filmed at the Cafe Brasil in New Orleans and shown as a TV movie on HBO in 2016. Audra McDonald stars as Holiday, also known as "Lady Day," the nickname given to her by saxophonist Lester Young. Lady Day performs in a seedy Philadelphia nightclub several months before her death. She is accompanied by Jimmy Powers (Shelton Becton) on piano. Holiday shares stories and quips between numbers, while sipping drinks and becoming increasingly intoxicated. "Jimmy keeps me in line. He makes sure I sing all the numbers I'm supposed to before I get too far juiced."

Billie Holiday died of complications from cirrhosis of the liver in 1959. She was cuffed to her hospital bed, under arrest on drug charges. Although she was virtually penniless, her recording catalog was rich, and reissues of her records followed. Posthumous Grammy Awards ensued, and Holiday became a legend to a modern audience, one all too familiar with performers who possess extraordinary talent and burn out rather than fade away.

Holliday, Kate
See: **Big Nose Kate (ca. 1850–1940)**

Hopper, Hedda (1885–1966)
See (mentioned in): **Lombard, Carole (1908–1942)**

Howard, Catherine (ca. 1524–1542)

Queen of England
Portrayed by: Angela Pleasence, Tamzin Merchant

Catherine Howard was the fifth of King Henry VIII's six wives, and the second, after Anne Boleyn, to be executed on trumped-up charges. Catherine had been a maid of honor to Anne of Cleves, Henry's fourth wife, and caught the king's attention at a time when he was eager to end his politically motivated fourth marriage. Henry was 49 years old and Catherine around 17, his "very jewel of womanhood," but one woefully inexperienced in the machinations of the royal court. So how did this vivacious young woman, held in such high esteem by a doting husband, end up with her head on the chopping block?

The details of Catherine's short life are difficult to sort out, but the main answers to that question involve love affairs Catherine allegedly had both before she met Henry and after they were married. Catherine was supposed to have been "chaste" before her marriage, but it is likely she had consummated her relationship with Francis Dereham, and her family had concealed that information from the king. Catherine, still a teenager, did not help her situation when she flirted with another man, Thomas Culpeper, at court, although both denied any sexual contact. Enemies, such as Archbishop Thomas Cranmer, were quick to take advantage of the rumors, and Parliament helped things along by passing the *Royal Assent by Commission Act 1541*, which made it high treason for any person who married the king to conceal their previous sexual history from him. King Henry VIII granted his royal assent to this act, and so his bride was executed for hiding her previous sexual history.

Angela Pleasence as Catherine Howard in *The Six Wives of Henry VIII* (PBS).

Historical assessments of Catherine have not been kind, at least until recent years. She has been viewed as oversexed, empty-headed, hedonistic, and more. *The Six Wives of Henry VIII* (Miniseries, 1970) certainly sees her as oversexed, but also adds volatile and conspiratorial to her list of faults. A dramatic change in demeanor occurs when Catherine (Angela Pleasence) confesses her sexual adventures to her cousin Anne Carey (Julia Cornelius), and Anne mentions them later, after Catherine has learned she has a chance to be the next queen. Catherine grabs her cousin violently by the hair and says, "If you so much as whisper anything to anybody, I swear I shall poison you."

In *The Tudors* (2007–2010), Catherine (Tamzin Merchant) is more the giggling, lusty teenager, although everyone is lusty on this show. Here her relationship with Thomas Culpeper (Torrance Coombs), one of Henry's favorites, is unambiguously sexual, although Catherine seems deeply infatuated with him. When she goes to her death, she defiantly proclaims, "I die a Queen, but I would rather die the wife of Culpeper."

Legend has it that the real Catherine said words to that effect, but historians believe she offered more traditional words, as apparently there were traditional words when one was executed by the king. One asked for forgiveness and accepted one's punishment, even when the king was your husband, the one who once thought you were his "very jewel of womanhood."

Humiston, Grace (1871–1948)

Attorney, Investigator
Portrayed by: Sarah Sokolovic

Grace Humiston isn't exactly a household name, but the television series *Timeless* tried to remedy that oversight with its episode "Mrs. Sherlock Holmes" in 2018. "Mrs. Sherlock Holmes" was the nickname given to the real Grace Humiston when she solved a cold case, the disappearance of a woman named Ruth Cruger in 1917, after the NYPD had closed their investigation without a result. After "Mrs. Holmes" located Cruger's body and fingered the killer, the New York City Police Department appointed Humiston as an investigator specializing in missing girl cases, prompting her to leave her law practice, the People's Law Firm, which had served poor immigrants in the city. Grace's work there had also led to her appointment as the first female United States District Attorney for her dogged investigations into missing immigrant laborers held in peonage (debt-induced servitude) down south.

Sarah Sokolovic portrays "Mrs. Sherlock Holmes" on *Timeless*, where time travelers Lucy Preston (Abigail Spencer) and Wyatt Logan (Matt

Lanter) meet her in 1919 New York. Lucy and Wyatt are there to make sure suffragist Alice Paul (Erica Dasher) catches the ear of President Woodrow Wilson (Bryan Scott Johnson) regarding passage of the 19th amendment, which would give women the right to vote in the U.S. When Paul is framed for murder, history professor Lucy seeks out Humiston and her prodigious skills of detection to get Paul off the hook, but things don't turn out as planned when Paul is murdered in prison. Humiston, who is initially reluctant, gives a speech that Paul was supposed to deliver, ensuring that women will receive the right to vote in 1920. Although a few historical inaccuracies are present, the bravery displayed by the suffragists is brought to vivid life, and, fair warning, there won't be a dry eye in the house as Humiston gives her speech in favor of women's suffrage.

Kudos to *Timeless* for introducing the TV audience to Grace Humiston, a real woman of accomplishment and determination, even if a few liberties were taken with the historical record. We know who Grace Humiston is now.

Ingalls, Laura
See: **Wilder, Laura Ingalls (1867–1957)**

Joan of Arc (ca. 1412–1431)
Warrior, French National Hero, Saint
Portrayed by: Sarah Churchill, Julie Harris, Geneviève Bujold, Leelee Sobieski, Christina Cox, Jeanne Simpson, Yancy Butler, Vanessa Hudgens

Joan of Arc is one of the most famous women in history, not a queen, nor a poet, nor a scientist, just an uneducated girl who lived during the Middle Ages. It's easy for people to take what they want from Joan's story, whether it's her feminist appeal as a warrior, her spiritual pull as a mystic and miracle worker, or her emotional resonance as hero and martyr. Then, too, there's her dramatic demise with its indelible image of her being burned at the stake, a picture vivid enough to awaken even the most habitual snoozer in history class.

Known as "The Maid of Orléans," Joan became famous within her own lifetime, brief as it was, for saving France from English conquest. Spurred by what she believed were visions of saints, she made her way to the Royal Court for a meeting with the heir to the French throne, Charles, later Charles VII, who was embroiled in a nasty business called the Hundred Years' War. For an unknown farm girl, Joan was surprisingly persuasive, convincing Charles to send her with a relief army to the Siege of Orléans, where she lead the French army to a momentous victory. Joan's military good fortune lasted about a year, until she was captured by a rival French faction and turned over to the English. She was put to death after a sham trial for heresy, but people never forgot her courage or her devotion to France.

The *Hallmark Hall of Fame*, a television anthology series, devoted three different programs to Joan, beginning with *Joan of Arc* (1952), starring Sarah Churchill as Joan. Five years later, it mounted another production entitled *The Lark* (1957), based on a 1952 play by Jean Anouilh, where Julie Harris reprised her 1956 Tony Award–winning role as Joan, while Boris Karloff and Basil Rathbone rounded out the stellar production. (Imagine seeing that for free on your black-and-white TV screen.). In 1967, the Hall of Fame adapted a different play about the teen warrior, *Saint Joan*, by George Bernard Shaw, with another all-star cast, including Geneviève Bujold as Joan, Roddy McDowall, and Raymond Massey.

With the exception of the miniseries *Joan of Arc* (1999), with Leelee Sobieski as the French hero, interpretations after the *Hallmark Hall of Fame* productions became more imaginative and less reverent. In a 1992 episode of *Forever Knight* entitled "For I Have Sinned," present-day vampire Nicholas Knight (Geraint Wyn Davies) recalls his 15th-century encounters with Joan (Christina Cox), who refused Knight's offers of immortality via neck bite, even when it meant she would die at the stake.

More unusual still is the tale recounted in "Bone of Arc," a 1995 episode of the Peabody Award-winning children's series *Wishbone*, wherein a dog tells the story of Joan of Arc (Jeanne Simpson), while imagining he is her page Louis. *Witchblade* (2001–2002) continued the trend of placing Joan in the fantasy realm, envisioning her as an earlier, look-alike incarnation of present-day New York detective Sara Pezzini (Yancy Butler), both of whom wield an ancient, supernatural weapon called the Witchblade. *Drunk History* brings Joan (Vanessa Hudgens) back to reality (sort of) as a "16-year-old girl in a 16-year-old world," and a girl with plenty of attitude at that, in "The Middle Ages" (2018).

The country of France holds a national festival each year on the second Sunday in May to celebrate Joan of Arc's life and legacy. Such an honor seems fitting and fair for a young woman whose courage helped to preserve the nation for which she sacrificed her life.

Johnson, Katherine (1918–2020)

Mathematician
Portrayed by: Nadine Ellis

The inspiring story of Katherine Johnson had flown under the radar for decades until the theatrical film *Hidden Figures*, starring Taraji P.

Henson as Johnson, leapt into the public consciousness in 2016. The film was based on a 2016 nonfiction book, *Hidden Figures: The American Dream and the Untold Story of the Black Women Who Helped Win the Space Race*, by Margot Lee Shetterly, who had sold the movie rights before the book was completed.

In the early days of the space program, back when it was known as NACA (National Advisory Committee for Aeronautics), Katherine Johnson was a member of the "West Computers," a group of African American women who excelled at mathematics and performed complex calculations for the program's engineers. When NACA was subsumed by NASA, Johnson worked on the Mercury program and, at astronaut John Glenn's request, verified the accuracy of an electronic computer's calculations for his historic orbit of the Earth in 1962. Her later work helped send astronauts to the moon on Apollo 11 in 1969, and she received the Presidential Medal of Freedom in 2015 from President Barack Obama.

Portrait of Katherine Johnson, 1983 (NASA).

Scripted television offered its own tribute to Johnson in 2016 on a memorable episode of *Timeless*, aptly titled "Space Race." Nadine Ellis portrays Johnson here, and she's called upon to rescue the entire Apollo 11 mission, when time-traveling terrorist Garcia Flynn (Goran Visnjic) and company insert a virus into NASA computers, disrupting all communication with the astronauts. Working with Lucy Preston (Abigail Spencer), a professor of history, and Rufus Carlin (Malcolm Barrett), an engineer and programmer, both of whom are pursuing Flynn as civilian time-cops, Johnson is able to get NASA's mainframe back online, saving the astronauts and preserving the timeline.

Fanciful, yes, but also a reverent and rousing introduction to the life of a true American pioneer.

Joliot-Curie, Irene (1897–1956)
See (mentioned in): **Curie, Marie (1867–1934)**

Keckley, Elizabeth (1818–1907)
See (mentioned in): **Lincoln, Mary Todd (1818–1882)**

Keller, Helen (1880–1968)
Author, Educator, Activist
Portrayed by: Patty McCormack, Melissa Gilbert, Hallie Eisenberg, Mare Winningham, Moira Kelly

Helen Keller was an author, educator, and disability rights advocate, who was deaf and blind from the age of 19 months. Her education began at the age of seven, when she met Anne Sullivan, a 20-year-old teacher from the Perkins Institution for the Blind in Boston. Keller learned to read, first from words spelled out on her palm, and later from raised words on cardboard. She spent winters at the Perkins Institution learning Braille, and learned to speak with the help of Sarah Fuller of the Horace Mann School for the Deaf, also in Boston. Keller later attended Radcliffe College and became the first deaf-blind person in the United States to earn a bachelor of arts degree. Anne Sullivan was at her side during these educational triumphs, and remained with Keller until October 1936, when Sullivan died.

In 1956, William Gibson wrote a teleplay especially for *Playhouse 90*, called "The Miracle Worker," based on Keller's autobiography *The Story of My Life* (1903). The production, which aired in 1957, starred Patty McCormack as Helen and Teresa Wright as Sullivan, and depicted several months in Helen Keller's childhood. Anne arrives to live with the Kellers and begins her job of teaching Helen immediately, as Helen embraces a doll Sullivan has brought in her suitcase. Sullivan spells out the letters D-O-L-L on Helen's hand, and Helen's education, as well as their test of wills, begins in earnest.

This least famous production of *The Miracle Worker* was the start of something big. Gibson adapted his teleplay into a three-act play, which premiered on Broadway in 1959, starring Anne Bancroft as Sullivan, in a Tony Award-winning performance, and Patty Duke as Helen. Gibson then wrote a screenplay based on the play, which became the 1962 film of the same title, with Bancroft and Duke on board again. Both women would go on to win Academy Awards for their performances in the film. But Duke still wasn't done with *The Miracle Worker*. In 1979, she turned the tables, portraying teacher Sullivan in a TV movie of the same title, with Melissa Gilbert as Helen Keller. Duke won the Emmy Award this time around.

All of these productions, and a 2000 version of *The Miracle Worker* for *The Wonderful World of Disney*, with Hallie Eisenberg as Helen, tell the story of Keller's initial wild state and Sullivan's persistence in teaching her. The story is encapsulated in a famous scene at a water pump in the yard of the Keller home. Having been splashed by Helen with a pitcher of water at the dinner table, Sullivan pulls the girl outside to refill it. As the water from the pump splashes over Helen's hands, a realization finally dawns and she says one syllable, "wa." Sullivan uses finger symbols on Helen's palm to confirm, and suddenly Helen is running to learn other words, ground, pump, step, etc. Sullivan calls Helen's parents outside, and Helen recognizes them as "mother" and "papa." Sullivan cries out triumphantly, "She knows!" Then Helen wants to know the word for Annie, and Sullivan spells into her palm, "teacher."

Two later TV movies leave the Helen of *The Miracle Worker* behind to concentrate on her early adult life. *Helen Keller: The Miracle Continues* (1984) stars Blythe Danner as Sullivan and Mare Winningham as Keller in a story based on the book *Helen and Teacher: The Story of Helen Keller and Anne Sullivan Macy* (1980) by Joseph P. Lash. The story begins as Sullivan and Mr. Gilman (Alexander Knox) argue over which of them is best suited to prepare Keller for her education at Radcliffe. Helen's mother (Vera Miles) arrives to sort things out, and soon finds that Gilman, although a professional educator, is seeking fame, while Annie has Helen's best interests at heart, as she always does.

Helen does attend Radcliffe, with Sullivan by her side, but their lives become more complicated, if that's possible, when John Macy (Perry King) arrives. Macy has come to help Helen write articles about her life for *The Ladies Home Journal*. Sullivan ends up marrying Macy, but she is devoted to Keller, leaving her husband on the outside looking in. Helen has romantic problems of her own, when she meets a young suitor, Peter Fagan (Jeff Harding), but her mother and Sullivan thwart an elopement plan.

Monday After the Miracle (1998) covers similar territory, beginning with Helen's attendance at Radcliffe and emphasizing the romances of both women. Based on a play of the same title by William Gibson, the production stars Roma Downey as Sullivan and Moira Kelly as Keller, both in fine performances, although the women are a bit too glamorous for their time and circumstances. Macy (Billy Campbell) enters the picture and the women's household, trying to cope with Helen's special needs and Anne's own need to shelter Helen, but ultimately decides he's "tired of coming in third." Helen's suitor, Fagan (Mike Doyle), is scared off by her mother (Christina Pickles), who tells him that his love for Helen "…will turn to duty, and duty will turn to resentment." Sullivan and Keller are alone again, but Helen says, "…we have our work ahead of us." A voice-over at the end speaks of some of that work. "Helen lobbied on behalf of women's suffrage, lent her voice against racism and segregation, and, with Annie, raised millions of dollars for the American Foundation for the Blind."

The bond between Helen Keller and Anne Sullivan lasted until Sullivan passed away, and no person or circumstance was ever able to rupture it.

Kelly, Grace (1929–1982)
Actress, Princess of Monaco
Portrayed by: Cheryl Ladd

Grace Kelly came to the world's attention in the 1950s as a beautiful actress, but in her line of work, beauty is nothing unusual. What made Grace Kelly stand apart were her elegance and quiet dignity, qualities not usually associated with a business that has the word "show" in front of it.

Kelly began her acting career in New York with theatrical productions, but soon found a home in the live "playhouse" dramas of television's first golden age. When the big screen beckoned, she gained attention in films such as *High Noon* (1952) and *Mogambo* (1953), before going on to win an Academy Award for Best Actress in *The Country Girl* (1954). It was her films for Alfred Hitchcock, however, which raised her to the status of icon, especially *Rear Window* (1954), where her role as a fashion model brought her elegant brand of glamour to the forefront. While attending the Cannes Film Festival, Kelly met Prince Rainier III of Monaco in May of 1955. She made the transition from screen queen to bona fide princess one year later, when she married Rainier, acquiring over 130 additional titles in the process.

Cheryl Ladd is radiant in the title role of *Grace Kelly*, a 1983 television movie which follows Kelly from her childhood through her fairytale wedding. Young Grace learns to be content sitting on the sidelines, while the other members of her athletic, overachieving family get all the attention, especially her domineering father Jack (Lloyd Bridges). Grace inherited some of Daddy's determination, however, and she insists on pursuing an acting career, much to Jack's displeasure. The real Jack thought acting wasn't much better than streetwalking, but movie Jack is more decorous, saying, "The theater is no place for … my daughter." Grace knows better than Dad, though, and continues her independent streak throughout an illustrious, albeit brief film career, until she meets the other important man in her life, "Prince Charming" (Ian McShane, also radiant here). Before the end credits, the producers acknowledge "the assistance of Princess Grace of Monaco in the preproduction of this film…."

Alas, Princess Grace was never to see the completed film. She died on September 14, 1982, from injuries sustained when she experienced a mild cerebral hemorrhage and lost control of her car. Princess Grace had never returned to acting, although not for lack of offers, but she had anonymously assisted theater, dance, and film artists in America over the years. After her death, her husband established the Princess Grace Foundation–USA to continue her work in support of emerging performers. Princess Grace wanted to be "remembered as someone who accomplished useful deeds, and who was a kind and loving person." Her many charitable works throughout her life ensure that legacy.

Kennedy, Jacqueline "Jackie" (1929–1994)
First Lady
Portrayed by: Jaclyn Smith, Blair Brown, Ginnifer Goodwin, Francesca Annis, Joanne Whalley, Sally Taylor-Isherwood, Emily VanCamp, Jill Hennessy, Jacqueline Bisset, Karen Ingram

Photographer, wife, mother, first lady, fashion icon, book editor, legend. Jackie Kennedy was all of those things and more, so it's no surprise that TV programs about her life abound.

Born Jacqueline Lee Bouvier in affluent Southampton, New York, young Jackie pursued interests in horseback riding, painting, and writing. After graduating from George Washington University in 1951, she took a job as an "Inquiring Camera Girl" at the *Washington Times-Herald*. As told in *Jacqueline Bouvier Kennedy* (TV movie, 1981), Jackie (Jaclyn Smith) soon meets politically ambitious Jack Kennedy (James Franciscus), teaching him how to eat fancy foods instead of bologna sandwiches, while their attraction builds. As their respective regional accents come and go, JFK makes his way to the White House, where Jackie struggles with the lack of privacy and finding a required role beyond wife and mother.

She finds her mission in renovating and restoring the crumbling White House, hiring a curator to catalog the mansion's holdings. When she's finished, Mrs. Kennedy takes the nation on a televised tour of the first family's home, a smashing TV success not only in America, but around the world. After that, the film winds inexorably to its conclusion, as the president and first lady board Air Force One for Dallas, but spares us the horror of watching JFK's assassination, which is referenced by the sound of a single gunshot as the plane flies into the sun.

A week after the assassination, historical Jacqueline Kennedy was interviewed in Hyannis Port by Theodore H. White of *Life* magazine. The movie uses a recreation of this conversation as its final scene, and Jaclyn Smith is affecting here, as Mrs. Kennedy tells White (Will Hunt) about her memories of the assassination and her husband's place in history. She says that Jack would play records every night, and that his favorite was from the musical *Camelot*, especially the last lines when King Arthur urges that the "one brief shining moment" known as Camelot should never be forgotten. Mrs. Kennedy says, "There'll never be another Camelot again." The legend of Camelot was thereafter associated with the "brief shining moment" that was the Kennedy administration.

Other productions focus on the period leading up to JFK's assassination, but are not Jackie-centric. *Kennedy*, a 1983 miniseries, is a "biography" of John F. Kennedy's presidency, starring Martin Sheen as the president and Blair Brown, who may have most resembled Mrs. Kennedy among the many actresses who portrayed her on TV. *Killing Kennedy* (TV movie, 2013) tracks the assassination of JFK from two vantage points, telling the stories of both JFK's presidency and Lee Harvey Oswald's growing disaffection, with Rob Lowe as the president, Will Rothhaar as suspected assassin Oswald, and Ginnifer Goodwin as Jackie Kennedy.

After retreating from public life in 1964, Jackie slowly re-emerged, only to be confronted with the assassination of another family member, her brother-in-law Robert F. Kennedy, in June 1968. In October of the same year, she married her longtime friend Aristotle Onassis, a development which met with much public disapproval. Jacqueline's image as a dignified, grieving widow had been etched into the American consciousness, and her union with a wealthy, divorced man who owned a private island seemed at odds with that picture.

Onassis: The Richest Man in the World (TV movie, 1988), covers some of this territory, when Jackie (Francesca Annis) appears in the second half, just after Bobby Kennedy's shooting. She says, "They're killing Kennedys. I don't want my children living here anymore." Good friend Aristotle Onassis (Raul Julia) has the solution, a home with him in Greece, and the two promptly marry. It seems like true love at first, but acute acquisitiveness is a pitfall for both of them. Ari's always buying Jackie things and telling her to go shopping, she's always buying herself things and overspending, he wants to show he has the most sought-after woman in the world, etc. The relationship deteriorates until Jackie is spending most of her time in New York, and it ends, not with divorce, as Aristotle would prefer, but with his passing.

After the death of her second husband in 1975, Jackie worked as a book editor in New York City, reaching the position of senior editor at Doubleday. She continued her interest in landmark preservation, playing a significant role in saving the Grand Central Terminal in New York. She never remarried, but maintained a close relationship with Maurice Tempelsman during the last 12 years of her life. The relationship is depicted at the start of *Jackie Bouvier Kennedy Onassis* (TV movie, 2000) as Jackie

(Joanne Whalley) and Maurice (Jerry Adler) visit Arlington National Cemetery, the site of JFK's grave. As they drive away, Jackie says, "I find myself thinking constantly of the past these days." The story of her life then unfolds, with a little help from Sally Taylor-Isherwood as Jacqueline at 8 and Emily VanCamp as Jackie at 13.

There are more televised Jacquelines. Jackie (Jill Hennessy) as part of the Kennedy wives' club in *Jackie, Ethel, Joan: The Women of Camelot* (TV movie, 2001), Jackie (Jacqueline Bisset) as the mother of JFK Jr. in *America's Prince: The John F. Kennedy Jr. Story* (TV movie, 2003), Jackie (Karen Ingram) as the wife who is saved from dying alongside her husband in the *Quantum Leap* episode "Lee Harvey Oswald—October 5, 1957–November 22, 1963: Part 2" (1992). And there are still others.

The most powerful image of Jacqueline Kennedy, however, was the one that TV transmitted on November 25, 1963. Wearing a sheer black veil, standing between her two children, Mrs. Kennedy whispered to her son, prompting him to salute his father's casket as it departed St. Matthew's Cathedral in Washington, D.C. Such a moment, such a life will always defy imitation.

Kenney, Annie (1879–1953)

See (mentioned in): **Pankhurst, Emmeline (1858–1928)**

King, Coretta Scott (1927–2006)

Civil Rights Activist, Author
Portrayed by: Carmen Ejogo, Cicely Tyson, Angela Bassett

Born in Heiberger, Alabama, Coretta Scott attended racially segregated schools. She was valedictorian of her high school class, and continued her studies at Antioch College, where she became involved in political causes on campus, including race relations, civil liberties, and peace. Scott earned a scholarship to the New England Conservatory of Music, where she studied voice, and while there she met Martin Luther King, Jr., who was working on his doctorate at Boston University. The couple married in 1953, but Coretta signaled that she didn't intend to be a traditional '50s wife, editing their vows to remove the one about obeying her husband.

After completing her degree, she moved with Martin to Montgomery, Alabama, where he had accepted an invitation to be the pastor of Dexter Avenue Baptist Church. Their lives took on new complexities and even dangers, as Martin became leader of the Montgomery bus boycott, a civil rights demonstration to protest segregated seating on buses. When the King residence was bombed while Coretta and ten-week-old daughter

Yolanda were at home, Coretta showed her bravery and resolve by refusing to relocate, even when pressured to do so by her father and father-in-law. She took a stand in the fight for freedom and made a commitment to support her husband in the burgeoning civil rights movement.

The Montgomery bus boycott, with an emphasis on the work of Dr. Martin Luther King, Jr. (Jeffrey Wright), is the subject of *Boycott*, a TV movie from 2001. Carmen Ejogo portrays Coretta Scott King, who is often seen with an apron on in the kitchen, keeping the home fires burning, so to speak. As Martin takes leadership of the protest movement, his life and those of his loved ones are threatened. The bombing of the King home is crosscut with a scene of a choir performance at a service that Martin is attending. Coretta hears a thud against the door, and moves to the back of the house and the baby's room. The viewer doesn't see the explosion. Instead we see someone deliver the message of the bombing to Martin.

Coretta's immediate reaction to the explosion and its impact on her are missing. The story is Martin's reaction. When Martin's father (Mike Hodge) later urges him to move to Atlanta, where the family will be safe, he asks Coretta to help convince Martin. She says, "Baby, what do you want to do?" Martin says, "I'm staying here." Coretta replies, "Then so am I."

The real Coretta Scott King once said, "I am made to sound like an attachment to a vacuum cleaner, the wife of Martin, then the widow of Martin, all of which I was proud to be. But I was never just a wife, nor a widow. I was always more than a label." This movie, while telling an important story, and even winning a Peabody Award in the process, takes the "vacuum cleaner attachment" approach to Coretta's life during the boycott.

Cicely Tyson brings Coretta to life in *King* (Miniseries, 1978), which tells her husband's story from their courtship in Boston through his assassination in 1968. When Coretta accepts a blind date with Martin (Paul Winfield), and he is overly enthusiastic and flattering, she says, "You're making me feel a little self-conscious." Coretta is less than impressed with this self-assured young man, and she offers a few subtle eye rolls. As the date ends, she lets herself out of the car, ignoring an established gender custom of the '50s, where the man comes around to open a car door for a lady. Martin accepts this lapse in etiquette with good humor.

Coretta talks about some of her experiences with discrimination as a student, and says, "Well, I know that I'm going to have to put up with this for the rest of my life, but nobody is going to make me feel that it's right." Later, after they are married, when Martin has begun to fight against the type of discrimination Coretta was talking about, he is arrested and dragged away by two uniformed officers. Coretta is right there in the mix, trying to pull the cops off of her husband.

King generated not only low ratings, but also lots of controversy. Some thought Martin Luther King, Jr., was portrayed as too meek and cowardly. Others complained that people important to the movement had been excluded. Still others thought the roles of Coretta et al. had been enlarged at the expense of more important players. The real Coretta Scott King was having none of it. She said, "*King* is a drama and not a documentary; therefore it should be judged as such."

Coretta's accomplishments in her own right come into full view in *Betty and Coretta*, a Lifetime television movie from 2013. Angela Bassett stars as Coretta Scott King, who, in the years after the passing of her husband, forms a friendship with Betty Shabazz (Mary J. Blige), wife of slain black activist Malcolm X (Lindsay Owen Pierre). In the words of on-screen narrator Ruby Dee, "…they were a sisterhood born of sorrow, yes, but they became a sisterhood of greatness." In the case of Mrs. King, she demonstrated her continued bravery and dedication to the cause of peace by leading a march in Memphis, the city where her husband was assassinated, just four days after his death, in hopes of healing the nation and averting riots.

She worked to establish a national holiday in honor of MLK, presenting to Congress a petition with 6 million signatures and leading the largest demonstration ever seen in Washington, D.C., to that time. The movie intersperses Ruby Dee's recollections, supplemented by actual documentary footage, with the story of the two widows, for a moving, albeit episodic presentation.

Coretta Scott King once said, "What most did not understand then was that I was not only married to the man I loved, but I was also married to the movement that I loved." We know this now, or at least we should.

Lady Day

See: **Holiday, Billie (1915–1959)**

Lamarr, Hedy (ca. 1913–2000)

Actress, Inventor

Portrayed by: Celia Massingham, Alyssa Sutherland

Behind-the-scenes tales about Hollywood's classic actresses tend to have a familiar ring—unrivaled beauty, multiple marriages, scandals, etc. But the story of Hedy Lamarr adds a feature that no other actor can lay claim to—the invention of a "secret communication system" that minimized the jamming of radio signals and was later incorporated into Bluetooth technology. That's right, the actress promoted as the "world's most beautiful woman" was a tech geek. Let that sink in.

Lamarr was typecast in roles requiring beauty and sensuality, but she wanted to do more, once famously saying, "Any girl can be glamorous. All you have to do is stand still and look stupid." An inventor in her spare time, Lamarr contacted composer George Antheil to help develop her idea for a frequency-hopping signal to assist Allied radio-controlled torpedoes during World War II. For their work, both Lamarr and Antheil were inductees into the National Inventors Hall of Fame in 2014.

Hedy Lamarr in *The Heavenly Body*, 1944 (MGM).

Scripted television first took note of Lamarr's beautiful brain in *Agent Carter* (2015–2016), with the Hedy-inspired character of Whitney Frost (Wynn Everett), a Golden Age actress who had used her scientific genius to help the Allies during World War II, but literally went to the dark side when she later absorbed Zero Matter, an unstable force of negative energy. *Legends of Tomorrow* brought us Hedy herself (Celia Massingham), whose acting and inventing careers are scuttled, when time-traveling Helen of Troy (Bar Paly) steals her thunder in "Helen Hunt" (2017). Lamarr (Alyssa Sutherland) receives another visit from time travelers in "Hollywoodland," a 2018 episode of *Timeless*, when she must help retrieve the only copy of the film *Citizen Kane*, which has been stolen in a plot to change history.

Time travel? That would have been right up Hedy Lamarr's alley.

Langtry, Lillie (1853–1929)

Actress

Portrayed by: Francine York, Francesca Annis, Jenny Seagrove, Dixie Carter

Lillie Langtry, born Emilie Charlotte Le Breton, was not a traditional woman by the standards of late 19th-century England. While her beauty and wit gave her entrée to London society, she caused a stir among the elite by becoming a stage actress, unheard of in that milieu, making her West End debut in the comedy *She Stoops to Conquer* in 1881. Lillie became interested in the business side of the theater as well, leasing, renovating, and managing London's Imperial Theatre for several years, beginning in 1900. Although women weren't allowed to register horses for thoroughbred racing at the time, Lillie maintained a successful racing stable at Newmarket. While married herself, she had affairs with noblemen and royalty, including the also married Prince of Wales, Albert Edward, who went on to become King Edward VII. And this doesn't even cover her adventures in America.

Death Valley Days touches on Langtry's American travels in "A Picture of a Lady" (1965). When Judge Roy Bean (Peter Whitney), a Texas saloon owner and justice of the peace, is captivated by a newspaper photo of the beautiful Lillie (Francine York), he begins to exchange letters with her in England. Langtry is flattered, especially when she learns that Bean has named his saloon "The Jersey Lilly," her popular nickname at the time. As his obsession builds, he renames the entire town Langtry, although the historical record indicates that Langtry, Texas is actually named after George Langtry, a railroad engineer. When Lillie finally makes it to town to see what Bean has created in her honor, she receives the sad news from Dr. Lathrop (Paul Fix) that the judge has passed. "A Picture of a Lady" is a surprisingly soft and romantic entry in the series, especially given Bean's reputation as the crusty "Law West of the Pecos."

Francesca Annis portrayed Lillie Langtry in two 1970s British productions. In the first, *Edward the Seventh* (Miniseries, 1975), known in the U.S. as *Edward the King*, Lillie is a minor character, one of Edward's many mistresses. In the second, Langtry is center stage, the subject of a 13-episode miniseries entitled *Lillie* (1978). The series begins on the island of Jersey, where Lillie grows up, but she seeks and gains escape by marrying Edward Langtry (Anton Rodgers), an apparently wealthy shipowner. Edward's fortune has been exaggerated, but Lillie's beauty has not, and one invitation to a dinner party leads to important social connections and work as an artist's model.

Soon a sketch of Lillie appears around London, and she becomes the belle of every ball, drawing the attention of royal suitors and Oscar Wilde (Peter Egan). The story continues through her extramarital affairs, transformation into an actress, American tours, and final days in Monaco. Francesca Annis, 39 years old at the time, aged from 15 to 76 as Lillie. Emphasizing Langtry's intelligence, will to succeed, and agency, she won a BAFTA (British Academy of Film and Television Arts) Award for her portrayal of Lillie in the miniseries.

After that, Langtry returned to supporting character status on television. In *Incident at Victoria Falls* (TV movie, 1992), Jenny Seagrove makes for a stunning Lillie, who exchanges secrets with an aging Sherlock Holmes (Christopher Lee), as the famous detective deals with the theft of a fabled diamond in South Africa. Dixie Carter portrays an ambiguously accented Langtry in *Gambler V: Playing for Keeps* (TV movie, 1994), where she tours the old west and runs into an old love, Brady Hawkes (Kenny Rogers), who's trying to save his son from a life of crime.

Lillie Langtry's storied life, the careers, the affairs, the fortunes won and lost, ended in Monaco, but she was buried on Jersey, her childhood home—her travels at an end.

Lincoln, Mary Todd (1818–1882)

First Lady

Portrayed by: Julie Harris, Elaine Bonazzi, Sada Thompson, Mary Tyler Moore, Lillian Gish, Donna Murphy, Karen Boles, et al.

Mary Todd's life started out happily enough, with success at finishing school, popularity among the gentry of Springfield, Illinois, and marriage to a country lawyer and member of the Illinois House of Representatives named Abraham Lincoln. After her husband's election as the 16th president of the United States, Mary Todd Lincoln became first lady on March 4, 1861. Alas, it was not to be a halcyon era for the couple or the country, as the nation plunged into the American Civil War a scant few weeks later. The war was not to be their only trial, however, as William Wallace Lincoln, the 11-year-old son of Mary and Abraham, died of typhoid fever at the White House in 1862. His passing deeply affected Mary, who remained in bed for three weeks.

As the future looked brighter a few years later, with the end of the Civil War in view, Mary was at her husband's side, holding his hand during a performance of *Our American Cousin* at Ford's Theatre. There, on April 15, 1865, President Lincoln was shot by an assassin's bullet, and Mary held him for the last time.

While the character of Mary Todd Lincoln appears in several TV productions focused on her husband's life, Mary herself is the subject of two programs dealing with the difficult years after her husband's assassination. Julie Harris won a Tony award for her portrayal of the former first lady in the Broadway play *The Last of Mrs. Lincoln*, and she reprised the role in a 1976 production of the same title for PBS's Hollywood Television Theatre. The teleplay follows Mary's life after the assassination for the 17 years until her death. In that time, she deals with the death of another son, Tad (Robby Benson), and institutionalization after proceedings prompted by her remaining son, Robert (Michael Cristofer). She later finds her way to a village in France, where she says, "I live from dream to dream." Who could blame her?

The institutionalization proceedings for Mrs. Lincoln are the basis for a nontraditional piece of televised historical fiction, *The Trial of Mary Lincoln*, a 1972 opera in one act commissioned for National Educational Television and shown on PBS. Mezzo-soprano Elaine Bonazzi portrays the first lady in the production, which takes place in May of 1875 at the Cook County courthouse in Chicago during a trial to determine whether Mary is sane. The real Mary Lincoln suffered from a host of conditions, including headaches, hallucinations, angry outbursts, a possible shopping addiction, and the sexism of many of the men around her. As the opera begins, the judge (Fred Stuthman) refers to evidence of "…eccentric and unusual behavior, suggesting an unsound mind." Mary's son Robert (Wayne Turnage) is the plaintiff, and his mother's behavior during past events is revealed in flashbacks. Anne Howard Bailey wrote the libretto, and received an Emmy Award for Outstanding Writing for a Variety Series.

Two TV miniseries about Abraham Lincoln, based on books by well-known American authors, featured the character of Mary Todd Lincoln, as interpreted by popular actresses of the time. The first, *Sandburg's Lincoln* (1974–1976), from Carl Sandburg's six-volume biography, featured Hal Holbrook as Abraham and Sada Thompson as Mary. In the six-part television series, we meet a folksy, saintly Abe, who is patient and adept at handling the problems caused by his sometimes overwrought and pushy wife. While Mary is supportive and loving, she does have her issues, such as excessive spending. When Abraham confronts her over a large bill, she replies, "It was only a few things I needed."

Heavily made-up Holbrook as Abe goes on to itemize the few things, "…20 handpainted Japanese fans, 12 pairs of silver dancing slippers, 15 lace shawls of varying designs, two dozen pairs of ladies' kid gloves…." Mary says she's trying to combat comments about how countrified they are, and their not belonging in Washington society. She then accuses him of not loving her, but he brings her around with a bouquet of flowers from the garden. It's a weird sitcom touch, amidst the personal and national tragedies they endure.

The second miniseries, *Lincoln* (a.k.a. *Gore Vidal's Lincoln*, 1988), based on *Lincoln: A Novel* (1984) by Gore Vidal, starred Sam Waterston as Abraham and Mary Tyler Moore as Mary Lincoln. Moore's Mrs. Lincoln is a chatterbox, nattering on about this and that, when she meets her new dressmaker, Elizabeth Keckley (Ruby Dee), a free black woman who has fled the South. "The vampire press is always ready to spring at me," says Mary Lincoln. She callously describes her knowledge of slavery,

Sada Thompson as Mary Todd Lincoln with Hal Holbrook as the president in *Sandburg's Lincoln* (NBC).

telling Keckley of a woman she knew who "beat to death seven slaves that we knew of," this while Lincoln gathers material and a pattern for the dress Keckley is to make. Then Mrs. Lincoln points out how poor she and her husband are, and concludes with, "...no matter what you may read in the press, I am the one who wants slavery destroyed." Mary Tyler Moore is effective and surprisingly natural as Mary Lincoln, although she doesn't physically resemble Mrs. Lincoln in any way.

Another book, *The Day Lincoln Was Shot* (1955) by Jim Bishop, was the basis for two TV productions filmed more than 40 years apart, but using the same title as the book. The first, shown as part of a series of monthly specials anthologized under the title *Ford Star Jubilee* (1956), boasted the all-star cast of Raymond Massey as Abraham Lincoln, Lillian Gish as Mary Todd Lincoln, and Jack Lemmon as assassin John Wilkes Booth. The second, a 1998 TV movie, featured Lance Henriksen as Lincoln, Donna Murphy as Mary, and Rob Morrow as Booth.

There are more Mary Lincolns, including one with demon-fighting powers, as portrayed by Karen Boles in the *Sleepy Hollow* episode "Columbia" (2017). The real Mary Todd Lincoln turned to spiritualism after the death of her son Willie, and even hosted séances at the White House. Hers was a life filled with tragedy and complicated by health issues. We may never truly understand the interaction of those forces upon her life.

Lister, Anne (1791–1840)

Diarist, Landowner

Portrayed by: Julia Ford, Maxine Peake, Suranne Jones

Often referred to as "the first modern lesbian," Anne Lister was a wealthy British landowner who pursued love affairs with women starting in her boarding school days, and documented the romances in her diaries. Anne kept her life as a lesbian a secret, due to the unenlightened times she lived in, but revealed all in her diaries, protecting sensitive passages from prying eyes by writing in a code of her own devising. She created her "crypthand," as she called it, by using letters from the Roman and Greek alphabets, punctuation marks, numbers, and mathematical symbols.

Julia Ford portrays Lister in "A Marriage," a 1994 episode of *A Skirt Through History*. This combination drama/documentary opens with the statement, "The words spoken by the people in this film are from their own writings." Dressed in her signature black, a color normally reserved for men of the time, Anne faces the camera, saying, "I love and only love the fairer sex…." She begins an intense affair with Mariana Belcombe (Sophie Thursfield), who later marries Charles Lawton (David Bacon), but the relationship between the two women continues sporadically for two decades. Although historical Lister considered herself married to Ann Walker, with whom she took communion and exchanged vows in 1834, *A Skirt Through History* brushes off the marriage as "not a fulfilling relationship." The emphasis in this rather dry production is on Lister's love for Belcombe.

A fuller picture of Lister's relationship with Walker emerges in *The*

Secret Diaries of Miss Anne Lister (TV movie, 2010). In voice-over, Lister (Maxine Peake) begins by telling us, "I was not born to live alone. I must have someone with me, and in loving and being loved, I could be happy." The immediate object of her affection is Mariana Belcombe (Anna Madeley), but living together becomes an impossibility when Mariana marries rich widower Charles Lawton (Michael Culkin). Anne starts to search for her ideal relationship elsewhere, but retains hope that Mariana will come around.

Years later, Lister begins a business partnership with Ann Walker (Christine Bottomley), a pretty, but shy woman, and the two embark upon the unlikely enterprise of running a coal mine on Lister's land. A romance proceeds slowly from the business arrangement, culminating in an exchange of wedding rings. When Mariana suddenly appears, finally ready to leave her husband, Lister says of her marriage to Walker, "We suit each other … and I like her very much." While not exactly professing undying love for her wife, Lister tells Mariana, "you made your choice," and returns to her greenhouse work. A coda to the film adds, "Anne Lister died of a fever, aged 49, while traveling with Ann Walker in the Caucasus Mountains."

Gentleman Jack (2019-), which takes its title from a local nickname for Lister, gives its subject the full TV series treatment. The story commences in 1832, when Lister (Suranne Jones) returns to her ancestral home of Shibden Hall in West Yorkshire, which she has recently inherited. Soon she will court Ann Walker (Sophie Rundle), but the emphasis here is not just on romance, as Lister also locks horns with an unscrupulous family, the Rawsons, her competitors in the coal trade. As Lister restores the estate, deals with intimidation from the Rawsons, and copes with Walker's mental health challenges, a portrait of her as an intelligent, capable, and energetic woman emerges.

In 2011, the *Diaries of Anne Lister* were added to the UK Register of the UNESCO Memory of the World Programme. The entry for the diaries describes Lister as a "remarkable landowner, business woman, intrepid traveller, mountaineer and lesbian." While noting the value of the diaries for their wealth of information about politics, business, religion, etc., the entry continues, "It is her comprehensive and painfully honest account of lesbian life and reflections on her nature, however, which have made these diaries unique. They have shaped and continue to shape the direction of UK Gender Studies and Women's History."

Little Britches (1879–?)

Outlaw
Portrayed by: Gloria Winters, Anne Helm

The story of Little Britches, like so many tales of the Old West, has only a passing acquaintance with the facts. Born Jennie Stevenson in southwestern Missouri, "Little Britches," as she came to be known, was attracted to the outlaw life at an early age, possibly inspired by stories of the Bill Doolin gang written by dime-novelist Ned Buntline. Jennie had married twice by the age of 16, but neither marriage lasted long, giving her the chance to answer the siren call of adventure. Along with her friend Cattle Annie (born Anna Emmaline McDoulet), Jennie finally connected with her heroes, the Doolin gang.

The two teens became known throughout the Oklahoma Territory, although their roles within the gang remain unclear. Both were sharpshooters, and Little Britches wore two six-guns and a cartridge belt over her men's trousers or "britches." Jennie and Annie sold alcohol to the Osage and Pawnee tribes, then a crime, and stole horses, eventually landing before a federal trial judge, who sentenced the women to two years in prison. Not much is known about Little Britches after her early release from prison for good behavior.

Characters based on Little Britches have appeared on *Stories of the Century* in "Little Britches" (1954) and on *Death Valley Days* in "Girl with a Gun" (1962). Both presentations were almost completely fictionalized, ignoring the few facts that we do know about Jennie. Perhaps in a tacit acknowledgment of the high levels of fabrication, both teleplays changed Jennie's last name while retaining her nickname of Little Britches. In *Stories of the Century*, Jennie McCall (Gloria Winters), already called Little Britches because of her habit of wearing pants, falls instantly in love with train robber Dave Ridley (James Best), leaving home with him to embark upon a life of crime.

In *Death Valley Days*, Jennie Metcalf (Anne Helm) seeks revenge against Marshal Hobe Martin (Ken Mayer), who killed her father (Garry Walberg). She joins an outlaw gang, where she is christened "Little Britches," and ultimately finds redemption by saving the marshal's life. Narrators for both series manage to find their way to one historical fact—that Jennie was imprisoned in a federal reformatory in Massachusetts. But they veer back into fiction by saying that she went on to settlement house work in New York after her release. Apparently helping the poor was the only proper penance both shows could envision for a young woman who wore pants and ran with outlaws.

Lombard, Carole (1908–1942)

Actress
Portrayed by: Sharon Gless, Denise Crosby, Vanessa Gray

Lombard, Carole

Born Jane Alice Peters in Fort Wayne, Indiana, Carole Lombard grew up to be both the queen of screwball comedy and a feminist trailblazer in Hollywood contract negotiation. Lombard was discovered at the age of 12, when her "tomboy" good looks and baseball acumen caught the eye of director Allan Dwan, who promptly gave her a small part in his film *A Perfect Crime* (1921). After some minor roles in silent films of the '20s, Lombard's big break came in *Twentieth Century* (1934), a film which pioneered the screwball comedy genre. Lombard's almost impossible mix of sophisticated glamour and down-to-earth spunkiness was a perfect match for the new genre, and she found success in later films such as *My Man Godfrey* (1936) and *To Be or Not to Be* (1942).

While characters based on Carole Lombard appear in three different TV movies, Lombard is not the focus of any of these programs. Sharon Gless plays Carole in *The Scarlett O'Hara War* (TV movie, 1980), a film about the legendary search for an actress to play Scarlett O'Hara in *Gone with the Wind* (1939), a role which ultimately went to Vivien Leigh (Morgan Brittany). The juiciest action occurs at a lavish party thrown by David O. Selznick (Tony Curtis), where many of the actresses up for the part are in attendance. Lombard describes the scene she encounters, while arriving at the gala with her boyfriend Clark Gable (Edward Winter): "We're up to our butts in Scarletts here."

Some of the women are still eager for the role, while others have grown tired of the competition and Selznick's procrastination, intentional or otherwise. Tallulah Bankhead (Carrie Nye) later prompts Carole to join her in dumping their soup bowls on Selznick's head, while proclaiming in unison, "Frankly, my dear, we don't give a damn." You won't get to know Carole Lombard or any of the other famous folk depicted in this movie, because it rarely ventures beyond caricature.

Lombard also pops up in two biopics about other women. Denise Crosby portrays her in *Malice in Wonderland*, a 1985 TV movie about Hollywood gossip columnists Louella Parsons (Elizabeth Taylor) and Hedda Hopper (Jane Alexander). Vanessa Gray is Lombard in *Lucy* (TV movie, 2003), a film about Lucille Ball (Rachel York, Madeline Zima), which covers Lucy's life from her early days in New York through the end of her marriage to Desi Arnaz (Danny Pino). Lombard's free-spirited ways are encapsulated in a brief scene, where she saves a Ball/Arnaz party from social disaster by being the first to serve herself from a large pile of spaghetti which has fallen to the floor.

While Carole Lombard was the equivalent of a bit player in these TV movies, she became a star in real life, a life that was cut tragically short by a plane crash in 1942. President Franklin Roosevelt sent his condolences to Clark Gable, who had become Carole's husband in 1939: "She brought great joy to all who knew her and to millions who knew her only as a great artist.... She is and always will be a star, one we shall never forget...."

Lovelace, Ada (1815–1852)
Mathematician, Computing Pioneer
Portrayed by: Lily Lesser, Emerald Fennell

Born Augusta Ada Byron in Middlesex, England, Ada Lovelace was the daughter of poet Lord Byron, although she never knew her father, who abandoned his family shortly after she was born. Ada married William King, who became Earl of Lovelace in 1838, making Ada the Countess of Lovelace. Privately educated in mathematics and science, Ada developed a working relationship with mathematician Charles Babbage, particularly intrigued by his plans to produce the Analytical Engine, a mechanical computer. Ada created a program for Babbage's proposed machine, thereby becoming, in the eyes of many historians, the world's first computer programmer.

A character based on Ada Lovelace appears in three episodes of *The Frankenstein Chronicles* (2015–2017), a crime drama which takes its inspiration from Mary Shelley's *Frankenstein*. Lily Lesser portrays Ada, here with the surname Byron, who in series 2 works with Frederick Dipple (Laurence Fox) to create a life-sized automaton. In "Seeing the Dead" (2017), Ada questions Dipple's belief that a man who builds and commands machines has more power than God. She's not averse to the holding of power per se, at least when it comes to increasing the power of women in the world. But she has no desire for man to have power over God, quoting Percy Bysshe Shelley: "Power, like a desolating pestilence, pollutes whatever it touches. And obedience, bane of all genius, virtue, freedom, truth, makes slaves of men, and of the human frame ... a mechanized automaton." Ada's use of this real-world quote is brilliant, as it turns the very subject of discussion, mechanized automatons, inside out, where people have become the automatons.

Lovelace appears again in "The Green-Eyed Monster," a 2017 episode of *Victoria*, a series which follows the early life of Queen Victoria. As its title suggests, the episode is more interested in romantic jealousy than science, as Ada (Emerald Fennell) and Charles Babbage (Jo Stone-Fewings) attend a palace function at the invitation of Prince Albert (Tom Hughes). Albert's wife, Queen Victoria (Jenna Coleman), is jealous of her husband's interest in Ada, but the queen is reassured by former premier Lord Melbourne (Rufus Sewell) that Albert likes Ada only for her science.

Ada Lovelace Day, observed on the second Tuesday of October every year since 2009, acknowledges the work of this computing pioneer, and honors the contributions of women to science, technology, engineering, and mathematics. Celebrated around the world, Ada Lovelace Day is a fitting commemoration of the woman Babbage called "the Enchantress of Number."

Ludington, Sybil (1761–1839)
Revolutionary War Hero
Portrayed by: Juno Temple

"Listen, my children, and you shall hear of the midnight ride of" ... Sybil Ludington? While Paul Revere and his ride to muster colonial militia were immortalized in the poem by Henry Wadsworth Longfellow, Sybil Ludington, who completed a similar mission at the age of 16, has suffered in the publicity department, at least until recently. On April 26, 1777, Ms. Ludington rode 40 miles through the night to rouse local troops in Putnam County, New York, warning nearly 400 militiamen under the command of her father, Colonel Henry Ludington, that the British were marching toward Danbury, Connecticut.

Drunk History does a surprisingly stirring retelling of Sybil's ride (with the usual anachronisms) in "New York City" (2014). Juno Temple stars as Sybil, who sets out alone in the dark when her father, Henry (Paul Scheer), realizes someone must rally the troops because "it's not like you can send an e-vite out." As Sybil races in the rain, she grabs a big stick, which she uses to bang on the houses she passes, rousing their inhabitants. By the time she returns home at daybreak, she has gathered 400 militiamen, who will follow her father into battle. Weeks later, George Washington himself appears at the Ludingtions' door to give Sybil his personal "huzzah!" Narrator Suzi Barrett concludes by saying, "Twenty miles is what Paul Revere rode, and then double it, and that's what Sybil Ludington did...."

Although some, such as historian Paula D. Hunt, have questioned the accuracy of details surrounding Sybil's ride, the United States government recognized her achievement by issuing a stamp in her honor as part of its "Contributors to the Cause" Bicentennial series in 1975. She has been immortalized in a statue sculpted by Anna Hyatt Huntington, which stands in Carmel, New York, with smaller versions of the statue located in places like Danbury, Connecticut, and Murrells Inlet, South Carolina. She is commemorated in children's books, the chamber opera *Sybil of the American Revolution*, and even an ultramarathon that approximates her historic ride, the Sybil Ludington 50K Run in Carmel, New York.

Long may you ride, Sybil!

Macphail, Agnes (1890–1954)
See (mentioned in): **Haile, Margaret (?–?)**

Madison, Dolley (1768–1849)
First Lady
Portrayed by: Casey Wilson

In "First Ladies," a 2014 installment of *Drunk History*, narrator Jenny Johnson describes Dolley Madison as "a big party monster." While that's not the most felicitous phrasing, it does point to Dolley's political importance as White House hostess for her husband, the fourth president of the United States, James Madison. The role of the president's wife, not yet called "First Lady," was still new, and Dolley did much to establish customs for the women who would follow her. Dolley's legendary hospitality and social graces led not only to "monster" bashes, but also to political amity, as she invited members of both parties, Federalists and Republicans, to her events in hopes of creating good will.

Dolley Madison's biggest claim to fame, however, is not as a Washington party girl, but as an American patriot during the War of 1812. *Drunk History* tells the story, mostly accurately, with Casey Wilson as Dolley and Ian Roberts as James Madison. When the British invade Washington, President Madison goes off to fight, while Dolley remains at the White House, refusing to leave, even though everyone else is fleeing the capital. Finally convinced that the situation is dire, Dolley agrees to depart, but won't leave the Gilbert Stuart portrait of George Washington behind to British desecration. When a servant wants to roll up the painting for easier transport, Dolley says, "It's not a Jimi Hendrix poster!" (The real Dolley probably never said that.) For good measure, Dolley also grabs a copy of the Declaration of Independence. Narrator Johnson says, "Dolley Madison takes all the important things that meant something to this country...." The British then burn the White House.

Dolley Madison's steadfastness under siege and behind-the-scenes political acumen made her a legend, but her legacy in popular culture became increasingly complex and peculiar. Beginning in the 1880s, her name and image began to appear on manufactured goods, including china plates, dolls, cigar wrappers, and desserts. Pop Dolley soon reflected not her own era or beliefs, but the values of the times in which her "products" were consumed.

Nowadays you can buy Dolly (with no "e") Madison "Zingers," small iced cakes in various flavors, at Amazon.com. As Dolley was well-known for balancing democratic and elitist tendencies in her work and life, she might have been just fine with Dolly Madison "Zingers."

Magoffin, Susan Shelby (1827–1855)
Diarist
Portrayed by: Linda Marsh

Susan Shelby Magoffin was the first woman to write an account of traveling the Santa Fe Trail, her diary finally published 70 years after her death as *Down the Santa Fe Trail and into Mexico: The Diary of Susan Shelby Magoffin, 1846–1847* (1926). Scholars have used the journal as a primary source for histories of the era, relying on its inside look at the Mexican-American War (1846–1848), Magoffin's descriptions of trade on the Santa Fe Trail, stories of people she met, and details of landscape and wildlife. Although Susan traveled in relative comfort with her husband, Santa Fe trader Samuel Magoffin, the rigors of the trip led to poor health, including a miscarriage, possibly caused by a carriage accident, and yellow fever during a second pregnancy, leading to the death of another child. Although she was able to return to her Kentucky home, later moving to Missouri, she never fully regained her health after the expedition, and died at the age of 28 after the birth of a fourth child.

Death Valley Days tells part of Magoffin's story in "No Place for a Lady" (1965). Linda Marsh stars as Magoffin, who is traveling with her husband Samuel (Simon Scott) on the Santa Fe Trail, when they meet William Bent (Ronald Reagan), a fellow trader. Susan, with the help of her maid Martha (Maidie Norman), sets out a surprisingly lavish dinner for Bent in a multi-colored tent, but William is upset that Susan has made the trip with her husband, as the men are on an important mission for the U.S. government. Bent says, "A woman is charming until she begins to get ideas."

Susan appears to be even more of an impediment when she has a miscarriage at Bent's Fort (how dare she), but she refuses to stay behind, insisting on continuing with her husband to Santa Fe. Just when the "stupid whim of this girl" looks like it might lead to the death of the entire party, Susan saves them all by brandishing a couple of guns at some Mexican outlaws. William suddenly changes his tune, saying "I never saw anything so brave in all my life." Susan replies, "I've been hoping there might be a way to be of some help, Mr. Bent."

Susan Shelby Magoffin was "of some help," of course, especially in writing her diary for posterity, but her appeal as a fabricated pistol-packing mama appears to have been too much for the episode's creators to resist. Had they looked more closely, they might have seen the real bravery that had been part of her story all along.

Marie Antoinette (1755–1793)
Queen of France
Portrayed by: Monique LeMaire, Elizabeth Berrington, Jayne Meadows

Little girls love to dress up as princesses for all the magic the title implies, but the life of a princess and later a queen wasn't a fairy tale for Marie Antoinette. Born Maria Antonia Josepha Johanna in Vienna, the new archduchess was the daughter of Empress Maria Theresa, ruler of the Habsburg Empire, who married off Maria Antonia at the age of 14 to the heir to the French throne. Maria, now Marie Antoinette, became queen of France in 1774, when her husband ascended the throne as King Louis XVI. The queen didn't make a favorable impression on her subjects, given her Austrian birth, her inability to conceive a child, at least initially, and rumors of profligate spending and extramarital affairs.

As the country's debt skyrocketed, not solely because of the queen's expenditures, and her subjects grew poorer, the French Revolution became inevitable, leading to the overthrow of the monarchy in 1792. Marie Antoinette died at the guillotine in 1793, after a guilty verdict for crimes against the state. Although she is famous for her alleged disregard for the plight of her starving subjects, as evidenced by the line, "Let them eat cake," there is no evidence she ever uttered the words.

For a notorious queen, Marie Antoinette hasn't made a big impact on the small screen. In "Reign of Terror," a 1966 episode of *The Time Tunnel*, the queen (Monique LeMaire) plays a tiny part in the story of two time travelers who fall (literally) onto the dangerous streets of Paris during the French Revolution. Time travelers Tony Newman (James Darren) and Doug Phillips (Robert Colbert) hatch a plan to see Marie, who is being held prisoner after the execution of her husband. She tells them that she has committed no crimes against her adopted country, but she is beyond saving at this point, giving them a document to help them escape the city. In return, they agree to assist her son, who is being held elsewhere, and they eventually save his life. Although Marie is a minor character in the teleplay, LeMaire portrays her with dignity and sympathy.

You would think a series called *Let Them Eat Cake* (1999) would have Marie Antoinette at its center, but the focus of this short-lived British comedy series is a countess who collects secrets for Marie at the Palace of Versailles in 1782. The queen herself (Elizabeth Berrington) puts in an occasional appearance, as in "The Pox," where Marie, in a white fright wig, thinks she is in Austria and proclaims her love for rats. In "Making Voopee," the Voopee in question is an Austrian delicacy, and Marie is treated to the farts of her royal snoop, Countess Colombine (Jennifer Saunders). That gives you a hint of Marie's DQ (dignity quotient) here.

The queen's DQ is higher in *Meeting of Minds*, an innovative and award-winning series from Steve Allen that ran on PBS stations from 1977 to 1981. In "Marie Antoinette, Sir Thomas More, Karl Marx, Ulysses S. Grant" (parts one and two, 1977), Jayne Meadows portrays the queen in full regalia, including a mammoth wig of curls, and discusses the French Revolution with Allen in this "tonight show" for historical figures. The queen talks about her background and beliefs, adhering to historical accuracy as much as possible.

The story of the revolution and royal response is long and complicated, but Marie Antoinette, who proved to be stronger and more decisive than her husband, often was judged as a symbol of the monarchy rather than as Marie Antoinette herself. While she was not blameless in her actions before and during the revolution, she was an easy scapegoat for anyone with a grievance, and she died bravely. "Courage! I have shown it for years; think you I shall lose it at the moment when my sufferings are to end?"

There's your replacement for "let them eat cake."

Jayne Meadows as Marie Antoinette in *Meeting of Minds* (PBS).

Mary I (1516–1558)

See (mentioned in): **Elizabeth I (1533–1603)**

Mary, Queen of Scots (1542–1587)

See (mentioned in): **de' Medici, Catherine (1519–1589)** and **Elizabeth I (1533–1603)**

Mata Hari (1876–1917)
Exotic Dancer, Spy
Portrayed by: Vanessa Hudgens, Phyllis Davis, Domiziana Giordano

Mata Hari, born Margaretha Zelle in Leeuwarden, Netherlands, was an exotic dancer and courtesan, who was executed by a French firing squad during World War I. The charge against Mata Hari was spying for Germany, although the facts of her case remain uncertain, and the German government publicly proclaimed her innocence in 1930. Recently released French documents also appear to clear her, with subsequent speculation that France had been looking for a scapegoat due to unacceptable military losses. Mata Hari's unconventional approach to life and work, with her semi-nude dancing, numerous lovers, some of whom were paying customers, and general disregard for the customs of the time, made her an easy target during a hypocritical time.

Drunk History takes some pains to flush out the real story of Mata Hari, although narrator Sugar Lyn Beard's inability to hold her inebriated self upright is a distraction in "Femme Fatales" (2019). A stunningly beautiful Vanessa Hudgens portrays Mata, who takes Paris high society by storm as an exotic dancer beginning in 1903. In this overly simplified story, Mata is doing the "girls just want to have fun" thing in France and Germany, but keeps running into military men, who want her to spy for them. Georges Ladoux (Dermot Mulroney), who works for French counterintelligence, wants to find a spy he can turn into a scapegoat, and hires Mata so he can use the information she collects against her. There was a real Ladoux, who worked for the Deuxième Bureau, France's military intelligence agency, and probably went so far as to tamper with the evidence against her, leading to her trial and execution.

Fantasy Island ventures into the fantasy realm, not surprising given that title, with its Mata Hari tale in "The Magic Camera/Mata Hari/Valerie" (1982). Phyllis Davis stars as Martha Harris, the great-, great-granddaughter of Mata Hari, who wants to learn the truth about her notorious ancestor. With the help of fantasy guide Mr. Roarke (Ricardo Montalban), Martha time travels to 1915 France, where she slips into the body of Mata Hari, while retaining her own sense of identity. Mata/Martha is a spy for the French, working with her lover Captain Claude Dumarque (George Chakiris), who sports perfect, blow-dried, '80s hair, while wearing a presumably accurate period uniform. But M/M might also be a spy for the Germans, romancing a man from the other side, Walter Lukas (Monte Markham). Mata/Martha is mock-executed with the assistance of Claude, and Martha, in later conversation with Mr. Roarke, concludes that the real Mata Hari was safely smuggled out of France. So much for the accuracy of history textbooks on Fantasy Island.

The Young Indiana Jones Chronicles makes some allusions to Mata Hari's possible espionage activities, but is mostly concerned with the coming-of-age story of its protagonist in "Paris, October 1916" (1993). Indiana Jones (Sean Patrick Flanery), a 16-year-old American who has joined the Belgian army using fake credentials, travels to Paris on leave, looking for "adventure of the softer and sweeter kind." He gets more than he bargained for when he meets Mata Hari (Domiziana Giordano), and they become lovers, unaware that they are under surveillance. Eventually Indy is arrested and questioned, still the innocent, oblivious to the larger events unfolding around him.

In the late 1970s, Bally released a pinball game called Mata Hari, which seems like a macabre choice for a game, especially once you've learned the real story behind the legend. Then again, given Mata Hari's iconoclasm and desire for the spotlight, maybe she would have loved it after all.

Meir, Golda (1898–1978)

Prime Minister of Israel
Portrayed by: Judy Davis, Ingrid Bergman

Born Goldie Mabovitch in Kyiv, then part of the Russian Empire, Golda Meir immigrated to Milwaukee, Wisconsin, with her family in 1906. She became interested in socialist, labor, and Zionist causes in high school, participating in youth organizations and speaking at public meetings. After marrying Morris Myerson in 1917, she became Goldie Myerson, later Hebraizing her name to Golda Meir. The couple immigrated to Palestine, then under British mandate, in 1921, where they joined a kibbutz, and Meir started her gradual ascent in politics. In 1948, Meir, still using the name Myerson, was a signatory of Israel's independence declaration, becoming the new government's minister to Moscow. She served as the state of Israel's fourth prime minister from 1969 to 1974, and was the first woman to hold that position, as well as only the fourth elected female head of state in the world.

Ingrid Bergman received posthumous Emmy and Golden Globe Awards for her portrayal of Meir in the 1982 TV movie *A Woman Called Golda*. Originally broadcast in two parts, the film begins in 1977, as Meir visits her old grade school in Milwaukee, where the students ask questions about her life, and her story unfolds. She flashes back to a night in Russia when her family hid in their house with the lights out, while mobs searched the street for Jews. She tells the children, "…human beings just can't live in such choking, terrible fear.…"

After reaching adulthood in America, Golda, here played by Judy Davis, receives a marriage proposal from Morris (Leonard Nimoy), but she won't accept his proposal unless he agrees to go to Palestine and live in a kibbutz. She tells him about her dream for the future, "...the dream that we can have the same peace and security other people have. The only way we're ever going to get it is in a Jewish homeland." The couple eventually makes it to Palestine in 1921, but kibbutz life is hard, especially when Morris catches malaria.

Later life for Golda in Jerusalem as an impoverished housewife and mother of two isn't much better. When she accepts a full-time job as secretary of the Women's Council of Histadrut (the General Federation of Labour), her marriage to Morris is effectively over. As 10 years pass, signaled by some documentary footage, Golda has advanced in the Histadrut to the executive committee, and Ingrid Bergman has become Golda Meir.

As Bergman takes the Meir role, the political story overtakes the personal one. Golda and the committee oppose the British position that Palestine must not become a Jewish state, but she must work with the very same British government in the fight against Hitler. The narrative moves through Israel's declaration of independence, its first government with Meir as minister of labour, the war with the Arab states, and her

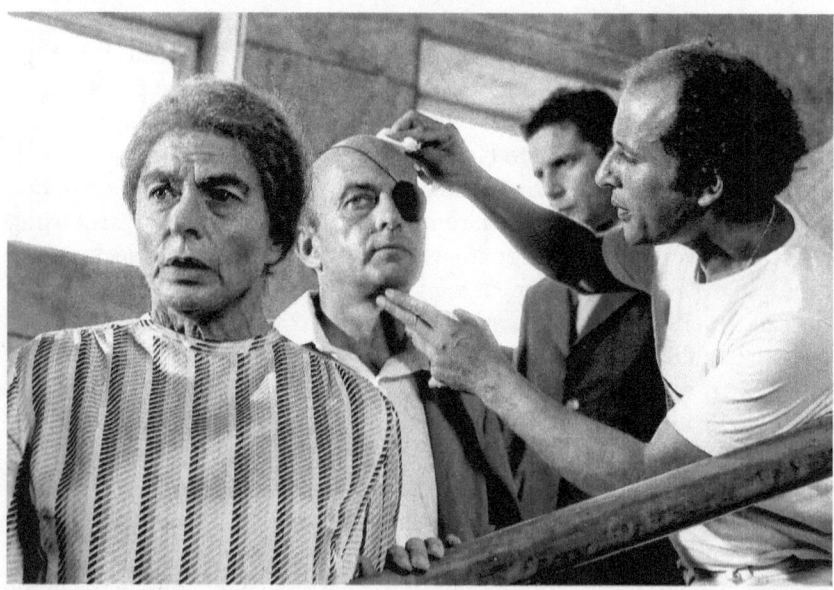

Ingrid Bergman as Golda Meir and Yossi Graber as Moshe Dayan in *A Woman Called Golda* (photograph by Yoni S. Hamenachem, CC BY-SA 3.0).

appointment seven years later as foreign minister. A lymphoma diagnosis leads her to retire from the ministerial post, but she answers her country's call to duty again in 1969, when she is elected Prime Minister, although her health is no better. Bergman finds the warmth in this real person, while portraying the larger-than-life figure that was Golda Meir in a performance called "remarkable" and "indelible" by television critics.

Mercer, Lucy (1891-1948)
See (mentioned in): **Roosevelt, Eleanor (1884-1962)**

Monroe, Marilyn (1926-1962)
Actress
Portrayed by: Ashley Judd, Mira Sorvino, Tracey Gold, Catherine Hicks, Poppy Montgomery, Kelli Garner, Susan Griffiths, Madonna, Juno Temple, et al.

Marilyn Monroe is an icon of American culture. The reasons she holds that distinction are complex and even contradictory, as are views on Marilyn's life and work. Was she a good actress or merely a sex goddess? Was she a victim of the male-dominated film industry or a savvy sculptor of her public image? Did she kill herself or was she murdered?

Norma Jean & Marilyn (TV movie, 1996) literally splits Monroe into two characters to deal with some of these dichotomies. Based on the book *Goddess, the Secret Lives of Marilyn Monroe* (1985) by Anthony Summers, the film features Ashley Judd as dark-haired Norma Jean Dougherty, the real, inner Marilyn, and Mira Sorvino as Marilyn Monroe, the blonde bombshell, who becomes a superstar, but struggles to find love and happiness. The two women appear together in scenes, where Norma Jean mocks Marilyn or the two visit a psychiatrist. The film places Monroe firmly in the victim camp, where she engages in plenty of weepy self-pity. It also subscribes to the suicide theory, as alter ego Norma Jean tells Marilyn she is "a cheap piece of trash," and pushes her over the edge to an overdose of pills. Lots of grim sensationalism in this one.

A more traditional biopic with a balanced portrait of Monroe came earlier with *Marilyn: The Untold Story* (TV movie, 1980). Based on the book *Marilyn: A Biography* by Norman Mailer, the film chronicles Monroe's life from childhood through her death. Tracey Gold portrays young Norma Jean, who must cope with foster care and a troubled mother (Sheree North), while Hollywood beckons just outside her window, giving her dreams of a better life. Catherine Hicks takes over as adult Norma Jean, who escapes factory work by becoming a photographer's model, and later becomes the protégée and mistress of agent Johnny Hyde (Richard Basehart). Norma Jean colors her hair platinum blonde, adopts a sashay, and gets her nose fixed, becoming Marilyn Monroe, film starlet.

The filming of Marilyn's famous number "Diamonds Are a Girl's Best Friend" from the film *Gentlemen Prefer Blondes* (1953) reveals many of her burgeoning issues, including insecurities about her looks and talent, a habit of showing up hours late on set, and frustration that she isn't allowed to offer input on how she should do a scene. Marriage to baseball great Joe DiMaggio (Frank Converse) doesn't bring happiness, as Joe objects to the cheesecake photos required by her career and especially to the famous subway grate scene, with air blowing up the skirt of her white dress, filmed for *The Seven Year Itch* (1955). The marriage quickly dissolves, and Marilyn is heartbroken. Marilyn Monroe, sex symbol, wasn't a problem just for DiMaggio, but for Marilyn herself, both professionally, as she sought more substantial acting roles, and personally, as she wrestled with issues of identity and self-esteem.

More books about Marilyn Monroe meant more TV biographies. *Blonde* (2000), a novel by Joyce Carol Oates, was the basis for a 2001 TV movie of the same title, which mixed fiction with fact, as had the predecessor novel, and starred Poppy Montgomery as Monroe. *The Secret Life of Marilyn Monroe* (Miniseries, 2015), based on the 2009 book of the same title by J. Randy Taraborrelli, featured Kelli Garner as Marilyn and Susan Sarandon as her mother, Gladys Pearl Baker.

Episodic television also found fascination in Monroe's story. In "Goodbye Norma Jean—April 4, 1960," a 1993 episode of *Quantum Leap*, time traveler Sam Beckett (Scott Bakula) must save Monroe (Susan Griffiths) from a barbiturate overdose in 1960, only to learn that she met that fate anyway in 1962. *Saturday Night Live* featured several MM skits, including a tasteless one on November 9, 1985, where Monroe, as portrayed by Madonna, is visited by John F. Kennedy (Randy Quaid) and his brothers, who plan to end her life so she won't tell all about her affairs with them. *Drunk History* chose the high road in emphasizing the positive impact Marilyn Monroe (Juno Temple) had on the career of Ella Fitzgerald (Gabourey Sidibe) in a touching vignette on "Legends" (2016).

There are more TV Marilyns, and fictionalizations of her life will no doubt continue. In "Marilyn Monroe, the Eternal Shape Shifter" (*Los Angeles Times*, August 5, 2012), historian Lois Banner says, "Monroe's multiple transformations allow each generation, even each individual, to create a Marilyn to their own specifications." While the fascination with Marilyn Monroe, however one perceives her, may always exist, the real Marilyn will forever remain elusive.

Montez, Lola (1821–1861)

Dancer, Actress

Portrayed by: Paula Morgan, Yvonne Cross, Patricia Medina, Rita Moreno

Lola Montez lived a lot of life in her scant 39 years on Earth. Born Eliza Rosanna Gilbert in Ireland, she took the stage name Lola Montez after a failed marriage in her teens, becoming a "Spanish" dancer, with successful performances in Europe. Men were mesmerized by Montez, especially famous ones, and she reportedly had affairs with composer Franz Liszt and author Alexandre Dumas. Her most notorious liaison was with King Ludwig I of Bavaria, who was so smitten by her beauty that he made her countess of Landsfeld, granting her a large annuity. Montez's involvement in other affairs, those of state, did not go as well, and Ludwig abdicated in 1848, while Lola fled the kingdom. In 1851, she answered the call of a new life in the United States, performing as a dancer and actress, eventually moving to San Francisco in 1853.

Lola's adventures in California had an Old West appeal, which attracted producers of television westerns of the '50s. The most complete, albeit over-the-top, version of her life is told in a scant 30 minutes by "Lola Montez," a 1955 episode of *Death Valley Days*. Paula Morgan is arrestingly beautiful as Montez, who speaks to the camera and narrates her life in a story that seldom rises above caricature. After her affairs with Liszt and Ludwig, Lola sails to California and meets Patrick Hull (Baynes Barron), a newspaperman. She explains to him how she got the name Montez. "I just took it, as I have taken anything I wanted." The two marry, settling in the gold

Portrait of Lola Montez, 1851 (Metropolitan Museum of Art, New York).

camp of Grass Valley, but Hull becomes jealous of the male attention she receives, and they quickly separate.

Later, Lola uses a bullwhip on the author of an unfavorable review of her dancing, a true story except for its location, which was Australia rather than California. At the end of her rope, she finds herself in New York, working at a rescue mission for outcast women in 1858. The conclusion of the story reflects an apparently true religious conversion experienced by real-life Lola before her passing.

Death Valley Days had visited the historical figure of Lola Montez once before in "Lotta Crabtree" (1954). Here Lola (Yvonne Cross) is in her Grass Valley period, and she takes a young girl, Lotta Crabtree (Sharon Baird), under her wing, teaching her to dance and sparking in her a love of performance. Lola isn't at the center of this story, but it shows her giving rather than taking, a glimmer of her future self after her religious conversion.

Lola's sojourn on the West Coast is the focus once again in "Lola Montez," a 1958 episode of *The Californians*. Patricia Medina portrays Montez in this highly fictionalized account of the dancer's arrival in San Francisco, where a large throng of men awaits her appearance at the docks. She makes no secret of the fact that she is looking for a husband, saying, "I have married everyone else. Why not an American?" Despite lots of male attention at a ball she throws for the elite of San Francisco, she fails in her quest to find a mate, although she says, "There is enough of Montez for all of you." Marshal Matt Wayne (Richard Coogan) doesn't want to become "just another notch" on her wedding ring, while newspaperman Jack McGivern (Sean McClory) is married, and his wife, Martha (Nan Leslie), decides not to give him up without a fight. Lola fails even to land a "patron," and Wayne blackmails her into leaving when he mentions her bigamy trial in England, another event plucked from the life of historical Lola.

All the foregoing episodes lacked most of the trappings of traditional westerns, but Lola's final appearance on '50s TV, "Lola Montez," a 1959 episode of *Tales of Wells Fargo*, had more recognizable Western elements. Rita Moreno portrays Montez, who is barricaded with fellow stagecoach passengers at a relay station during an Apache attack. The episode's title notwithstanding, the story is not Lola-centric, and involves a dispute between the Apaches and railroad agent Jim Hardie (Dale Robertson) over who has the greater right to pursue justice against a murderer.

Despite lots of available information, it's hard to get a handle on who the real Lola Montez was, sometimes because that information is conflicting. These TV presentations don't add much to our understanding, but one thing is clear. Lola Montez lived life on her own terms, not an easy feat for a woman of the mid–19th century.

Montgomery, Lucy Maud (1874–1942)
Author
Portrayed by: Alison Louder

Lucy Maud Montgomery was a prolific Canadian author, who wrote novels, short stories, poetry, and essays, but is best known for her first novel, *Anne of Green Gables*, published in 1908. Calling upon Montgomery's own experiences growing up on Prince Edward Island in Canada, the novel sings the praises of rural life on the island, while telling the story of an imaginative orphan named Anne Shirley, who finds a home with a middle-aged brother and sister. Writing as L.M. Montgomery, Maud, as she was called, was "…frankly in literature to make a living out of it," defying the turn-of-the-century notion that female authors should be anonymous and unconcerned about remuneration or celebrity. Anonymous Montgomery was not, as *Anne of Green Gables* became an immediate hit, making the author famous in her own lifetime, spawning sequels, as we would say nowadays, and eventually selling more than 50 million copies worldwide.

Maud Montgomery leaves the rural simplicity of P.E.I. for a visit to the big city of Toronto in "Unlucky in Love," a 2016 episode of *Murdoch Mysteries*. Alison Louder portrays the author, who finds herself in a writing class taught by Constable George Crabtree (Jonny Harris), who isn't much of a teacher. Sweet, pretty, and perky, Maud tells Crabtree that she has had success with poetry and stories, but now is keen to crack the novel form. Crabtree's review of *Anne of Green Gables* over a meal at a restaurant is hilarious, criticizing just about everything other than the author's "exemplary" use of the English language.

He finds the nature stuff overdone, Anne's red hair and freckles overstated, and, come to think of it, the character's gender poorly chosen, because if she were a boy, she could have real adventures. Maud is disappointed, but when they meet again, she says, "Half the world is made up of women. I suspect there should be a large readership for a novel with a female protagonist." She later learns she must return to the island to care for her grandmother, an action the real Maud took in 1898, but she also wants to devote herself to writing.

Montgomery and Crabtree spend one night together, and he inspires Maud to make the character of Anne an orphan, just like he is. A disclaimer is appended to the end of the program, stating, "Despite the story you have just seen there is no evidence to suggest Lucy Maud Montgomery met constable George Crabtree or that her work was influenced by him. (He's not real)." Since the line between fact and fiction is blurred in such shows, a clear statement of what's real and what isn't is appreciated, as is a sense of humor.

Morris, Esther Hobart (1814–1902)
Suffragist, Justice of the Peace
Portrayed by: Bethel Leslie

In "A Woman's Rights," a 1960 episode of *Death Valley Days*, we meet Esther Morris (Bethel Leslie), a woman living with her husband John (Dean Harens) in South Pass, Wyoming Territory, in the year 1869. Those few facts of the real Esther Hobart Morris's story are true, but most of what follows is made out of whole cloth. TV Esther, who is about 20 years younger than her historical counterpart of the same period, loses her husband to gunplay, and when it looks like his killer will get off scot-free, she decides to visit the governor. Esther and Lucretia Mott (Hope Summers), who appears in need of some *Voyagers!*-style help, because she has wandered badly off her historical course, interrupt a meeting on women's suffrage led by Governor Lee (Frank Wilcox).

Esther speaks passionately about her fellow women: "…they will bring to politics in this territory the point of view of those interested in building up, not tearing down, of preserving not destroying. Gentlemen, give women a chance to fight for what they believe in." The governor is impressed by Esther's words, and even appoints her as a replacement for the corrupt judge in South Pass who was about to let her husband's killer go free.

The real Esther Morris was, indeed, the first woman to hold the position of justice of the peace in the United States, serving in that capacity for almost nine months in South Pass City. Although Morris lacked legal experience, none of the cases she decided during her tenure were later reversed. But the death of Morris's husband played no part in setting her on the road to her appointment as a judge. In fact, historical Esther left behind her very-much-alive but ne'er-do-well husband, when she moved to Laramie to live with one of her sons in 1871.

In 1960, Wyoming officials presented a statue of Esther Hobart Morris to the National Statuary Hall at the U.S. Capitol in Washington, D.C. An "Overlooked No More" obituary of Morris in the 2018 *New York Times* noted: "One of just nine women represented in the collection in Washington, Morris is—as she was during her pioneering days in Wyoming—surrounded mostly by men."

Mott, Lucretia (1793–1880)
See (mentioned in): **Morris, Esther Hobart (1814–1902)**

Nation, Carrie (1846–1911)

Temperance Activist
Portrayed by: Valerie Buhagiar, Vanessa Bayer

Born Carrie Moore in Garrard County, Kentucky, Carrie Nation was deeply affected by the alcoholism of her first husband, Charles Gloyd, which ruined their brief marriage and later led to his death. In 1877, Carrie (sometimes spelled Carry) married David Nation, and the couple eventually settled in Kansas, where Carrie joined the temperance movement in 1890. Nation began protesting alcohol sales at saloons, which were flourishing, although Kansas was on the books as a dry state. At first, Nation used mostly words and prayers in her demonstrations, but in 1900, acting on directions from what she believed to be the voice of God, she upped her game, using rocks to smash up several saloons. Later she graduated to a hatchet as her tool of destruction, and her "hatchetations," as she called them, landed her in jail more than 30 times. She paid her fines from lecture tour fees and sales of souvenir hatchet pins, which read, "DEATH TO RUM."

"The Local Option," a 2015 episode of *Murdoch Mysteries*, gives us a glimpse of the Carrie behind the hatchetations. Nation (Valerie Buhagiar) finds herself on the periphery of an investigation into the murder of an anti-temperance politician in Toronto. While staying with Inspector Thomas Brackenreid (Thomas Craig) and his wife Margaret (Arwen Humphreys), Nation displays some of her typical tactlessness, when finding that the Brackenreids haven't lived up to her high ideals of sobriety. "May God have mercy on

Carrie Nation, ca. 1903, by White Studio (National Portrait Gallery, Smithsonian Institution).

your damnable souls," she tells Margaret, upon departing the home of her hosts. Earlier, Nation had shown her streak of fanaticism when discussing the assassination of President William McKinley, whom she suspected had been a secret drinker. "The Lord had no choice but to put that bullet right through President McKinley's heart." This comment reflects sentiments shared by the real Carrie Nation in 1901 that "the brewer's president" had gotten what he deserved.

Historical Carrie, who didn't seem to have much of a sense of humor, would have been appalled to learn that her next televised portrayal occurred on *Drunk History* in the 2016 episode "Bar Fights." Narrator Amber Ruffin boozily celebrates the work of Nation (Vanessa Bayer) in this vignette, which concentrates mostly on the temperance leader's saloon smashing. At the end, Ruffin and host Derek Waters drunkenly smash beer bottles in Carrie's name, a nice gesture, but one that lends a surreal feel to this already ironic entry in the series.

If there is an historical figure ripe for caricature, it is Carrie Nation, with her floor-length dress, her spectacles, and her hatchet. But we shouldn't forget that Nation truly cared about the lives of women, advocating for women's suffrage and establishing a shelter for the wives and children of alcoholics. Nation used the income from her autobiography *The Use and Need of the Life of Carry A. Nation* (1904) to care for her alcoholic daughter. While we remember Carrie's shiny hatchet, we should also consider the factors that led her to wield it.

Nevada, Emma (1859–1940)
Operatic Soprano
Portrayed by: Erin O'Brien

Emma Nevada, née Wixom, an operatic coloratura soprano, was born in a mining camp in Alpha, California, spending her early childhood in nearby Nevada City. Wixom took her stage name from her hometown, as well as from the state of Nevada, where her family later moved, residing in Austin. Emma trained as a singer in Europe, debuting in London, and later touring throughout France, Germany, and Italy. She became recognized as one of the great coloratura sopranos of her day, and was a favorite of Queen Victoria, who presented the singer with a diamond necklace, reported to be worth $100,000. In 1885, Emma returned to America, touring the country and performing for silver miners in her beloved Austin.

The necklace and Emma's visit to Austin are the inspirations for an episode of *Death Valley Days* titled "Emma Is Coming" (1960). Erin O'Brien portrays Emma, who is treated like a favorite daughter upon her return to Austin and is delighted to perform for the people who had supported her in the early days. Emma plans to wear the valuable necklace given to her by Queen Victoria, but Duke Clayton (Rick Jason), a local bad boy, steals the necklace before the performance. Emma covers for Clayton and sings without the necklace, while Duke, transformed by her singing, returns the necklace to her dressing room. Saccharine, yes, but this O. Henryesque tale is also surprisingly affecting.

Nightingale, Florence (1820–1910)
Nurse, Social Reformer, Statistician
Portrayed by: Sarah Churchill, Julie Harris, Janet Suzman, Jayne Meadows, Jaclyn Smith, Laura Fraser

One of history's most recognizable names, Florence Nightingale is associated with compassionate care for the sick, but few know of her accomplishments as a social reformer and statistician. While her work during the Crimean War sealed her image as the "Lady with the Lamp," who tended to wounded soldiers during the night, she also established base standards of care and sanitation, psychological counseling services, and better supply acquisition at the Barrack Hospital in Scutari (present-day Üsküdar, Turkey) in 1854. Upon her return to England, Nightingale provided statistical data and analysis to two Royal commissions, one of which examined the military medical systems which Nightingale had found so inadequate during her war experience. In 1860, she instituted the Nightingale School of Nursing at St. Thomas's Hospital in London, making nursing a viable option for women at a time when work outside the home was not considered respectable.

Florence Nightingale, ca. 1860, by Henry Hering (National Portrait Gallery, London).

Nightingale, Florence

Fictional characters based on Florence Nightingale have been appearing on TV screens for over 50 years. *Hallmark Hall of Fame* got the ball rolling with *Florence Nightingale* (1952), starring Sarah Churchill as the nursing pioneer in a 30-minute presentation which focused on her work during the Crimean War. The Hall of Fame returned to the subject of Nightingale in the oddly named *The Holy Terror* (1965), starring Julie Harris in a more thorough examination of Nightingale's life. The telecast opens with a jolt, as young Florence jumps from her bed, speaking to an unseen presence. As her father (Alan Webb) enters the room, he suggests she has been dreaming, but she insists that she has spoken to the angel of God, who has called her to God's service. Eventually that service will lead her to reform the inhumane conditions at the barracks in Scutari, but will also take its toll, as she becomes a victim herself of Crimean fever (brucellosis) and must do much of her fighting from her sickbed.

The '70s saw more productions about the Lady with the Lamp. Janet Suzman portrayed her in the British TV movie *Miss Nightingale* (1974), which covered the reformer's life from childhood to bedridden old age, when she receives the Order of Merit from an emissary of the king.

Julie Harris portrays Florence Nightingale in *The Holy Terror* (NBC).

Jayne Meadows picks up the mantle in "Florence Nightingale, Plato, Martin Luther, Voltaire" (parts one and two), a 1978 episode of *Meeting of Minds*, Steve Allen's "talk show" for historical figures. In a masterful performance as a geriatric Florence, Meadows puts meat on the bones of the reformer's remarkable story. She explains parental opposition to Nightingale's nursing aspirations in this way: "…nurses were recruited from women of the lowest class. Many of them were alcoholics or prostitutes. Except for members of religious orders, no decent woman would think of becoming a nurse."

She describes how she set out to change the nursing profession as well as the positively harrowing (and stomach churning) conditions of hospitals at the time. She even adds some historical perspective on the value of news reporting. "For the first time in history, war correspondents had accompanied an army, and were sending dispatches back home, telling what it was like for the British soldier to fight a war, to be wounded, and to die of those wounds because of the stupidity of inadequate or barbaric treatment." The impact of those reports back home helped her to revolutionize military medical care and nursing itself.

In later decades, style became more important than substance in the portrayals of Florence Nightingale. Jaclyn Smith played the title character in *Florence Nightingale* (TV movie, 1985), probably the most glamourous TV nurse ever to make rounds in a wartime military hospital, and certainly the most glamourous to hear the words "better maggots than gangrene." Laura Fraser stars in yet another *Florence Nightingale* (TV movie, 2008), as a Flo with lots of modern spunk, who narrates her story looking straight into the camera.

Florence Nightingale lived long enough to leave a vocal recording for posterity, which was captured by a representative of the Thomas Edison Company in July of 1890. At that point, even 34 years after the Crimean War, Nightingale was still thinking about the welfare of those with whom she had served. "When I am no longer even a memory, just a name, I hope my voice may perpetuate the great work of my life. God bless my dear old comrades of Balaklava and bring them safe to shore. Florence Nightingale."

Nonhelema (ca. 1718–1786)

Shawnee Leader
Portrayed by: Karina Lombard

The TV series *Timeless* once again does its homework, bringing another overlooked historical figure into the spotlight with Shawnee Chief Nonhelema in "Stranded" (2016). Karina Lombard steals the show in a brief, but riveting performance as Nonhelema, whose people have unknowingly captured three time-travelers in 1754 during the French and Indian War. Historian Lucy Preston (Abigail Spencer) immediately recognizes "very beautiful and super-intimidating" Nonhelema, who isn't fond of the British, and doesn't much care for the French either. Nonhelema can see that these strangers are lying about their identities and sentences Lucy and her colleague Wyatt Logan (Matt Lanter) to death, but spares the third member of their party, Rufus Carlin (Malcolm Barrett), an African American and, she assumes, their slave. Rufus tells Nonhelema as much of their truth as he can, pleading for the lives of his friends, and Nonhelema releases them all because of "this man's honor."

The real Nonhelema held to her dislike of the British, siding with the colonists in the American Revolutionary War, which had come to her lands in eastern Ohio. While other Shawnee tribes backed the British, Nonhelema, called "The Grenadier Squaw" for her imposing height and battle skills, warned Americans of impending attacks at Fort Randolph and Fort Donnally in West Virginia. For her wartime service, Nonhelema later petitioned the new Congress for a land-grant in Ohio, instead receiving a pension of daily rations and an annual allotment of blankets and clothing.

It would take almost two centuries for Nonhelema to receive some small recognition with a monument to her legacy in Ohio's Logan Elm State Park.

Oakley, Annie (1860–1926)

Sharpshooter
Portrayed by: Gail Davis, Mary Martin, Ethel Merman, Diane Civita, Jamie Lee Curtis, Reba McEntire, Sarah Strange

Annie Oakley, born Phoebe Ann Mosey, endured a troubled childhood, but the shooting skills she developed beginning at the age of eight led to later international stardom when she joined *Buffalo Bill's Wild West* show in 1885. At just five feet tall, Oakley, a.k.a. "Little Sure Shot," astounded audiences with her feats of marksmanship, such as splitting a playing card on its edge from a distance of 30 paces. Her husband, Frank Butler, whom she had bested in a shooting match when she was just 15, managed her act and served as her assistant during stunts, such as her famous trick where she shot a cigarette from Frank's lips. Oakley was a big hit on the show's overseas tours, performing for the crowned heads of Europe, and was the star of an early short film from Thomas Edison's studio, *The "Little Sure Shot" of the "Wild West," an exhibition of rifle shooting at glass balls, etc.* (1894).

Historical Annie is not much recognizable in *Annie Oakley* (1954–1957), a syndicated series starring Gail Davis in the title role. Davis's Oakley is a sharpshooter, to be sure, but there's no Frank Butler in her life or performances in Buffalo Bill's show. Instead Annie, in Davis's iconic blonde braids and fringed skirt, helps Deputy Sheriff Lofty Craig (Brad Johnson) catch bad guys, when she's not keeping an eye on her younger brother Tagg (Jimmy Hawkins). In "Desperate Men" (1956), Lofty interrupts Annie's cake decorating to ask for help. "Better get your gun, Annie." Oakley removes her apron and she's off to search for an outlaw, later using some fancy shooting to save Lofty from two ambushers. Although this Western adventure fictionalized historical Oakley, it showed audiences a skilled, independent woman doing the usual job of a man, just as *Buffalo Bill's Wild West* show had done 60 years earlier with the real Annie Oakley.

Annie Get Your Gun (TV special, 1957) brings Frank Butler back from the oblivion of the Davis series in a live telecast of Irving Berlin's hit musical. Mary Martin portrays an energetic Annie, who is smitten with Frank (John Raitt) when she meets him at a shooting competition. She joins Buffalo Bill's show to be near him,

Annie Oakley in the 1880s, by Baker's Art Gallery (Heritage Auctions).

but Frank is jealous of Annie's marksmanship. Annie, Frank, and company sing some well-known songs, including "Anything You Can Do" and "There's No Business Like Show Business," as the two try to find their way towards love.

The song remains the same in a later version of *Annie Get Your Gun* (TV special, 1967), this time with Ethel Merman as Annie and Bruce Yarnell as Frank. Alas, no known video copies exist of this production, except for one color clip of "I Got the Sun in the Mornin'," as performed by Merman.

Annie is a headliner once again in "Annie Oakley," a 1985 episode of *Tall Tales & Legends* (1985), part of Shelley Duvall's anthology series about American folklore. Jamie Lee Curtis is radiant as Annie in this story of her life that covers more ground than the musicals. The tale begins when Annie is a young girl (Anne Marie McEvoy), who finds she has "uncanny aim," in narrator Duvall's words, while shooting grouse to feed her family. Annie later meets Frank Butler (Cliff De Young) in Cincinnati, who isn't

Annie Oakley's Gail Davis, wearing her signature braids, sits with the show's executive producer Gene Autry (Archives of Ontario).

much interested in a shooting competition with her. "This isn't the stuff that a little girl could do."

Annie shows Butler just what a skilled "little girl" can do during target practice, and the two begin their lifelong relationship together. The most touching scene of the production comes when Oakley meets Lakota Sioux Leader Sitting Bull (Nick Ramus), who names her "*Watanya Cicilla*" or "Little Miss Sure Shot," and asks Annie to be his honorary daughter, in a reasonable approximation of the historical record.

Televised Oakley isn't always front and center, however, sometimes landing in other people's stories. In "Buffalo Bill and Annie Play the Palace," a 1983 episode of *Voyagers!*, a feminist Annie (Diane Civita) performs for Queen Victoria (Lurene Tuttle) in 1887, while assisting two time travelers who are trying to fix a historical aberration. *Buffalo Girls* (Miniseries, 1995) finds Annie (Reba McEntire) on tour in England again, this time with Calamity Jane (Anjelica Huston), who is the focus of this production about "the last of the Wild West times." *Murdoch Mysteries* catches up to peripatetic Annie (Sarah Strange) in Toronto, where Oakley flirts with a married police inspector during the course of a murder investigation in "Mild Mild West" (2009).

During her professional life, Oakley gave her considerable earnings to family and charitable organizations, such as those benefiting orphans. She offered this advice about achieving success: "Aim at the high mark and you will hit it."

Annie Oakley hit the high mark.

Onassis, Jacqueline Kennedy
See: **Kennedy, Jacqueline "Jackie" (1929–1994)**

Pankhurst, Christabel (1880–1958)
See (mentioned in): **Pankhurst, Emmeline (1858–1928)**

Pankhurst, Emmeline (1858–1928)
Suffragist, Activist
Portrayed by: Tatiana Maslany, Sandi Toksvig, Siân Phillips

The name Emmeline Pankhurst is synonymous with the women's suffrage movement, especially in England, the country of her birth. Pankhurst founded the Women's Social and Political Union (WSPU) in 1903, an organization dedicated to "deeds, not words" in the fight for British women's right to vote. As the years passed, the group's "deeds" became more militant, sometimes involving arson of mailboxes and unoccupied public buildings. Pankhurst was imprisoned repeatedly, enduring a cycle of arrest, hunger strike, release, and rearrest. She continued to give speeches and participate in marches, during which she was harassed and/or apprehended by police. Keeping Pankhurst safe became one of the group's priorities, so the women became pathfinders in personal protection as well.

Drunk History focuses on this part of Pankhurst's story in "Civil Rights" (2018). Tatiana Maslany stars as Pankhurst, who seeks the help of Edith Garrud (Maria Blasucci), an expert in jujitsu and self-defense, to train a special unit of 30 women within the WSPU. This cadre comes to be known as "the Bodyguard," which uses both hand-to-hand combat, termed "suffrajitsu," and deception techniques to keep Pankhurst out of police hands. The Bodyguard engages in a battle royale with Scottish police, who try to prevent Pankhurst from speaking, a real event sometimes called, "The Battle of Glasgow." *Drunk History* stages the confrontation like a cool action movie, with slow-motion moves and amped up music.

Narrator Kirby Howell-Baptiste tells us that all the attention Pankhurst's arrests received led to public sympathy and ultimately the passing of a bill in 1918 giving British women the right to vote. The actual history was more complex, as the 1918 bill, the Representation of the People Act, granted the vote to women over the age of 30. It wasn't until 10 years later, in 1928, that women received the same voting rights as men, with both eligible to vote upon reaching the age of 21.

Who would have thought that the subject of Emmeline Pankhurst would be such fodder for comedy writers? A second series, *Up the Women*, also found humor in Mrs. Pankhurst's suffrage work in "The Poem" (2013). Pankhurst (Sandi Toksvig) is treated with (much) less reverence here, as the Banbury Intricate Craft Circle Politely Requests Women's Suffrage group invites her for a visit in hopes of being inducted into the WSPU. Needless to say, things don't go according to plan, especially since one of the group members, Helen (Rebecca Front), has an unpleasant history with Emmeline, whom she had known at school.

Pankhurst enters in an oversized hat, resembling an ornate lampshade, and refers to herself in the third person. This Emmeline is a bully and a diva, prompting Helen to taunt her with, "Meanie, meanie Emmeleanie." There are a few funny moments here, but if you're looking to learn something about the suffrage movement, you'll get more from the show's stirring opening credits, which show historical photos of suffrage activists, some being hauled off by police, to the tune of "Nana Was a Suffragette" by Jules Gibb.

Shoulder to Shoulder (Miniseries, 1974) is a TV production which takes the suffrage movement and Pankhurst more seriously. Told in six installments, *Shoulder to Shoulder* highlights key figures within the British suffrage movement, including Emmeline (Siân Phillips), her daughters [Estelle] Sylvia (Angela Down) and Christabel (Patricia Quinn), and Annie Kenney (Georgia Brown). It shows that the women weren't always happy sisters in arms, however, as differences in philosophy and strategy lead to rifts, both within the Pankhurst family and the WSPU itself. The episode "Outrage!" chronicles the increasingly militant tactics used by the group and the brutal treatment members received at the hands of the police, including force-feedings during hunger strikes.

The screams of the women during the horrifying procedure haunted historical Pankhurst for the rest of her life. She wrote, "I shall never while I live forget the suffering I experienced during the days when those cries were ringing in my ears."

Pankhurst, Estelle Sylvia (1882–1960)

See (mentioned in): **Pankhurst, Emmeline (1858–1928)**

Parker, Bonnie (1910–1934)
Bank Robber, Outlaw
Portrayed by: Tracey Needham, Holliday Grainger, Jacqueline Byers

During her short life, Bonnie Parker became famous as an outlaw, the accomplice of her lover Clyde Barrow, both wild, young people, who robbed and shot their way through the midsection of the United States in the early 1930s. Bonnie and Clyde became legendary, for their love, their willingness to die, and the image of freedom they represented, always taking what they wanted, at a time of deprivation during the Great Depression. It is not clear whether Bonnie herself killed anyone, but Clyde certainly did, as did other members of their gang, which racked up a death toll of at least nine police officers and four civilians. There's not much romantic about that, so it's not surprising that TV producers chose to soften their story, emphasizing star-crossed love over sociopathic impulse.

You've got to admire the chutzpah of an historical fiction film that dares to use the subtitle, "The True Story," as in *Bonnie & Clyde: The True Story* (TV movie, 1992). But the film takes chutzpah one step further by immediately issuing an ironic apology. "Some composite characters and time compression have been employed for dramatic reasons." Okay, then. As the story opens in 1922, young Bonnie (Jennifer Thomas) is sweet and full of promise, winning the Cement City, Texas, spelling bee with the word "Chihuahua." The narrative quickly flashes forward to 1929, where Bonnie (Tracey Needham) is already an unhappily married wife, whose husband Roy (Michael Hannon) storms out because he thinks his spouse is uppity for wanting better things in life.

Soon Bonnie meets Clyde Barrow (Dana Ashbrook), who is her match in smooth-skinned beauty. Clyde sets up unwitting Bonnie as his "wheel man" in the robbery of a small store, and she is furious. Bonnie tries to stay away from this charming, but restless man for a month, but she is lonely, and desperate to get away from the Great Depression in general, and her dead-end job as a waitress at the local café in particular. She escapes with Clyde, but he and his buddy W.D. (Billy Morrissette) soon descend into armed robbery and murder. Bonnie is again upset, but feels trapped with no options left. Parker is seen as a victim here, saying to Clyde, "How did this happen to me?"

Bonnie & Clyde (Miniseries, 2013) doesn't purport to be the true story, but its original airing on the History Channel gave it a patina of accuracy. As it turns out, this telling gives Bonnie (Holliday Grainger) such a fame fetish that she pushes Clyde (Emile Hirsch) back into a life of crime even when he wants to get out. When Barrow's dark premonitions make him ready to leave their glory days behind, Bonnie says, "If you're demanding we stop this thing we're doing, then, I don't know, maybe I'm gonna have to find some other way to get where I'm supposed to be." Grainger's Bonnie is a narcissist rather than a victim of circumstance, like Needham's Parker.

History has a way of twisting in new directions on the TV series *Timeless*, and does so again in "Last Ride of Bonnie & Clyde" (2016). The show's time travelers are after a gold key, stolen from Henry Ford, which Bonnie (Jacqueline Byers) is wearing around her neck. Bonnie and Clyde (Sam Strike) are very much in love, and are soon to meet their end, but not in the hail-of-over-100-bullets way that historical Bonnie and Clyde did. Frank Hamer (Chris Mulkey) is still leading the posse here, but the lovers are surrounded at their hideout rather than being ambushed on the road. Hamer shoots Clyde, who dies after two more shots. Lovestruck Bonnie had wanted to go out in a blaze of glory with Clyde, so she aims her gun at one of the posse members, knowing she will be killed. Her final words are heard in voice-over, reciting the last stanza from the real Bonnie's poem "The Trail's End" also known as "The Story of Bonnie and Clyde" (1934).

> Some day they'll go down together
> they'll bury them side by side.
> To few it'll be grief,
> to the law a relief
> but it's death for Bonnie and Clyde.

Parks, Lillian Rogers (1897–1997)

See (mentioned in): **Roosevelt, Eleanor (1884–1962)**

Parks, Rosa (1913–2005)

Civil Rights Activist

Portrayed by: Lisa Bonet, Chardé Manzy, Angela Bassett, Vinette Robinson

In 1999, Rosa Parks received the Congressional Gold Medal, which bore the legend, "Mother of the Modern Day Civil Rights Movement." Parks, once a seamstress at a department store, had just been awarded the highest honor given by the U.S. Congress.

Her journey to that moment began on a bus in Montgomery, Alabama. The date was December 1, 1955. On that day, Parks refused to give up her seat to a white passenger. People later speculated that she had refused out of simple weariness, but Parks set the record straight. "…the only tired I was, was tired of giving in." She was arrested for violating the city's segregation law, but her civil disobedience quickly galvanized a movement within the black community to boycott all Montgomery buses, an action which lasted for 381 days.

Rosa Parks was not the first to refuse to relinquish her seat on a segregated bus, nor the first to be arrested, a point driven home by the *Drunk History* episode "Montgomery, AL" (2014). Narrator Amber Ruffin tells the story of Claudette Colvin (Mariah Wilson), a 15-year-old student who was arrested for refusing to give up her seat on a segregated Montgomery bus nine months before the Parks incident. That fact is true, and it was Colvin's case, with five other plaintiffs, that eventually led to a United States Supreme Court ruling in *Browder v. Gayle* that bus segregation was unconstitutional. But the episode goes on to portray the Parks protest as a planned, copycat stunt hatched by the local office of the NAACP for maximum public relations value and to gain white sympathy.

The NAACP group, as portrayed here, thinks Parks (Lisa Bonet) is a better symbol for the movement, since she is married and has a lighter complexion than Colvin. Historical documents, including Rosa's written accounts, do not support the contention that her protest was planned, although, as an NAACP secretary, Parks was aware of Colvin's arrest.

While the accomplishments of Rosa Parks are downplayed in *Drunk History*, they are highlighted in *The Rosa Parks Story* (TV movie, 2002). The film focuses not only on her famous act of civil disobedience and its aftermath, but also on the forces that shaped her early life and brought her to that point. Young Rosa (Chardé Manzy) attends the Montgomery Industrial School for Girls in 1924, and has an answer when another student questions why black girls should be bothering with education given their menial employment prospects. Rosa says, "We bother so we can be equal to everybody else."

When adult Rosa (Angela Bassett) sits on a Montgomery bus and is arrested for refusing to give up her seat to a white man, she says to the arresting officer, "Why do you all push us around?" The bus is crowded on a rainy night during Christmas season, but Parks is alone, with no one, black or white coming to her defense. She relinquishes her seat only when the officers escort her off the bus. Bassett is pitch-perfect in the role, and won the NAACP Image Award for her performance in the film.

The historical significance of Rosa Parks is also center stage in the *Doctor Who* episode "Rosa" (2018). Doctor Who (Jodie Whittaker), an alien time traveler, and her team arrive in 1955 Alabama and must stop a racist criminal named Krasko (Joshua Bowman) from altering the timeline. Krasko wants to prevent the arrest of Rosa Parks (Vinette Robinson), thereby extinguishing the spark which ignited both the Montgomery bus boycott and the civil rights movement. Doctor Who and her companions succeed in thwarting Krasko's plans, but they can't untangle themselves from the historical moment, and must witness the events on the bus firsthand as passengers.

When bus driver James Blake (Trevor White) says to Parks, "If you don't stand, I'm going to have you arrested," the time travelers are forced to sit in painful silence. They also witness Rosa's famous reply, "You may do that." The thirteenth doctor later points out the Rosa Parks asteroid on a viewscreen, explaining that Rosa "changed the world. In fact, she changed the universe." To say that this is moving and powerful television is an understatement.

Yes, the asteroid name is for real. "284996 Rosaparks." Who could have guessed one bus ride would have taken her so far?

Parsons, Louella (1881–1972)

See (mentioned in): **Lombard, Carole (1908–1942)**

Paul, Alice (1885–1977)

Suffragist
Portrayed by: Erica Dasher, Hilary Swank

In "Mrs. Sherlock Holmes," a 2018 episode of *Timeless*, we meet Alice Paul (Erica Dasher), a legendary American suffragist, who is framed for murder by reactionary forces out to change the course of American history. Although the good guys, timecops who include a historian, Lucy Preston (Abigail Spencer), try to rectify the situation, Paul is murdered in prison and thereby prevented from delivering a crucial speech that will ensure women receive the right to vote in 1920. Not only does *Timeless* kill off Alice Paul, but it erases her contributions to history, at least in the *Timeless* universe.

In our own world, history does record the prodigious accomplishments of Alice Paul, who lived a long life, fighting for women's rights, including the Equal Rights Amendment, until the end of her days. After graduating from Swarthmore College in 1905 and doing settlement house work in New York City, Alice Paul moved to England to pursue her postgraduate studies. Her life changed forever when she heard suffragist Christabel Pankhurst speak in Birmingham. Paul later moved to London, where she joined the Women's Social and Political Union (WSPU) led by Christabel and her mother Emmeline Pankhurst.

Alice quickly became adept at militant tactics, some of which led to arrest and imprisonment three times. She engaged in hunger strikes during each of her incarcerations to protest improper treatment and to call attention to the suffragist cause. During her last prison stay, she was force-fed, a ghastly process which led to both immediate and lasting health consequences for Paul. While in London, Paul also met Lucy Burns, who would become her partner in the fight for women's suffrage in the United States.

The work of Alice Paul and Lucy Burns in bringing about passage of the 19th amendment to the U.S. Constitution is the focus of *Iron Jawed Angels*, a television film from 2004. Hilary Swank stars as Paul, who is outraged by the treatment of women in the United States. She says, "We don't make the laws, but we have to obey them like children." Paul's goal is a constitutional amendment which would give women the right to vote, while the National American Woman Suffrage Association (NAWSA), led by Carrie Chapman Catt (Anjelica Huston), prefers a state-by-state approach to enfranchising women. Further disagreements about tactics and finances lead Paul and Burns to leave NAWSA and create the National Woman's Party (NWP), dedicated to one thing, and one thing only, obtaining a national women's suffrage amendment.

In January of 1917, the NWP stations "silent sentinels" at the White House from dawn to dusk every day until a constitutional amendment is passed. After Alice is arrested at the picket line, she refuses to make a plea, because she has had no say in the making of the laws affecting her. When she is placed in solitary confinement for breaking a window to protest prison conditions, Alice refuses to eat. When she is sent to a prison psychiatric ward for a competency assessment, Alice tells her inquisitor, "The hunger strike was a tradition in old Ireland. You starve yourself on someone's doorstep until restitution is made and justice is done."

The real Alice Paul was willing to starve herself to see that justice was done for women in the United States. As newspapers began to report on the hunger strikes, the suffragists and their cause gained sympathy, forcing President Woodrow Wilson to support the suffrage amendment as a "war measure." The 19th amendment was ratified in 1920, but Alice Paul thought obtaining the vote for women was just the beginning of the battle for gender equality. She earned three law degrees, and wrote the Equal Rights Amendment (ERA) in 1923, which has yet to be ratified. The profound impact of a woman, Alice Paul, on the course of American history is itself a strong statement in favor of gender equality.

Pavlichenko, Lyudmila (1916–1974)

See (mentioned in): **Roosevelt, Eleanor (1884–1962)**

Place, Etta (ca. 1878–?)

Outlaw
Portrayed by: Elizabeth Montgomery, Katharine Ross

Place, Etta

Etta Place is one of those figures known to the public not from history books, but because of a famous cultural depiction. The iconic film *Butch Cassidy and the Sundance Kid* (1969), starring Paul Newman and Robert Redford in the title roles and Katharine Ross as Etta, not only spoke to a generation looking for new types of movie heroes, but also gained accolades for artistic significance, eventually landing on the U.S. National Film Registry. It's hard to replace the image in our minds of schoolteacher Etta, the natural beauty who rides on the handlebars of Butch's bicycle, but it would be easier if we had a clear picture of who the real Etta was. Alas, her history is so obscure that she is often referred to as a "mystery woman."

Etta was born in Utah or not-so-nearby New York. The little that is known of her comes from the Pinkerton detective agency's files and an article in the *San Antonio Light* newspaper. She appears to have met Butch Cassidy and Harry Longabaugh, alias the Sundance Kid, in 1899, while working at a brothel in San Antonio. She went on to marry Sundance in December of 1900. Some accounts place her at the scene of Butch and Sundance's robberies, where she remained outside, holding the horses and keeping watch.

Who was this woman who seems to have dropped into the Old West out of nowhere? One prominent theory held that Etta was actually Ann Bassett, a cattle rustler and known associate of Butch Cassidy's Wild Bunch. Photographic comparisons done at Los Alamos National Laboratory appeared to confirm that identification, but the known facts of the women's timelines do not coincide.

The mysteries of Etta Place do not end with her origins. While Butch and Sundance are generally believed to have died in a shootout with Bolivian soldiers, as depicted in the 1969 movie, nothing is known about Etta after 1906. In that year, she settled in San Francisco after leaving South America and her life on the run with Sundance and Butch.

But people have theories, LOTS of theories, about what happened to Etta, and television couldn't help but offer some glosses of its own. The first came in *Mrs. Sundance*, a 1974 TV movie starring Elizabeth Montgomery as Etta Place. Etta has been working as a teacher, Miss Johnson, for three months, as the film opens, but there's a price of $10,000 on her head for robbery, treason, and other crimes. Famed Lawman Charles Siringo (L.Q. Jones) is on her trail, and when he comes to town, Etta leaves her quiet, comfortable life in a hurry. Lured by a story that Sundance didn't die in South America, Etta sets out to look for Butch Cassidy's old gang, not realizing that Siringo has set a trap for her. The movie has a wistful tone, as Etta searches for her true love, and death is a recurring theme. As in the real world, the mystery of Etta lives on here. Not only does she ride off into the sunset, but this TV movie pilot didn't sell as a weekly series despite Montgomery's affecting performance as Mrs. Sundance.

20th Century–Fox Television, producer of *Mrs. Sundance*, decided to give Etta Place one more chance in *Wanted: The Sundance Woman* (TV movie, 1976). Katharine Ross, everyone's Etta from 1969, stepped in for Montgomery who had stepped in for her. Not only is Montgomery erased, but all of the events of *Mrs. Sundance* as well. *Wanted* starts the clock again with a brief scene of the shoot-out in Bolivia that killed Butch and Sundance. The setting quickly shifts to Arizona, where Etta has been working as a general store clerk for what she calls "a happy year."

When two detectives show up, Etta escapes, but her boss and friend Dave Riley (Michael Constantine) is jailed for helping her. She then seeks the help of Mexican revolutionary Pancho Villa (Hector Elizondo), suggesting a sort of mutual aid agreement, his help with breaking Dave out of prison, for hers in robbing a train filled with arms. Villa is portrayed as a ladies' man, who doesn't get far with Etta because of her continued love for Sundance. Of course, Charlie Siringo (Steve Forrest) is hot on Etta's trail, but she will eventually ride off into whatever mysterious future awaits her.

The remainder of the real Etta's life is indeed a mystery. No rest home, no grave marker, Etta is forever young and beautiful, the woman who lived outside of society's bounds and got away with it.

Pleasant, Mary Ellen (ca. 1814–1904)
Entrepreneur, Abolitionist
Portrayed by: Lisa Bonet

Mary Ellen Pleasant has lots of origin stories. She was born a slave on a Georgia plantation or a free woman on Barley Street in Philadelphia. Her father was a Hawaiian merchant or a white slaveholder. She was black or she was white. (At least she allowed people to believe she was white.) It's hard to pin Mary Ellen Pleasant down, which suits her life to a tee, as a woman who never let people know what she was really about, and with good reason. Working as a domestic servant and cook, Pleasant amassed a fortune, some inherited from her first husband, but some earned on her own. She eavesdropped on her wealthy employers, ever invisible in the background, gaining useful information which she parlayed into good investments. Pleasant used that wealth to assist others, especially former or escaped slaves, and served as a conductor on the Underground Railroad, helping slaves to reach freedom in Canada.

Lisa Bonet portrays Pleasant in the *Drunk History* episode "San Francisco" (2013). While the piece is unfocused and doesn't do Pleasant justice, you can't take your eyes off Bonet, who is beautiful and riveting in the short amount of screen time she receives. Narrator Artemis Pebdani calls Pleasant "the mother of civil rights in California," but the segment doesn't do much to explain that appellation. The story centers on Mary Ellen's time in the Golden State, beginning in 1852, as she opens restaurants, boarding houses, and laundries, always making sure to hire black employees. At some time, presumably in the late 1850s, Pleasant gives $30,000 to abolitionist John Brown "for guns and stuff."

Pebdani tells us that "John Brown gets caught," but she doesn't say for what. Historical Brown used the "guns and stuff" to attack the United States Arsenal at Harpers Ferry, Virginia (later West Virginia) in hopes of inciting and arming a slave revolt. When Brown is hanged for murder and treason, a note is found in his pocket. The *Drunk History* version says, "Hey, I'm in support of you and I'm going to keep being in support of you." The note is signed with the initials M.E.P., which are misread as W.E.P. and Pleasant is never caught as a result.

The real letter from Mary Ellen Pleasant read, "The ax is laid at the foot of the tree. When the first blow is struck, there will be more money to help." The identity of the writer remained a mystery for decades, until Pleasant dictated her autobiography to journalist Sam Davis. She said, "I wish to clear the identity of the party who furnished John Brown with most of his money to start the fight at Harpers Ferry and who signed the letter found on him when he was arrested."

For Mary Ellen Pleasant, identity was and had to be a slippery concept. Nothing was ever etched in stone, not even on her gravestone. That too needed revision, when a line she had requested on her deathbed was finally added 60 years later: "A Friend of John Brown."

Pompadour, Madame de (1721–1764)

Patron of the Arts
Portrayed by: Sophia Myles, Jessica Atkins

Born Jeanne Antoinette Poisson in Paris, Madame de Pompadour became the official chief mistress of King Louis XV in 1745. Educated and intelligent, the Marquise de Pompadour, as she was officially titled, also served as the king's private secretary, but she is most famous for her role as Louis's advisor in matters both political and aesthetic. She made lasting contributions to the arts as both patron and creator, supporting a royal porcelain factory at Sèvres, helping to plan the Place Louis XV (now the Place de la Concorde) in Paris, engraving gems herself, and so much more.

Pompadour's romantic entanglement with King Louis doesn't stop her from falling in love with a time traveler in "The Girl in the Fireplace," a fascinating 2006 episode of *Doctor Who*. Seven-year-old Reinette (Jessica

Atkins), the future Madame de Pompadour, receives a visit from the Doctor (David Tennant), who steps through a spaceship's time window into her 18th-century bedroom. He saves the girl from a clockwork android, but after a quick exit and return to check on her, Reinette (Sophia Myles) is now a young woman. She kisses him, and after she departs with her mother, he realizes just who she is, reciting her resume as "uncrowned queen of France, actress, artist, musician, dancer, courtesan, fantastic gardener."

A later encounter reveals that the droids are actually after Reinette's brain to run their ship, the SS *Madame de Pompadour*. The automatons return again, this time at a royal costume ball, when Reinette is finally Pompadour. Though they take her hostage, she is not afraid, saying, "You are merely the nightmare of my childhood, the monster from under my bed. And if my nightmare can return to plague me, then rest assured, so will yours." As if on cue, the Doctor, now on horseback, crashes through a large mirror to save Reinette yet again. Ever a woman of refinement, Madame de Pompadour introduces Louis, saying, "Oh, this is my lover, the King of France." The Doctor replies, "Yeah, well, I'm the lord of time," possibly the best royal putdown ever. Reinette is prepared to throw over the king of France for the lord of time, but, in a sad irony, the lord of time returns to find that seven years have passed and Pompadour has died.

"The Girl in the Fireplace" won the 2007 Hugo Award for Best Dramatic Presentation, Short Form. Madame de Pompadour, a woman of so many artistic achievements, might have appreciated the invention and visual style of this stimulating science fiction work.

Robinson, Sylvia (1936–2011)
Singer, Record Producer
Portrayed by: Retta

Born in the Harlem neighborhood of New York City, Sylvia Robinson (née Vanderpool) entered the music business at age 14, recording under the stage name Little Sylvia. As half of the duo Mickey and Sylvia, she scored a big hit in 1957 with "Love Is Strange," which reached number one on the R&B chart and number 11 on the Billboard pop chart in 1957. She achieved later solo success under the name Sylvia with a song she co-wrote, "Pillow Talk," which topped the charts in 1973 with its breathy vocals, suggestive lyrics, and enticing rhythms. Her biggest fame, however, came not as a singer, but as a record producer and executive, where her contributions led to her being dubbed "the mother of hip-hop."

Drunk History explains how Robinson became a pioneer of the new form called rap in "American Music" (2014). Retta stars as Sylvia, who attends a New York City party in the late '70s, and hears something revolutionary, a performer who speaks rhymes over instrumental breaks in the records being played. Robinson gets the inspiration to make an album of this hybrid form, "rap," but all the performers she asks refuse, saying that rap is all about live performance. Undeterred, Sylvia finally meets a "rapping pizza guy," Big Bank Hank (Da'Vone McDonald), who likes the idea, and with two others, forms the Sugar Hill Gang, named after an artistic community in Harlem. The resulting recording, "Rapper's Delight," produced by Sylvia, becomes a hit, and, in the words of narrator Colton Dunn, "…created a genre of music and blazed the path for all other hip-hop."

In 2022, Sylvia Robinson received the Ahmet Ertegun Award, given by the Rock & Roll Hall of Fame. Her Hall of Fame essay by Alan Light states, "Sylvia Robinson played many roles in the music world—artist, producer, and most notably, record executive. But as the founder and leader of the pioneering Sugar Hill label, she revealed herself to be something even rarer. She was a visionary."

Roebling, Emily Warren (1843–1903)
Engineer, Builder, Businesswoman
Portrayed by: Taylor Schilling

The story of the Brooklyn Bridge is the story of the Roebling family, father John Augustus Roebling and his son Washington, but especially the story of Washington's wife Emily Warren Roebling. Emily saw the bridge through to completion at a time when women didn't manage business projects, let alone the construction of the world's longest-span suspension bridge. After John had died of tetanus and Washington had become bedridden by decompression sickness, both illnesses related to their work on the bridge, Emily took over day-to-day operations at the site. She began as Washington's messenger to his team, but eventually Emily became proficient in all the duties assigned to her husband, the chief engineer, dedicating herself to the bridge's construction for over a decade.

Drunk History takes an expletive-laden approach to telling the story of the Brooklyn Bridge and the Roeblings in "Landmarks" (2016). Taylor Schilling portrays Emily, who doesn't take any, shall we say, baloney, from the men at the construction site, smacking them on the head with rolled blueprints when they refuse to take orders from a woman. She says, "hell, yeah," when Washington asks her to be the first to cross the bridge by carriage, and she wears a rooster on her shoulder as a symbol of victory, although the bird is a stuffed animal in the fictional version. Amidst all the drunken irreverence, there is actual reverence for Emily's accomplishments.

In 2018, *The New York Times* published a belated obituary of Emily Warren Roebling in its "Overlooked" section. The piece quoted Emily's own words, written in a letter to her son, which serve as a fitting epitaph: "I have more brains, common sense and know-how generally than have any two engineers, civil or uncivil, and but for me the Brooklyn Bridge would never have had the name Roebling in any way connected with it!"

Thanks, Emily, for that beautiful bridge.

Rogers, Maggie (1874–1953)

See (mentioned in): **Roosevelt, Eleanor (1884–1962)**

Roosevelt, Eleanor (1884–1962)

First Lady, Diplomat, Human Rights Activist
Portrayed by: Jane Alexander, Mackenzie Phillips, Jane Curtin, Eileen Heckart, Ellen Geer, Cynthia Nixon, Busy Philipps, Jean Stapleton

A niece of President Theodore Roosevelt, Eleanor Roosevelt married her fifth cousin once removed, Franklin Delano Roosevelt, in 1905. Although stricken with polio in 1921, which left him unable to walk or stand without support, FDR went on to win four terms as U.S. president thanks in major part to Eleanor's efforts. Since the president and his advisors took great pains to hide FDR's condition from the public, Mrs. Roosevelt made speeches and public appearances on her husband's behalf, while pursuing her own interests in social reform.

Eleanor held regular White House press conferences for female correspondents, a practice which forced wire services to employ women or face the prospect of missing out on breaking news. She wrote a daily syndicated newspaper column, "My Day," and fought injustice where she found it. In 1939, when the Daughters of the American Revolution refused to let black singer Marian Anderson perform at Constitution Hall, Mrs. Roosevelt publicly resigned her membership, using her "My Day" column as a platform. Anderson later performed her concert in front of 75,000 people at the Lincoln Memorial.

Jane Alexander portrays this larger-than-life historical figure in *Eleanor and Franklin*, a 1976 miniseries based on Joseph P. Lash's 1971 book of the same title. The story begins in 1945 as Eleanor is called from a public appearance back to the White House, where she is informed that Franklin (Edward Herrmann) has passed away. She travels to the Little White House in Warm Springs, Georgia, where the president had suffered his fatal cerebral hemorrhage. As she sits with her husband's body, Mrs. Roosevelt begins to remember the pivotal events of their lives, which appear in flashbacks.

A shy, 14-year-old Eleanor (Mackenzie Phillips) renews her acquaintance with distant cousin Franklin (Ted Eccles) at a party hosted by Uncle Teddy Roosevelt (William Phipps). After an awkward dance, the teens compare notes on ambition. Eleanor says, "..I just can't see any point in just living and dying and not leaving any mark on the world, as if you hadn't lived at all." Franklin, although more lighthearted than Eleanor, agrees with her worldview, and the two pledge to keep in touch.

Keep in touch they do, as later memories reveal their courtship, marriage, and children. The title of the miniseries is indicative of its personal nature, as the world of politics is shunted mostly to the sidelines. Instead the couple's major crises at home take center stage, FDR's affair with Lucy Mercer (Linda Kelsey) and his paralytic illness. The two-part miniseries ends with Franklin's election to the U.S. presidency in 1932, as the Great Depression is deepening.

Alexander and Herrmann reprised their roles the next year in *Eleanor and Franklin: The White House Years* (TV movie, 1977), based on the same book by Lash. The story begins as the happily engaged couple arrives at the White House for Teddy Roosevelt's inauguration. The scene quickly shifts to FDR's inauguration, and the story picks up where the miniseries left off. Newsreels play, newspaper headlines fly, as we learn about the issues confronting Roosevelt's presidency, including the Great Depression and World War II. There is still time for the personal here, however, as Eleanor confides what she told herself when she learned FDR was in love with Lucy Mercer. "If we stay together for whatever reason, the children, your career, even if we spend the rest of our lives together it can never be as it was. We can never be lovers again."

Jane Alexander as Eleanor Roosevelt in *Eleanor and Franklin: The White House Years* (ABC).

But they do stay together, and Eleanor travels the world to advance the interests of her husband and the United States during the war. She tours England, where she draws enthusiastic crowds, and the South Pacific, where she visits American troops and boosts morale. The film ends where the miniseries began, with FDR's death in 1945.

Anyone looking for a break from Mrs. Roosevelt's reverential treatment in *Eleanor and Franklin* would have found it in the *Saturday Night Live* sketch "What If Eleanor Roosevelt Could Fly?" (November 4, 1978). Here a "panel of experts" considers what the impact on World War II might have been if the first lady had possessed the power of flight. Professor Sylvia Reed (Laraine Newman) notes that Mrs. Roosevelt was "perhaps our most outstanding first lady even without the ability to fly." George Temple (Garrett Morris) of the Lockheed Corporation takes an engineer's perspective: "We performed wind tunnel tests on elderly women and we found that they are basically unwieldy."

The most telling part, of course, is the dramatization, where Eleanor Roosevelt (Jane Curtin), arms outstretched, flies over Germany ahead of a squadron of B-17 bombers and is attacked by German antiaircraft. The panel draws the erudite conclusion that had Mrs. Roosevelt possessed the ability to fly, her special power would have had no bearing on the outcome of World War II. Good to know.

Eileen Heckart received two Emmy nominations as Outstanding Supporting Actress for portrayals of Eleanor Roosevelt. In *Backstairs at the White House* (Miniseries, 1979), based on a 1961 memoir by White House seamstress Lillian Rogers Parks, we view Eleanor and Franklin (John Anderson), as well as the first families from the Taft through Eisenhower administrations, through the eyes of Parks (Leslie Uggams) and her mother Maggie Rogers (Olivia Cole), a White House maid and hairdresser. It's back to the White House for Eleanor (and Heckart) in *F.D.R.: The Last Year* (TV movie, 1980), where efficient Mrs. Roosevelt helps FDR (Jason Robards) win a fourth term as president, as World War II winds down and the Yalta Conference with Churchill and Stalin beckons.

Eleanor Roosevelt had a fruitful public life after Franklin's passing, but most productions continued the trend of ignoring her later years. In "Destiny's Choice," a 1983 episode of *Voyagers!*, Ellen Geer portrays Eleanor, whose husband Franklin (Nicholas Pryor) ends up as a movie director in 1928 Hollywood, but is set on the right historical path by two time travelers. *Warm Springs* (TV movie, 2005) spotlights Franklin Roosevelt's use of mineral springs in Georgia as therapy for his polio, with Kenneth Branagh as FDR and Cynthia Nixon as Eleanor Roosevelt. The story of the relationship between Eleanor (Busy Philipps) and Soviet sniper Lyudmila Pavlichenko (Mae Whitman), who traveled the United States together to drum up support for American intervention in Europe during World War II, is the focus of a vignette in "The Roosevelts," a 2016 episode of *Drunk History*.

At last we come to a production that acknowledges some of Mrs. Roosevelt's post–FDR accomplishments in *Eleanor, First Lady of the World* (TV movie, 1982). Jean Stapleton leaves her ditzy *All in the Family* character behind for a woman with a sharp intellect, focusing on the former first lady's role as a delegate to the United Nations. Answering a call from President Harry S. Truman (Richard McKenzie), Eleanor emerges from her life as a private citizen to step again onto the world stage. She is undaunted by the tasks ahead, although even she acknowledges that her high-pitched "school girl" voice gets in the way of people taking her seriously. When John Foster Dulles (E.G. Marshall) tries to hide her away on a human rights committee, he's in for a surprise when Eleanor takes on the job of convincing member countries of the United Nations to ratify the first worldwide declaration of human rights.

After her husband's death, Eleanor Roosevelt accumulated a substantial résumé on her own. In addition to her work on the UN Commission on Human Rights, Roosevelt chaired the Presidential Commission on the Status of Women during the Kennedy administration. *The New York Times* said in her obituary, "When she entered the halls of the United Nations, representatives from all countries rose to honor her. She had become not only the wife and widow of a towering president but a noble personality in herself."

Sacagawea (ca. 1788–?)
Explorer
Portrayed by: Angela Dorian, Vanessa Rare, Aubrey Plaza, Dayana Rincon

Sacagawea gives her name to more mountains and natural features than any other North American woman, yet historians disagree on what her name actually was, and on other important facts of her life (and death). But whether her name is Sacagawea, Sakakawea, or Sacajawea, the accomplishments that make her life important to American history, women's history, and Native American history are clear and profound.

Sacagawea was a Lemhi Shoshone woman, who at the age of 16 or 17 helped Lewis and Clark explore the Louisiana territory. She accompanied the expedition, called the Corps of Discovery, as an interpreter and guide, helping the explorers to interact positively with native peoples. She also searched for edible plants, made clothing, and even rescued the expedition's journals from a capsized boat, an action which prompted

Lewis and Clark to name the Sacagawea River in her honor on May 20, 1805.

Death Valley Days continues the story in "The Girl Who Walked the West" (1967), with Angela Dorian as Sacagawea, who advises Lewis (Richard Simmons) and Clark (Don Matheson) on how to approach the Shoshone for the horses they desperately need to continue the trip. Sacagawea, who cares for her baby on the journey, counsels them to send only one leader and not to bring guns, so the Shoshone will not mistake them for a war party. Eventually the two groups come together to negotiate a trade, and Sacagawea realizes that the Shoshone chief is her long-lost brother Cameahwait (Steven Marlo). Lewis and Clark, who call Sacagawea "Janey," receive their horses with Janey's intercession. She unexpectedly departs with them, telling her brother, "This is my home, my valley, my people, but they are my friends."

Most of the teleplay is faithful to the historical record, although the characters are painted with broad strokes, especially Sacagawea's husband, Toussaint Charbonneau (Victor French). Charbonneau mistreats Sacagawea and is jealous of her friendship with golden-boy Clark, a rivalry that appears never to have happened in real life. Fighting illness, the terrain, and the elements to find the first overland route to the Pacific Ocean was certainly enough conflict, but Charbonneau was elected antagonist with a capital "A."

Sacagawea makes surprisingly few scripted television appearances after *Death Valley Days*, and they are small ones at that. *Jack of All Trades* catches up with Sacagawea (Vanessa Rare), "a well-known guide just in from the states," who will lead woefully lost Lewis (Patrick Wilson) and Clark (Peter Rowley) from a South Pacific island back to Oregon in "Up the Creek" (2000). "Nashville," a 2013 episode of *Drunk History*, casts Aubrey Plaza as the explorer in a vignette that focuses on Lewis (Tony Hale) and Clark (Taran Killam), and treats Sacagawea mostly as a tagalong. *Sleepy Hollow's* "Sick Burn" (2017) features Dayana Rincon in a brief appearance as Sacagawea, who is searching for supernatural evil rather than the road west, working with Davy Crockett (Daniel Parvis), Samuel "Uncle Sam" Wilson (Rick Espaillat), and others.

Sacagawea died in 1812, while still married to Charbonneau, although some oral traditions claim that she went to live among the Comanches, passing in 1884. Her posthumous honors include the Sacagawea dollar coin struck by the U.S. Mint in 2000 and the title of Honorary Sergeant, Regular Army presented by President Bill Clinton in 2001.

Sacagawea walked the West and then walked into the history books, leaving a footprint that time has not erased.

Sampson, Deborah (1760–1827)
Revolutionary War Soldier
Portrayed by: Evan Rachel Wood

In "Heroines," a 2018 episode of *Drunk History*, narrator Paget Brewster, in a boozy, breezy style, shares the remarkable story of Deborah Sampson (Evan Rachel Wood), a patriot who disguised herself as a man so she could join the Continental Army during the American Revolutionary War. As usual, *Drunk History* gets most of the major historical details right, while fudging a few others for dramatic effect. As a young girl, Sampson becomes an indentured servant in Massachusetts, but she grows up to be an "incredible bad ass," a description that will be applied to her repeatedly throughout the vignette.

Sampson decides to join the war effort, sewing her own uniform, cutting her hair, and wrapping her breasts in fabric. As Robert Shirtliff, she enlists in George Washington's army, becoming a supersoldier until she is wounded at Tarrytown. Since seeking medical assistance might reveal her sex, Sampson removes a musket ball from her own thigh, but later develops a fever and lands in the hospital. Her secret is ultimately revealed, but "Robert" receives an honorable discharge from the service, while Deborah becomes "the first woman to take a bullet for America." Wood, with her perfect makeup and sculpted brows, probably wouldn't have passed for a man in the gender-conforming 18th century, but this is "drunk" history, where vision isn't always the clearest.

The real Deborah Sampson was about five foot nine, making her much taller than average women of her time and even some men. Her height added to the illusion she created, allowing her to join an elite unit of light infantry, whose members were chosen for their height and strength. Sampson carried a musket ball in her leg for the rest of her life, and, through the intercession of Paul Revere, was awarded a disabled veteran's pension by Congress.

While Sampson embellished some of the details of her service in later years, the major points of her story are fully documented. Not only was she the equal of men on the battlefield, but she carried the burden of potential discovery wherever she was assigned. In 1802, she embarked upon a lecture tour, to talk about her experience: "…I burst the tyrant bonds which held my sex in awe…."

Shabazz, Betty (1936–1997)
Educator, Civil Rights Activist
Portrayed by: Mary J. Blige

Betty Shabazz experienced life from both sides. Born Betty Dean Sanders, she was abused by her mother, but at age 11 found refuge with a prominent black couple in Detroit, the Malloys, who raised her in a caring and comfortable home. Sheltered from race problems by her foster parents, Betty was unprepared for the racism she encountered in Alabama, when she attended the Tuskegee Institute to study elementary education. Frustrated and unhappy in that environment, Betty moved to New York City, where she attended the Brooklyn State College of Nursing in 1953. Through a friend she became interested in Nation of Islam activities, and at a dinner party, Betty met Malcolm X, a minister and rising black nationalist. The two married in 1958, and took the last name Shabazz after leaving the Nation of Islam in 1964.

Betty and Coretta (TV movie, 2013), starring Mary J. Blige as Betty and Lindsay Owen Pierre as Malcolm, picks up the story from there. The couple's split from the Nation of Islam has not been amicable, and Malcolm, who has been receiving threats, tries to prepare Betty for his eventual death. Malcolm's demise comes all too quickly, when he is gunned down during a speech at the Audubon Ballroom in Manhattan, as Betty and their young daughters watch in horror. After her husband's assassination, Betty makes the safety of her six daughters the first priority, eventually moving from the city to the suburbs, where she volunteers for educational causes, but stays away from divisive politics.

She decides to make an exception for the National Black Political Convention, which she attends to set the record straight on her husband's beliefs and legacy. While there, she shares the stage with Coretta Scott King (Angela Bassett), who convinces Betty that she is strong and has something to offer the world on her own. Betty returns to school, earning her PhD, and begins a teaching job at Medgar Evers College in Brooklyn. As Betty and Coretta become friends and the years roll by, Betty's daughter Qubilah (Shinelle Azoroh), the most affected by Malcolm's assassination, struggles to find her place in the world, leaving college, taking odd jobs, and raising a son named Malcolm. Betty says to Coretta prophetically, "When Malcolm was killed, it left a path of destruction I feel like I just can't ever fix."

Alas, that path of destruction eventually led to Betty Shabazz herself. In 1995, Qubilah was arrested for conspiring to murder Louis Farrakhan, whom the family blamed for the assassination of Malcolm X. Qubilah accepted a plea agreement, whereby she was required to undergo psychological counseling, during which her son Malcolm would live with Betty. Two years later, Malcolm, then 12 years old, set fire to his grandmother's apartment. Betty Shabazz suffered burns over 80 percent of her body and died three weeks later from those injuries.

While Betty Shabazz was never able to escape the legacy of Malcolm X's assassination, she did not let his violent death define her life. After she passed, civil rights leader Jesse Jackson said, "She never stopped giving and she never became cynical. She leaves today the legacy of one who epitomized hope and healing."

Shelley, Mary (1797–1851)
Author
Portrayed by: Tracy Keating, Evan Rachel Wood, Anna Maxwell Martin

Mary Shelley wrote *Frankenstein; or, The Modern Prometheus* (1818), one of the earliest examples of science fiction literature. The story of the novel's genesis is itself famous, providing inspiration for movies, such as *Gothic* (1986) and *Haunted Summer* (1988). In history's version, Shelley, then Mary Wollstonecraft Godwin, traveled with her lover, the poet Percy Bysshe Shelley, to Geneva in 1816. Their host, Lord Byron, suggested that they and his other guests "each write a ghost story" to pass the hours during an uncommonly wet summer.

The group turned out to be a horror writing workshop par excellence, producing two works which have resonance to this day. The first, "The Vampyre," a short story by John William Polidori, Byron's physician, was one of the earliest vampire stories and an inspiration for Bram Stoker's *Dracula*. Shelley's story-turned-novel, well known because of its many film adaptations, but more quiet and philosophical than most of them, created a horror sub-genre of its own with the story of a man-made man who struggled to find a place among humans.

Like cinema, television was captivated by the story of the novel's creation. *Highlander: The Series* offered a clever fantasy twist to the tale of Byron's ghost-story competition in "The Modern Prometheus" (1997). Tracy Keating stars as Mary, who, like her real-life namesake, initially struggles to find an inspiration for her story. While staying with Lord Byron (Jonathan Firth), Mary witnesses a "quickening," a lightning-filled extravaganza whereby an immortal, in this case Byron, dies and comes back to life. After the experience, Mary is moved to write a story about the "anguish of immortality" and "a man born of fire" which she will call *Frankenstein*.

Drunk History was also taken with the story of *Frankenstein*'s birth, and devoted an entire episode to it rather than its usual seven-minute vignettes in "Are You Afraid of the Drunk?" (2019). In this star-studded, but abrasive outing, narrator Rich Fulcher screams out the story, while repeatedly stumbling over the words "Wollstonecraft Godwin." Evan Rachel Wood portrays Mary, while Elijah Wood is Shelley, arriving to spend the summer with Byron (Jack McBrayer), during which many opium-fueled orgies will ensue. A nightmare is the catalyst for Mary's story, and she begins by telling us in not-so-nineteenth-century vernacular that Victor Frankenstein (Seth Rogen) is a nerd. The nerd creates a monster (Will Ferrell), and the monster creates a star, Mary, who will publish the story as a novel and make appearances at book signings.

Shelley is taken more seriously in *The Frankenstein Chronicles* (2015–2017), although she is not the show's protagonist. In 1827 London, someone is murdering children for, shall we say, Frankenstein-esque purposes, and a detective, Inspector John Marlott (Sean Bean), is charged with finding the perpetrator. Marlott seeks out Mary Shelley (Anna Maxwell Martin), now Percy's widow, on the chance that the murderer has some connection to Mary or her novel. It's even possible that the author herself is somehow involved. Mary asks, "What would we not do to defeat death, Mr. Marlott?"

While one might think that *Frankenstein* is Shelley's only novel, she wrote several others, including *The Last Man* (1826), an apocalyptic science fiction novel about the destruction of humanity by a mysterious plague in the late 21st century. Mary's work was overshadowed by that of her husband well into the 20th century, but she has come into her own in recent years as a woman of literary achievement and profound imagination.

Shippen, Peggy (1760–1804)

Revolutionary War Spy
Portrayed by: Flora Montgomery, Winona Ryder, Ksenia Solo, Annie Young

You've no doubt heard of Benedict Arnold, whose actions during the American Revolutionary War have made his name synonymous with "traitor." Lesser known is his wife Peggy Shippen, who may have convinced her husband to commit treason. What part did young Peggy, who married Arnold when he was 38 and she was just 18, play in the most famous defection of all time? Historians now believe that Shippen was at least complicit in Arnold's plans, and may, in fact, have instigated them.

Margaret "Peggy" Shippen came from a prominent Philadelphia family, which maintained a careful neutrality during the war, but whose sympathies leaned toward the British rather than the colonists. Only a month after Peggy married Benedict on April 8, 1779, her husband contacted a British officer, John André, Peggy's friend, not Arnold's, and the conspiracy began. Benedict, a general in the Continental Army, offered to pass along valuable military information that would help the British win the war. He later transmitted news of troop numbers and defensive arrangements at West Point, where he had become commander. Peggy wrote seemingly innocent letters to her friend André, which contained a cipher written in invisible ink by her husband.

It's difficult to know what happens in private moments between a wife and her husband, even when what transpires is of monumental importance to the public. Benedict ran into legal problems in Pennsylvania as its military governor and hoped to receive help from George Washington, commander-in-chief of the Continental Army, who refused to intervene. Was his public humiliation enough to drive him over the edge, or did his beautiful, young, loyalist wife give him a push?

In *Benedict Arnold: A Question of Honor*, a 2003 TV movie which portrays the Arnolds in a sympathetic light, the "push" theory holds sway. When Arnold is abandoned by Washington and insulted by the Continental Congress, Peggy (Flora Montgomery) asks her husband, "Where is Washington? You say he loves you as a father. Well, what father would not make all haste, all effort to rescue his son?" From there she proceeds to talk her husband into treason.

The *Drunk History* episode "Philadelphia" (2014) also espouses the "push" theory, but in broader (much broader) terms. Winona Ryder stars as pretty Peggy, "the it girl" of Philadelphia, in the words of narrator Erin McGathy. Peggy entices Benedict (Chris Parnell) to change sides in the war and is unequivocal in describing her part in the conspiracy. "I love being a spy. This is so great, because I love drama."

The Revolutionary War drama *Turn: Washington's Spies* (2014–2017) moves from speculation to outright fabrication in depicting Shippen's role in Arnold's defection. Here Peggy (Ksenia Solo) plots with her secret love John André (JJ Feild) to lure Benedict (Owain Yeoman) from the Patriot cause. When things don't turn out as planned, Peggy becomes engaged to Arnold, but holds out hope for rescue by André. All available evidence points to the fact that the real Peggy loved Benedict, and, even if she didn't, she thought the match a good one in terms of her social status in Philadelphia.

In "The Capture of Benedict Arnold," a 2016 episode of *Timeless*, events have moved to the point when Benedict's treason has been discovered. Benedict (Curtis Caravaggio) is more the leader than the follower here, as he tells Peggy (Annie Young) how to deal with the imminent arrival of George Washington (Damian O'Hare). "He needs to think you're innocent. You don't know anything, understand?" Peggy, nervous, though composed, and clasping her infant, stalls Washington, giving her husband time to escape. Historical Shippen had suffered a breakdown, real or feigned, at that point, convincing Washington and his officers that such a distraught woman must be innocent in the plot.

In November 1780, two months after Benedict's defection, Peggy joined her husband in New York, which was then held by the British. A year later, the Arnolds departed for England, where Peggy received a reward of £350 from King George for her services and an annuity of £100 from Queen Charlotte for each of her children. After Benedict died in 1801, Peggy worked to pay off the debts from his various business ventures, providing some financial stability for the five of her seven children who had survived past infancy. Shippen died of cancer in 1804 at the age of 44.

Drunk History's Peggy celebrated the drama of the spy game, but historical Peggy's life turned out to be anything but a glamorous romp.

Sophie (1901–1990)
Princess of Hohenberg
Portrayed by: Amalie Alstrup

The Young Indiana Jones Chronicles introduces viewers to a stunning girl named Sophie (Amalie Alstrup) in "Vienna, November 1908" (1993). Nine-year-old Indiana Jones (Corey Carrier) takes Sophie ice-skating without permission, almost causing a diplomatic incident, when his little friend is revealed to be the daughter of Archduke Franz Ferdinand (Lennart Hjulstrom), heir to the throne of Austria-Hungary. After the encounter, it's clear that Indy is smitten with Princess Sophie, and he stops at nothing to see her again, protocol be damned. Hiding in a carriage, Indy sneaks into the palace and presents Sophie with a snow globe, while she reciprocates with a locket containing her photo. The two share a kiss, each realizing the meeting is both the beginning and the end of their relationship.

This lovely tale of youth and innocence belies the turmoil of real-world events that would overtake Europe in general, and Sophie's family in particular, a scant six years later. The historical Sophie, just as beautiful as her fictional counterpart, and her younger brothers, Maximilian and Ernst, were the first orphans of World War I. Their father the Archduke and their mother, Sophie, Duchess of Hohenberg, were assassinated at Sarajevo in 1914, sparking the First World War. Sophie herself went on to live a long life, but war hadn't finished decimating her family, taking two of her sons as a result of the Second World War.

Back in the fictional world, Sophie's locket saves an older Indy's life during the Great War, stopping a bullet during an attack in "German East Africa, December 1916." On TV, happy endings, even in war, are easier to come by.

Starr, Belle (1848–1889)
Outlaw

Portrayed by: Marie Windsor, Carole Mathews, Jeanne Cooper, Jean Willes, Lynn Bari, Brooke Tucker, Florence Henderson, Elizabeth Montgomery, Melissa Clayton, Sheila E. Campbell

Although she doesn't have the marquee value of Calamity Jane or Annie Oakley, Belle Starr, "the queen of the outlaws," cut a swath through TV westerns over the decades, leaving lots of portrayals, but not a clear picture of who she was or even what she looked like. When the real Belle was fatally shot in 1889, she quickly became the stuff of legend, thanks to Richard K. Fox, who wrote her biography *Belle Starr, the Bandit Queen, or The Female Jesse James* (1889), which was billed as "a full and authentic history of the dashing female highwayman." Mr. Fox, publisher of the *National Police Gazette*, was given to embellishment, as when the *Gazette* captioned an 1886 drawing of Belle: "A wild western amazon. The noted Belle Starr is arrested on the border of Indian Territory and being released on bail vanishes on horseback." Fox set the trend for making Belle Starr anything you wanted her to be, and TV followed suit in the modern era.

Studio portrait of Belle Starr, 1880s (Battle of Carthage Civil War Museum).

We first meet Belle Starr on television in a 1954 episode of *Stories of the Century*, appropriately titled "Belle Starr." Marie Windsor, sporting frontier false eyelashes, portrays the outlaw, wearing Belle's characteristic plumed hat, but also buckskins, where the real Starr preferred to wear dresses and ride sidesaddle. Windsor's Belle is abrasive, constantly barking out orders, demeaning her Native American husband, Sam Starr (Ric Roman), and pushing people around. She engineers the theft of 100 or more U.S. cavalry horses consigned to a railroad depot in Fort Smith, Arkansas, and railroad detective Matt Clark (Jim Davis) investigates. Eventually Clark catches up with Belle after an exciting shootout on horseback, while the truth of her capture for horse stealing was decidedly less telegenic. In reality, noted black lawman Bass Reeves held the warrant for Starr's arrest, and she turned herself in quietly and without incident.

The real Belle and Sam Starr were indicted for horse stealing in 1883, ultimately receiving a short federal prison sentence from Judge Isaac C. Parker, the "hanging judge" of Fort Smith. The crime forms the basis for another, even more fictionalized telling, "A Bullet for the D.A.," a 1961 episode of *Death Valley Days*. Carole Mathews portrays Belle, whose husband Sam Starr (William Thourlby), is the one on trial for "horse thieving," while Belle has gone straight. The D.A. of the episode's title, Frank Clayton (Don Haggerty), reveals Sam's illiteracy during courtroom questioning, infuriating Belle, who is embarrassed by the public revelation.

Mrs. Starr becomes obsessed with seeking revenge against Clayton, and hatches a plan to shoot him during the reenactment of a stagecoach robbery. Sam saves the day at the last minute in a convoluted and unconvincing story of redemption that bears little resemblance to historical Belle's life. In fact, the real Sam died in a gunfight in 1887—no happily ever after for historical Belle and Sam.

Other westerns of the period simply invented their own crimes for Belle Starr to commit. In another "Belle Starr" episode, this one from 1957, another railroad detective, Jim Hardie (Dale Robertson), sets out to capture Belle (Jeanne Cooper), when she and her gang commit a train robbery right under his nose in *Tales of Wells Fargo*. A blonde Belle (Jean Willes) is one of 10 notorious outlaws, including her beau Cole Younger (Gregory Walcott), planning a major heist, but she isn't averse to flirting with Bret Maverick (James Garner), when the crew mistakes him for the mastermind of their caper in "Full House," a 1959 episode of *Maverick*. Using her maiden name, Myra Shirley, Belle (Lynn Bari) feigns serious illness to board a special run of the Overland Stage, which just happens to be carrying Cole Younger (Robert J. Wilke), who is in desperate need of escape from a U.S. Marshal (Tyler McVey) in "Perilous Passage," a 1960 episode of *Overland Trail*.

As the popularity of traditional westerns waned, children's shows managed to find kid appeal in the decidedly not G-rated story of Belle. In "They Went Thataway," a 1975 episode of *The Ghost Busters*, Brooke Tucker portrays Belle Starr, a ghost returned to our world to do some cattle rustling, in this kids' sitcom about bumbling ghost hunters. In 1977, Florence Henderson appeared as Belle Starr, decked out like a dance hall girl, and with a spittoon, booze, and empty shot glasses on her desk, in *Storybook Squares,* a version of the game show *Hollywood Squares* for children.

In 1980, Belle finally received the full TV movie treatment in, you guessed it, *Belle Starr.* Elizabeth Montgomery portrays Belle in the later years of her not-very-long life, seeking respectability for her daughter, here called Pearl Younger (Michelle Stacy), the daughter of Cole Younger (Cliff Potts). The real Belle's daughter was born Rosie Lee Reed, nicknamed Pearl, daughter of Belle and first husband Jim Reed, but unsubstantiated rumors about her parentage apparently were too much for the producers to resist. While Belle farms out Pearl to a proper lady who teaches the girl good manners and how to play piano, Belle tends to son Ed (David Nell), who is a wee bit obsessed with mom. In the meantime, Belle maintains her frontier chic look, as Younger and the James and Dalton boys show up to involve her in one last heist. She is shot in the back at her ranch, while the real Starr was ambushed by person or persons unknown while riding home.

Jean Willes as a blonde Belle Starr on *Maverick* (The Bureau of Industrial Service for ABC).

The list of shows with historical inaccuracies or healthy doses of dramatic license goes on, including "Baby Outlaws," a 1995 episode of *Dr. Quinn, Medicine Woman,* with Melissa Clayton as 14-year-old Belle, who would have been a married woman of 21 by 1869, the approximate setting of this season-three episode. *The Pinkertons* paint a sympathetic portrait of Belle in "Frontier Desperados" (2015), but have the decency to call her Belle Carson (Sheila E. Campbell) in their highly fictionalized tale, where she says she would take the name Belle Starr if she were truly an outlaw.

Lynn Bari as Belle Starr, with William Bendix (left) and Doug McClure in *Overland Trail* (NBC).

This Belle has her husband kidnapped by her partner Jesse James (John C. MacDonald) for ransom money paid by her father.

That's Belle Starr. The blonde/brunette, abrasive/refined Wild West Amazon and criminal mastermind of her time. Or a lady who stole some horses with her husband and ran with the wrong crowd. Or anyone you like.

Sullivan, Anne (1866–1936)
See (mentioned in): **Keller, Helen (1880–1968)**

Tarbell, Ida (1857–1944)
Journalist
Portrayed by: Shannon Woodward

Ida Tarbell was a muckraker. While that might sound like a dirty job or an epithet, Ida's kind of muckraking was noble and clean, exposing the corruption, fraud, and social hardships of her era, not with a rake, but with her pen. Tarbell was a pioneer of investigative journalism, who believed that finding and transmitting the truth could bring about important social change, and her work eventually led to the dissolution of John D. Rockefeller's Standard Oil monopoly.

As *Drunk History* tells her "superhero origin story" in "Underdogs" (2018), Tarbell (Shannon Woodward) is deeply affected by her father's loss of livelihood at the hands of "robber baron" Rockefeller (John Ennis), who works with railroads to drive smaller oil companies out of business. Choosing between an anachronistic Barbie doll and a pen, young Ida knows how she will right the wrongs done to society by people like Rockefeller. Her choice of the pen eventually leads her to work for *McClure's Magazine*, where she decides to write a major exposé about Standard Oil and Rockefeller.

Conducting research for two years, and gaining access via Mark Twain (Derek Waters) to an overly cooperative Standard Oil executive, Tarbell composes a 19-piece article for *McClure's* titled "The History of Standard Oil." Calling Rockefeller a "living mummy," Tarbell outlines his unethical business practices and turns public opinion against him. Finally, in 1911, the Supreme Court rules that Standard Oil's monopoly is illegal and the company is ultimately broken into two entities. Oft-belching narrator Jon Gabrus says of Tarbell's accomplishment: "So a woman who was unable to even vote was able via just writing to take down the richest man in the world."

Ida Tarbell didn't consider herself much of a writer, but she was a dogged researcher, a necessary skill when seeking out and examining hundreds of thousands of documents in the pre-Internet era. Tarbell used her pen to share the truths she unearthed in her research. While Rockefeller may have called her "that poisonous woman," history provides a different perspective. Tarbell's book based on her *McClure's* articles, *The History of the Standard Oil Company* (1904), is considered one of the best and most influential books ever written by an American investigative journalist.

Taylor, Elizabeth (1932–2011)
Actress
Portrayed by: Lindsay Lohan, Helena Bonham Carter, Casey Ahern, Sherilyn Fenn

Elizabeth Taylor lived her life in the spotlight, the quintessential star, drawing fans into her orbit even after her movie career had ended. Taylor began working in Hollywood as a child, soon achieving fame in *National Velvet* (1944), where she portrayed a 12-year-old girl who rides her horse in the Grand National steeplechase. Although child stars often have difficulty transitioning to adult roles, Taylor had no such trouble. At the age of 18, she starred in the comedy *Father of the Bride* (1950), and followed it up with the dark and disturbing *A Place in the Sun* (1951), finding critical acclaim. Her career elevator had only one button at that point, "UP," and major roles followed, in *Giant* (1956), with Rock Hudson and James Dean, *Cat on a Hot Tin Roof* (1958), with Paul Newman, and *Butterfield 8* (1960), for which she won her first Academy Award.

Scandals and tragedies surrounding Taylor's romantic life also became part of the public's fascination with her. Her list of marriages and divorces was ever growing, with a short marriage to Nicky Hilton, a longer marriage to Michael Wilding, and a short marriage to Mike Todd, which ended with his death in a plane crash. After the tragedy, came the scandals, including an affair with Eddie Fisher, who was still married to Debbie Reynolds, transforming Liz from sympathetic widow to callous homewrecker in the eyes of the public. Another affair with Richard Burton, while she was married to Fisher, increased the disapproval, but also the press attention. Taylor's stormy and storied relationship with Burton, whom she married twice, was professional as well as personal, leading to a collaboration on 11 films, including *Who's Afraid of Virginia Woolf?* (1966), for which Elizabeth won her second Academy Award.

The romance between Taylor and Burton is the subject of *Liz & Dick*, a Lifetime TV movie from 2012. Lindsay Lohan portrays Elizabeth to Grant Bowler's Richard, a beautiful, passionate couple, who can't stand living with or without each other. The film covers their years together, and the last day of Richard's life in 1984, during which he writes a letter to Elizabeth, signing it, "with my undying love." The letter-writing scene seems like the framing device for the movie, but then it cuts to a darkened studio, where Liz and Dick banter about their lives, and the flashbacks begin.

The film was savaged by most critics, who took particular aim at Lohan's performance. To be fair, playing one of the screen's greatest legends is a tall order for any actor. Even when Elizabeth Taylor appears as herself on a sitcom like *The Nanny*, she comes across as not quite one of us, somehow otherworldly. That's not a quality that's easy to capture, and Lohan leaves her Liz decidedly earthbound.

Liz and Dick are the subjects of another TV movie, *Burton and Taylor* (2013), but the focus here is on the couple after their divorce, when they are appearing together in the play *Private Lives* in 1983. Helena Bonham Carter portrays Taylor, who is struggling with substance abuse issues, while Dominic West is Burton, recovering from his own problems with alcohol and suffering from poor health. The play, by Noël Coward, about a divorced couple who realize they still have feelings for each other, is uncomfortably close to home for Richard, although you'd think that would have been obvious from the start. Liz is portrayed as more of the problem here, tempting Richard to drink (he refuses), arriving late for shows, and generally being difficult, which leads to a confrontation that comes to blows. Somehow Taylor and Burton still love each other, but they conclude that they must do their loving from afar.

Liz: The Elizabeth Taylor Story, a two-part miniseries from 1995, has more on its mind than Liz's relationship with Burton. It's a full biography, covering Taylor's life, beginning in 1942, when Elizabeth (Casey Ahern) auditions for *Lassie Come Home* (1943), and successfully emotes to a mop, which she uses to stand in for the famous collie. Sherilyn Fenn stars as the adult Elizabeth Taylor, and her breathtakingly beautiful looks, as well as her walk and manner, are as close to Elizabeth Taylor's as anyone is ever likely to get on screen.

Although the real Elizabeth Taylor sought an injunction to prohibit NBC from broadcasting this miniseries, claiming it would sully her name and invade her privacy, a Los Angeles judge disagreed with her. Perhaps Liz needn't have worried, as it is a sympathetic portrayal overall, its very first frame transmitting a positive message via a title card: "Elizabeth Taylor is one of the most recognizable women in the world. Having reached the pinnacle of her profession, much of her time and energy today is spent leading a compassionate struggle on behalf of AIDS victims."

Temple, Shirley (1928–2014)
Actress, Diplomat
Portrayed by: Ashley Rose Orr, Emily Anne Hart

A child was the top box office star of 1935. And 1936. And 1937. And 1938. Her name was Shirley Temple. Shirley's patented mix of singing, dancing, and dimples in films such as *Bright Eyes* (1934), *Curly Top* (1935), and *The Little Colonel* (1935) provided happiness and hope to moviegoers at a time when both were in short supply during the Great Depression. President Franklin D. Roosevelt once said, "…it is a splendid thing that for just 15 cents, an American can go to a movie and look at the smiling face of a baby and forget his troubles."

"Child Star: The Shirley Temple Story" (2001) is much like one of Shirley Temple's movies, with an adorable, sweet protagonist who spreads happiness wherever she goes. The movie-length presentation was shown as part of *The Wonderful World of Disney*, so a sunny, family-friendly view of reality is to be expected. Ashley Rose Orr portrays Temple for most of the film, which focuses on her big box office years, when she was America's pin-curled darling. Jay Gorney (Bruce Roberts) brings Shirley to Fox Films, where she shows what a prodigy she is, picking up complicated tap-dance routines instantaneously from professional dancers.

As Shirley's star continues to rise, a plan forms for her to dance with the best tap dancer in the world, Bill "Bojangles" Robinson (Hinton Battle), although Gorney expresses reservations about audience reaction. He says, "There's never been a black man dancing with a white girl on screen before." The project moves forward, more to make money than to make a point, and Temple performs her famous staircase dance with Robinson in *The Little Colonel*. After continued film successes follow, Shirley, now portrayed by Emily Anne Hart, is happily retired from the movies, without much explanation. She goes to a dance and later finds out from her mother (Connie Britton) that she is 14 rather than 13. This section seems sandwiched in at the end to no real purpose, and leaves the impression that Temple made a big comeback in films. The real Shirley Temple, however, never returned to her box office glory, officially announcing her retirement from films in 1950, at the ripe old age of 22.

True to the title "Child Star," the movie tells us nothing about Temple's later life, not her marriage at 17 to John Agar, or her popular television show in the '50s, or her later marriage to Charles A. Black. In fact, Temple, then known as Shirley Temple Black, had a dramatic career change later in life, becoming a diplomat during several Republican administrations. Her last official appointment was as United States ambassador to Czechoslovakia from 1989 to 1992, where she witnessed the fall of communism during the Velvet Revolution.

Shirley Temple clearly believed that there are second acts in American lives, and she had a remarkable one.

Theodora (ca. 497–548)

Empress of the Byzantine Empire
Portrayed by: Salome Jens

Theodora rose from humble beginnings to become one of the most powerful women in Byzantine history. As empress of the Byzantine

Empire by marriage to Emperor Justinian I, Theodora took an active role in her husband's affairs of state, leading some contemporaries to believe it was Theodora rather than Justinian who ruled the empire. At a minimum, Theodora was a trusted advisor to her husband, and Justinian himself once called her his "partner in my deliberations."

The Theodora we encounter in *Meeting of Minds*, as portrayed by Salome Jens, has a regal, silky voice, and wears an imposing, gem-studded headdress. In "St. Augustine, Empress Theodora, Thomas Jefferson, Bertrand Russell" (parts one and two, 1979), the empress is much affected by the poverty she experienced as a child, which led her into an early life of prostitution. She says to the other guests gathered for this talk show of historical figures, and especially to St. Augustine (Ivor Francis), "Yes, gentlemen, a prostitute by the time I was 13, and not by choice, Father, but as the price of poverty." She bristles as the men discuss politics and philosophy, thinking the conversation impractical. "Our bodies dictate our actions even more than our minds. The body has its hungers, and if those hungers are not met, then all your theories are vanities.... I was a product of poverty. I saw people starve, I saw them die in the gutter."

Historical Theodora's background influenced the social reforms of her husband's reign, which included laws to prohibit trafficking in young girls and divorce laws more favorable to women. Her name, in fact, is mentioned in many of the laws passed during the era. The empress also sponsored the creation of institutions for the poor, such as orphanages, hospitals, and a home for former prostitutes.

While often portrayed at the time as scheming and immoral, possibly by people with axes to grind, Theodora's keen intelligence and consummate political skill are her important attributes. The "Theodora ran things" theory is given some credence by the fact that little important legislation appeared between her death in 548 and the Emperor's passing almost 20 years later in 565.

Tubman, Harriet (ca. 1820–1913)
Abolitionist, Spy, Suffragist
Portrayed by: Ruby Dee, Cicely Tyson, Fay Hauser, Christine Horn, Octavia Spencer

History textbooks in earlier decades didn't include many women, but Harriet Tubman was always in them. Her brave story of escape from slavery in 1849 and subsequent work leading other slaves to freedom via the Underground Railroad was too remarkable and important to be ignored. Although illiterate, Ms. Tubman was ingenious in avoiding capture while conducting fugitive slaves to freedom, one time using her publicized illiteracy to advantage by pretending to read so she wouldn't be recognized. During the American Civil War, she was a spy and scout for Union forces, even leading a raid in South Carolina, which rescued almost 800 slaves. Due to that involvement, Tubman fought for years to receive a military pension from the U.S. Government, which was finally approved 30 years later through legislative action, but it recognized only her work as a nurse. In later years, Tubman promoted women's suffrage, traveling despite poverty and illness to speak at meetings and receptions of suffragist and women's organizations.

Television's earliest depictions of Harriet Tubman were biographical dramas. "Go Down, Moses" (1963), an episode of the short-lived historical anthology series *The Great Adventure*, stars Ruby Dee in a riveting performance as Ms. Tubman. The story begins as Tubman volunteers to be a conductor on the Underground Railroad in 1850 Philadelphia, and focuses on her trip to rescue enslaved relatives in Dorchester County, Maryland. The program hits emotional high notes, portraying the heartbreak of leaving her parents behind and the unbearable tension of surreptitiously passing through a slave patrol checkpoint.

More well-known is the 1978 miniseries *A Woman Called Moses*, starring Cicely Tyson as Tubman, a.k.a. "Moses," the nickname given to her in reference to the biblical prophet who led the Israelites out of Egyptian slavery. With its four-hour running time, the miniseries naturally covers more ground than "Go Down, Moses," beginning the story earlier, when young Harriet (Jean Foster) is hit on the head by an overseer, receiving an injury whose ramifications will plague her throughout her life, causing dizziness, narcolepsy, and visions she thought were sent by God. Later televised

Harriet Tubman, 1895, by Horatio Seymour Squyer (National Portrait Gallery, Smithsonian Institution).

Ruby Dee (center) stars as Harriet Tubman in *The Great Adventure* with (clockwise from left) Mimi Dillard, Ossie Davis, Brock Peters, and Gloria Calomee (CBS).

depictions added genre elements to Tubman's story, particularly the time travel trope. In "Created Equal," a 1982 episode of the series *Voyagers!*, Harriet Tubman (Fay Hauser) meets two time travelers who must restore history to its proper course by rescuing Tubman from captivity on a riverboat. The *Timeless* team has a similar, albeit graver, mission in "The General" (2018), assisting Tubman (Christine Horn) in a plantation raid during the Civil War, when evil forces attempt to subvert both her legacy and the Union's victory. Tubman's revelation that she had put her faith in the time travel team, because she had seen them, especially Rufus (Malcolm Barrett), in one of her visions, takes on a thrilling resonance when she clearly describes from memory what they know to be their ship, "the Lifeboat."

Drunk History adds alcohol and (almost) deleted expletives in its telling of Tubman's accomplishments, emphasizing her work as a Union operative in "Spies" (2015). Octavia Spencer portrays Tubman, who gathers intelligence about mines in South Carolina's Combahee River, later leading a Union Army raid to burn the neighboring plantations and free their slaves. This depiction might not be for everyone, especially those sensitive to expletives or the incessant sound of beeping to mock-delete them.

In December 2014, President Barack Obama signed into law a bill establishing the Harriet Tubman Underground Railroad National Historical Park in Dorchester County, Maryland.

(La) Tules
See: **Barceló, Maria Gertrudis (ca. 1800–1852)**

Tz'u-hsi
See: **Cixi (1835–1908)**

Valland, Rose (1898–1980)
Art Historian, Spy
Portrayed by: Busy Philipps

One of France's most decorated women, Rose Valland began her career in art history as a volunteer assistant curator at the Jeu de Paume Museum in Paris. While that unassuming position doesn't sound like a stepping stone to greatness, Valland made it one during World War II. When the Nazis used the Museum to collect, store, and ship valuable artwork they'd stolen from the nation of France and its Jewish citizens, Valland concealed her knowledge of German, while keeping track of the shipping destinations for the art. A woman of uncommon bravery, she risked her life to provide information to the French resistance about trains carrying the treasures, so their operatives wouldn't target the shipments for demolition.

Drunk History picks up the story from there in "Heroines" (2018).

Busy Philipps stars as Valland, who must fetch champagne for Reich Marshal Hermann Göring (Craig Cackowski), when he visits the Jeu De Paume to scoop up some treasures for himself. From October 1940 to December 1944, Valland surreptitiously takes notes on the stolen works and their destinations, until American James Rorimer (Derek Waters) visits the museum. Rorimer, who represents the Monuments Men (the Monuments, Fine Arts, and Archives program of the Allied armies), asks for Valland's help in locating the plundered treasures. Although reluctant to trust Rorimer at first, Valland eventually shares her secrets, sending allied troops to stop trains and invade salt mines, where they recover Europe's cultural heritage. Narrator Tiffany Haddish says, "She saved, like, over 60,000 pieces of culture. She's a heroine."

Rose Valland's valor and dedication resulted in numerous awards from her own country, including the Légion d'honneur, and the United States recognized her achievements as well with its Medal of Freedom in 1948. While her tale may sound familiar from *The Monuments Men*, a 2014 film directed by George Clooney, the name of the real-life art historian at the Jeu de Paume is not Claire Simone (Cate Blanchett), as in the movie. It is Rose Valland, the woman who saved much of the world's inheritance of modern art.

Victoria (1819–1901)
Queen of the United Kingdom
Portrayed by: Jane Connell, Jacquelyn Hyde, Lurene Tuttle, Patti Allan, Pauline Collins, Julie Harris, Patricia Routledge, Victoria Hamilton, Joyce Redman, Jenna Coleman, Michael Palin, et al.

For a woman who gave her name to a prim and inhibited era, Queen Victoria sure gets around ... the TV dial. From comedies to dramas, from fantasies to westerns, Victoria has made more appearances than she made children (and she made nine of them).

Victoria (Jane Connell) lands in a 1960s American suburb, of all places, when bumbling witch Clara (Marion Lorne) accidentally summons her majesty to the home of Samantha Stephens (Elizabeth Montgomery), Clara's witchy niece, in "Aunt Clara's Victoria Victory," a 1967 episode of *Bewitched*. Her majesty is off on an even wilder adventure in *The Wild Wild West Revisited* (TV movie, 1979), when clones replace kidnapped world leaders, including Queen Victoria (Jacquelyn Hyde), in a mad scientist's plot to take over the world. (If ever there were a time for Queen Victoria's famous, albeit apocryphal phrase, "we are not amused," it would have been here.)

Ever beleaguered, the queen (Lurene Tuttle) gets some help from two time travelers, thwarting a Russian plot and correcting an aberration in the timeline when "Buffalo Bill and Annie Play the Palace" in *Voyagers!* (1983). Then it's back to battling world domination plots in *The Secret Adventures of Jules Verne* (2000), when Queen Victoria (Patti Allan) dodges assassins in "Queen Victoria and the Giant Mole" and "The Victorian Candidate." The poor dear should have been exhausted by now, but Victoria (Pauline Collins) must deal with warrior monks who plan to sic an alien werewolf on her in "Tooth and Claw" (*Doctor Who*, 2006).

Queen Victoria, 1882, by Alexander Bassano (National Portrait Gallery, London).

But it's not all time travel and royal clones when it comes to televised depictions of Victoria. Some movies and series treat her life with a dignity she might have appreciated. Julie Harris won an Emmy Award for her portrayal of the queen from her accession to the throne at age 18 through her diamond jubilee in *Victoria Regina* (TV movie, 1961), part of the *Hallmark Hall of Fame* anthology series. Patricia Routledge appeared in another production of *Victoria Regina*, also based on the 1935 play by Laurence Housman, a four-part Granada Television miniseries in 1964.

As its title suggests, *Victoria & Albert* (TV movie, 2001) focuses on the relationship between Queen Victoria (Victoria Hamilton) and her husband Prince Albert (Jonathan Firth), with Joyce Redman appearing as Victoria in her later years. And Victoria finally received the full TV series treatment in the eponymous *Victoria* (2016–2019), with Jenna Coleman as the young queen, who gives new meaning to the term "working mother," attending to crises such as war and famine, while producing six heirs by the age of 30.

There have been more televised portrayals of Queen Victoria,

James Donald and Julie Harris as Albert and Victoria in *Victoria Regina* (NBC).

including one by a man, Michael Palin, in "Michael Ellis" (*Monty Python's Flying Circus*, 1974), wherein Victoria repeatedly lapses into German during a poetry reading.

We ARE amused.

von Hohenberg, Sophie
See: **Sophie (1901–1990)**

Warne, Kate (1833–1868)
Detective, Spy
Portrayed by: Adrianne Palicki, Martha MacIsaac

In 1856, widow Kate Warne, 23 years old, presented herself at the Chicago office of the Pinkerton Detective Agency. Much to the surprise of agency founder Allan Pinkerton, Warne was not there to seek clerical employment, but was offering her services as a detective. Pinkerton wasn't impressed, but Warne made the case that women could go where men couldn't, and Pinkerton hired her, making her America's first female detective.

In a truth-is-stranger-than-fiction twist, it would take only five years for the fate of the entire nation to be placed in this young woman's hands. In 1861, the president of the Philadelphia, Wilmington and Baltimore Railroad hired the Pinkerton agency to investigate threats against the railroad. Evidence of a plot to assassinate president-elect Abraham Lincoln emerged, and Warne was one of five agents sent to Baltimore to investigate. Warne went undercover as a wealthy southern lady, infiltrating secessionist circles and gathering details of the assassination plot. Her initial pitch to Pinkerton of a woman's special worth in such matters turned out to be prophetic, as her flirtatious southern belle routine collected enough evidence to convince her boss that the assassination plans were imminent.

The plan, a.k.a. the "Baltimore Plot," called for Lincoln to be murdered while he switched trains in Baltimore on his way to Washington, D.C. The Pinkertons convinced a reluctant president-elect to make a slight modification to his schedule after his stop in Harrisburg, Pennsylvania. Thereafter Lincoln posed as a sick man, donning a soft cap and shawl, while Kate Warne posed as his caring sister and traveling companion, accompanied by Pinkerton and Lincoln's bodyguard, Ward Hill Lamon. Kate stayed awake all night, guarding Lincoln on the trip from Pennsylvania to Washington. The Pinkerton motto "we never sleep" is said to have been inspired by Kate's vigilance that night.

Drunk History briefly recounts the story of the Pinkertons' role in thwarting Lincoln's assassination in "Baltimore" (2014). The focus is mostly on Allan Pinkerton (Charlie Day), although Adrianne Palicki gets a couple of scenes as Kate Warne.

The Pinkertons (2014–2015) devotes an entire TV series to the cases of Kate Warne (Martha MacIsaac) after the Civil War, but only fleetingly alludes to her protection of Lincoln in "The Play's the Thing" (2014), where a flashback scene or an even an entire episode would have been preferable. Produced in cooperation with Pinkerton, now a global risk management agency, and based on some of the agency's actual cases, *The Pinkertons* finds Kate in 1865 Kansas City, where she is assigned to a case by Allan Pinkerton (Angus Macfadyen). When Allan's son Will (Jacob Blair) is having no luck solving a string of bank and train robberies, Allan decides to put his "best man," i.e., Kate, on the case, and eventually leaves the two in Kansas City as a mini-bureau for crime-solving, with Kate as Will's boss.

Although Kate can play the southern belle when the case warrants, she is no shrinking violet. She goes undercover as a cowboy, pulling her duds and a fake beard from her trunk of disguises, in "In Marm's Way" (2015). Kate can't sew, but she knows her way around the tools of the Old West, drawing a pistol on Jesse James in "Frontier Desperados" (2015), and jumping off a moving horse to catch a fleeing outlaw in "The Play's the Thing." But Kate isn't simply an action hero. She conducts forensic experiments in her home, even inventing a facial reconstruction procedure by forming clay over a skull in "On Account of Huckleberries" (2015). She is always dogged and dutiful, even when her principles take her to dark places, revealing that she had compromised her honor during the war to get important troop information from a confederate soldier.

Kate Warne died of pneumonia at the age of 34 or 35. Her death notice in the *Democratic Inquirer* acknowledged the groundbreaking nature of her accomplishments: "In her career while she lived she developed that her sex could do much more than had ever before been ascribed to their sphere." Warne had not only carved out a new role and career for herself, but also her success at her job led Pinkerton to establish an entire department of female detectives, with Warne as its superintendent. The *Inquirer* continued: "She leaves a void in the female detective department which it will be difficult ever to fill. As she lived, so she died, a strong, pure, devoted woman."

Washington, Martha (1731–1802)

First Lady
Portrayed by: Jane Connell, Elizabeth Appleby, Patty Duke, Lilli Birdsell

Martha Washington was the *first* first lady of the United States. As wife of George Washington, the first U.S. president, Mrs. Washington had no examples to follow, so she had to decide what her public role, if any, should be. Often addressed as "Lady Washington," Martha was drawn into her husband's political life, as the president's office was in their home, first in New York, and later in Philadelphia. Lady Washington served as hostess at social gatherings, which became known as "The Republican Court," where political figures and intellectuals, spouses included, debated matters of state and philosophy.

Lady Washington is less attracted to intellectual discourse than to modern kitchen appliances in "George Washington Zapped Here" (part two), a 1972 episode of *Bewitched*. Mrs. Washington (Jane Connell) time travels with her husband (Will Geer) to sixties suburbia, thanks to an accidental spell cast by clumsy witch Esmeralda (Alice Ghostley). Most of the emphasis in this outing of the popular sitcom is on George, who, what a surprise, cannot tell a lie, while Martha is the perennial tagalong.

Time travel is also a plot catalyst in "Wilmington," a 2018 entry in the *Outlander* series. Here George (Simon Harrison) and Martha (Elizabeth Appleby) are not the travelers themselves, but encounter time displaced Claire Fraser (Caitríona Balfe) and her hunky hubby Jamie (Sam Heughan) at a play. Claire is starstruck to meet the Washingtons, who later agree to give Jamie a lift, unaware he is involved in a robbery plot.

Martha is untouched by the vagaries of time displacement in *George Washington* (Miniseries, 1984), although some time travel shenanigans might have brightened the proceedings. Patty Duke (credited as Patty Duke Astin) first appears as recent widow Martha Custis, who receives a condolence visit from her acquaintance George Washington (Barry Bostwick). A later visit prompts his marriage proposal, and George sends a "Dear Jane" letter to pretty, married Sally Fairfax (Jaclyn Smith), ending their flirtation. After war between Great Britain and the newly minted United States comes to pass, Mrs. Washington visits her husband, now commander of the Continental Army, at Valley Forge. Conditions are poor for the soldiers in camp, and Martha assists when she can, helping a man to the sick hut, where she watches the amputation of his leg.

The real Martha Washington did indeed spend winters with George at his military encampments, not only enjoying private time with her husband, but also serving as his hostess and household manager. Dinners with officers were described as "elegant," socializing included singing, and the camp even produced a play performed by the officers. Mrs. Washington's presence boosted morale among the officers and inspired the wives who were present, although there is some question as to whether she actually visited the common soldiers, as depicted in the miniseries.

Patty Duke reprises her role as Martha Washington in *George Washington II: The Forging of a Nation* (TV movie, 1986). Like the original, this sequel is based upon James Thomas Flexner's Pulitzer Prize–winning biography *George Washington*, published in four volumes and later abridged as *Washington: The Indispensable Man* (1974). The two-part movie begins as George assumes the presidency after the ratification of the Constitution in 1788, and follows the Washingtons through his second term, ending in

1797. Audiences were apparently more attracted to the Washingtons in war than in peace, as this production pulled in only half the audience of its predecessor, and was deemed a "major disappointment" by CBS.

Martha makes two brief appearances in *Turn: Washington's Spies* (2014–2017), the story of the Culper Ring, a network of spies who fed General Washington information during the Revolutionary War. In one of the episodes, "Many Mickles Make a Muckle" (2016), the Washingtons attend a lavish ball hosted by soon-to-be-traitor Benedict Arnold (Owain Yeoman). While George (Ian Kahn) mulls a decision about Arnold's fate, Martha (Lilli Birdsell) teases that George is too concerned about being liked. The general disagrees, feeling that he's actually seeking respect, but Martha, an astute wife who knows her husband, insists that the issue is affection.

In all of these productions, Martha serves as an appendage to her husband. To be sure, George Washington is a towering figure in United States history, worthy of the attention scripted television has given him. At the same time, stories centered on Martha, a woman who set many of the standards for the position and influence of the U.S. First Lady, would be welcome. While such a task would be made more difficult by the fact that Martha Washington burned almost all of the couple's correspondence after George's death to maintain a private couple's privacy, some nuggets remain. For example, Martha wasn't a big fan of the restrictions her husband's public office placed on her life. She once wrote to a niece, "I think I am more like a state prisoner than anything else, there is certain bounds set for me which I must not depart from...." While Martha was amiable and tactful as first lady, a title coined after her death, and supported her husband's continued calls to serve his country, Martha's feelings of being a "state prisoner" might serve as a touchstone for a fascinating production about her life.

Watson, Ellen "Ella"
See: Cattle Kate

Wilder, Laura Ingalls (1867–1957)
Author, Farmer
Portrayed by: Melissa Gilbert, Alandra Bingham, Meredith Monroe, Tess Harper, Michelle Bevan, Kyle Chavarria

Millions know the name Laura Ingalls Wilder from the long-running television series *Little House on the Prairie* (1974–1984). Laura (Melissa Gilbert), called "Half Pint" by her father Charles Ingalls (Michael Landon), discovers the joys and hardships of a new life, when her family moves to Walnut Grove, Minnesota, in the 1870s. Laura begins the series as a young girl, who attends school, but isn't very studious, preferring to play with her dog Jack or go fishing. By the end of the show's run, Laura is a married,

Melissa Gilbert stars as young Laura Ingalls Wilder in *Little House on the Prairie* (NBC).

albeit still young woman in her late teens, who pursues the profession of teaching, while facing 19th-century challenges with husband Almanzo Wilder (Dean Butler). The show, which ran for nine seasons, is loosely based on the real Laura Ingalls Wilder's autobiographical children's novels, the best-selling Little House books, including *Little House on the Prairie* (1935), the third in the series.

Television Laura has some of the same adventures and troubles as her historical counterpart, including her husband's serious bout with diphtheria and the loss of their newborn son. The show took other liberties with the real Laura's story, however, such as setting her on the novel-writing path when she was still a young mother in "Once upon a Time" (1983). While this episode has a touching and memorable conclusion, where a little girl (Shawna Landon) runs into a modern library to read *Little House on the Prairie*, historical Laura didn't begin writing her Little House books until she was in her late 50s. The real Laura had gained experience writing articles for magazines, including a regular column in the *Missouri Ruralist*. Eventually she tried her hand at novel-writing, finding success in 1932 with the publication of her first book, *Little House in the Big Woods*.

While we might expect nine seasons and four TV movies of *Little House on the Prairie* to have exhausted Little House's appeal, television wasn't done with Laura Ingalls Wilder yet. In 2000, a two-part TV movie appeared, *Beyond the Prairie: The True Story of Laura Ingalls Wilder*, starring three different actresses as Laura, Alandra Bingham (age 3), Meredith Monroe (younger adult), and Tess Harper (older adult). A second movie followed in 2002, *Beyond the Prairie, Part 2: The True Story of Laura Ingalls Wilder*, featuring the same actors, except for Michelle Bevan as young Laura. The movies accurately place Laura and her family in South Dakota rather than Minnesota during her teens, and cover the last four books in the Little House series, including *The First Four Years*, discovered after Wilder's death and published in 1971. Adding the words "True Story" to the titles is a stretch, however, as the movies depict Laura as a blonde with a modern look and outlook, and, distort facts, such as misrepresenting the age of Laura's daughter Rose (Skye McCole Bartusiak) at the start of part 2.

It was back to the prairie once more for the six-part *Wonderful World of Disney* miniseries *Little House on the Prairie* (2005), based on Wilder's novels *Little House in the Big Woods* and *Little House on the Prairie*. Laura (Kyle Chavarria) is a girl in braids again, and older sister Mary (Danielle Ryan Chuchran) is at her side, while baby Carrie is mysteriously absent from the Ingalls family's journey from Wisconsin to Kansas.

The three presentations as a whole remind us that televised historical fiction, especially when adapted from other fictional works, is like viewing history through frosted glass. It's pretty, but you're not going to see very well.

Wilson, Edith (1872–1961)
First Lady
Portrayed by: Courteney Cox

In the *Drunk History* episode "First Ladies" (2014), narrator Jen Kirkman says that Edith Wilson was "the first female president of the United States." What? As described by a very drunk Kirkman, Edith Wilson (Courteney Cox) takes over for husband Woodrow (Derek Waters) after the president suffers a debilitating stroke. Edith energetically carries papers between Congress and the president, while Woodrow is bedridden, unable to move or speak, not even a puppet, more a rag doll as far as *Drunk History* is concerned. When the public begins to clamor for more Woodrow, Edith arranges a photo shoot, hovering over a propped up president, while he is staged in a document-signing pose. The resulting photo mirrors a real-life photo of Edith and Woodrow, who was paralyzed on his left side and needed help from his wife in holding the document steady.

While *Drunk History* portrays the president's condition in extreme terms for alleged comic effect, the idea that Mrs. Wilson was essentially the country's chief executive after his stroke is a popular view, one held even by some historians. Other scholars put more stock in Mrs. Wilson's own words in describing her contributions during the president's illness. "I myself never made a single decision regarding the disposition of public affairs.... The only decision that was mine was what was important and what was not, and the very important decision of when to present matters to my husband." Others note that Edith's gatekeeper role inevitably influenced policy, whether she intended to or not, simply by controlling what would reach the president and when.

Edith Wilson outlived her husband by 37 years, and spent the rest of her life preserving his legacy by collecting his papers, creating national shrines to his memory, and working with his biographer. While there may be questions about her official role during his illness, her status as devoted spouse is undeniable.

Windsor, Edie (1929–2017)
LGBTQ Rights Activist
Portrayed by: Sugar Lyn Beard

In the aptly titled episode "Love" (2019), *Drunk History* tells the story of Edie Windsor (Sugar Lyn Beard), who loves a woman named Thea Spyer (Alison Brie) for decades, mostly secretly, finally marrying her in 2007. Thea, who had been living with multiple sclerosis for years, dies in 2009, leaving Edie a significant estate. Since the marriage, which took place in

Canada, isn't recognized in the United States under DOMA (Defense of Marriage Act), Windsor must pay an estate tax of half a million dollars (in reality $363,053).

Windsor seeks out legal help, but is turned down even by gay rights advocacy groups. At last, she connects with the right lawyer, Roberta Kaplan (Amanda Lund), who is delighted to accept the case. "You are what marriage is about.... You are the perfect example of what gay marriage can be." The case eventually reaches the Supreme Court, which finds the applicable section of DOMA unconstitutional in a landmark 5–4 decision. Narrator Alison Rich says, "Thanks to this one brave woman and her belief in the equality of her love, gay marriage became legal."

Legal proceedings are an unlikely place to find a story of true love, but the 2013 Supreme Court case of *United States v. Windsor* brought Edie and Thea's 40-year romantic partnership into the spotlight. After the ruling, Windsor said, "While Thea is no longer alive, I know how proud she would have been to see this day." Their relationship, which had bloomed in Greenwich Village during the 60s, showed in the new millennium that no one is second-class when it comes to love and marriage.

Wright, Katharine (1874–1929)
Aviation Pioneer, Teacher
Portrayed by: Jenna Fischer

You've heard of the Wright brothers, but have you heard of the Wright sister? *Drunk History* wants to make sure you have in "Siblings" (2016), with a vignette on Katharine Wright, the lesser known, but not necessarily less important sibling of aviation pioneers Orville and Wilbur. Jenna Fischer stars as Katharine, who makes a reluctant pact with Orville (Jason Ritter) and Wilbur (Derek Waters) never to marry. The episode hits hilarious high notes in depicting Orville's fixation with his sister, as when he presents her with a "brotherly" gift of a diamond ring upon her graduation from college. Katharine ultimately ignores the diamond, whatever it represents, when she marries later in life, and Orville promises never to speak to her again. Historical Orville actually kept that promise until Katharine was on her deathbed, arriving just one day before she succumbed to pneumonia.

While humorously effective in its emphasis on Orville's obsession with Katharine, the vignette misses most of her real contributions to the Wright brothers' success. It sees Katharine mostly as a cheerleader for the brothers, someone who picks them up with her intelligence and support, whenever they are floundering. But the real Katharine did much more than that, becoming "the third member of the team" in the eyes of contemporaries and scholars. Her biggest contribution came in working as the front person for the shy brothers, negotiating aviation contracts, meeting with foreign dignitaries, including the king of Spain, and dealing with the press. A graduate of Oberlin College, and more educated than her brothers, she gave up a career in teaching to help them develop a commercial aviation company from their invention of the practical airplane.

Along with her brothers, Katharine Wright received the French Légion d'Honneur (Legion of Honor) award, an early recognition that we should be thinking in terms of the "Wright Siblings" rather than the Wright Brothers, when we talk about the milestones of early aviation.

Zaharias, Babe Didrikson (1911–1956)
Athlete, Olympian
Portrayed by: Susan Clark, Emily Deschanel

One of the greatest athletes, male or female, of the 20th century, Babe Didrikson Zaharias won two gold medals in track and field at the 1932 Summer Olympics, and went on to become a world champion golfer, earning 10 LPGA titles. She stopped along the way to pitch in some Major League baseball exhibition games, and didn't let wearing a colostomy bag stop her from winning the U.S. Women's Open golf championship in 1954.

Babe (TV movie, 1975) chronicles her amazing life, her groundbreaking achievements in a sports world dominated by men, and her losing battle with cancer at the young age of 45. Susan Clark portrays Babe, who, as the story opens, enters a Beaumont, Texas, hospital with her husband (Alex Karras) in 1953. Flashbacks ensue, as flashbacks must, first in black-and-white to chronicle her early years. We meet multitalented Babe

Babe Didrikson Zaharias with husband George, ca. 1955 (MGM Television).

in high school, where she plays on the girls' basketball team, and is soon recruited for the Employers' Casualty basketball team, leading them to a national championship. Her true love is track and field, however, where she also excels, soon qualifying for the 1932 Olympics. She breaks records as she goes, and Clark is astonishing in these athletic scenes.

After her success at the Olympics, Babe turns her attention to golf, a sport she has never played. Suddenly the flashbacks are in color, and we see some of the prejudice Babe has endured as a female athlete. An onlooker thinks she's making a funny joke when she says of Babe's Olympics participation, "They tried to disqualify her for entering as a girl." In the meantime, flash-forwards reveal Babe's battle with colon cancer, and Clark is equally effective in these scenes. Susan Clark went on to win a 1976 Emmy Award for her portrayal of Babe, while the film itself won a Golden Globe Award for Best Motion Picture Made for Television.

Drunk History retells Babe's story more humorously and with a few anachronisms (a "dude" here and a smartphone there) in "Sports Heroes" (2014), but it gets the important details right. Emily Deschanel plays Didrikson Zaharias this time, showing Babe's pluck and determination to make a career for herself in sports at a time when such work wasn't considered "ladylike." "It would be much better if she and her ilk stayed at home, got themselves prettied up and waited for the phone to ring," said sportswriter Joe Williams in the *New York World-Telegram*, quoted (minus a word here or there) in the episode.

But Babe never sat at home waiting for the phone to ring—she made things happen. That's the legacy of the formidable woman with the incongruous name of "Babe."

Susan Clark as Babe Didrikson Zaharias in *Babe* (MGM Television).

Appendix A: Historical Women Hall of Fame—TV Programs

As the researching and writing of this book progressed, some programs stood out for their usefulness, inspirational value, high quality, or all of the above. The presentations listed below possessed some or all of those attributes.

1. *Timeless* (2016–2018, 28 episodes, USA)

Timeless is first on my list for many reasons, not the least of which is that it was part of the inspiration for this book. The main characters in this time travel drama, a historian, a tech genius, and a soldier, brought an irresistible enthusiasm to their encounters with historical figures, people who were like rock stars to them. Lucy Preston (Abigail Spencer), Rufus Carlin (Malcolm Barrett), and Wyatt Logan (Matt Lanter) join together for missions which take them back in time to keep history safe from terrorist Garcia Flynn (Goran Visnjic), who wishes to change historical events, thereby sculpting a new future. The intrepid time-cops soon learn, however, that there may be an even bigger threat to the past and future from a shadowy organization called Rittenhouse. As Lucy, Rufus, and Wyatt perform their assignments, they begin to question their roles, wondering if there is any point to preserving history, if lives must be lost in the process. If they can save Abraham Lincoln's life, should they?

During those sometimes heartbreaking, often dangerous travels, they meet well-known historical women, such as actress and inventor Hedy Lamarr (Alyssa Sutherland), abolitionist Harriet Tubman (Christine Horn), and physicist Marie Curie (Kim Bubbs). But this series does its homework, also bringing to light lesser-known historical women such as lawyer and investigator Grace Humiston (Sarah Sokolovic), Shawnee

Chief Nonhelema (Karina Lombard), and architect Sophia Hayden (Katherine Cunningham).

Timeless is particularly effective in conveying the excitement of its protagonists when they meet historical icons, as when Rufus, engineer, programmer, and pilot of their time-travel missions, meets one of his heroes: mathematician, NASA pioneer, and Presidential Medal of Freedom recipient Katherine Johnson (Nadine Ellis). The show delivers a thrill, a "*Timeless* tingle," that few other shows about history have been able to match.

2. *Death Valley Days* (1952–1970, 452 episodes, USA)

I didn't know when I began researching *Death Valley Days* for this book that I was in for a big surprise. I had vague memories of viewing the show as a child and being confused by the fact that different actors appeared each week, not understanding what an anthology format was, but beyond that it seemed like a dusty old western. I had no idea there would be stories focused on women, let alone women from many walks of life. I soon learned that the rather ominous-sounding title wasn't indicative of the variety of stories presented over the show's long-run.

In addition to the usual Old West suspects, like Calamity Jane (Fay Spain) and Belle Starr (Carole Mathews), *Death Valley Days* presented stories about women in the arts, like operatic soprano Emma Nevada (Erin O'Brien), modern dance pioneer Isadora Duncan (Kathy Garver), and California Poet Laureate Ina Coolbrith (June Lockhart). While the emphasis was on white, English-speaking women, *Death Valley Days* did include tales about pioneering Mexican businesswoman Maria Gertrudis Barceló, known as "La Tules" (Katy Jurado), and Lemhi Shoshone explorer and interpreter Sacagawea (Angela Dorian).

Given the anthology format, with contributions from so many different creators, the views presented about women were all over the place, accepting nonconformist women one week, and maligning them the next. That inconsistency, however, provides a glimpse into the push and pull of evolving views about women's roles during the 1960s and '70s.

3. *Drunk History* (2013–2019, 72 episodes, USA)

Drunk History gave substantial coverage to female historical figures, both prominent and obscure, making it the most valuable TV resource used for this book. Why, then, isn't it number one on my list? The answer, I'm afraid, concerns the "drunk" in *Drunk History*. While the premise of using drunk narrators to describe important moments of history sometimes plays out in humorous ways, it just as often comes off, at least to me, as annoying, puerile, and even a bit sad with its exercises in bad behavior—belches, screams, frequently "bleeped" expletives, and worse.

What *Drunk History* does well, however, is to remember the women of history, not just the first ladies and household names, but the women who weren't mentioned in history books, such as Deborah Sampson (Evan Rachel Wood), a patriot who disguised herself as a man so she could join the Continental Army during the American Revolutionary War; or pioneering aviator Bessie Coleman (Samira Wiley), the first African-American woman and first Native American to hold a pilot's license; or Dorothy Fuldheim (Mary Elizabeth Ellis), television's first female news anchor and intrepid interviewer of Adolf Hitler, who had been unaware that his interviewer was Jewish. *Drunk History*'s continued inclusiveness is where it really shines, setting a good example amidst all the bad behavior, simultaneously the "Goofus and Gallant" of historical TV shows.

4. *Meeting of Minds* (1977–1981, 24 episodes, USA)

Like *Drunk History*, *Meeting of Minds* is an innovative historical series, but the word "sober" would be appropriate in describing Steve Allen's imaginative program, which uses a talk show format to "interview" guests from world history. Allen serves as host, while well-known actors portray historical figures, using the words of the actual luminaries wherever possible. Each guest receives some time to describe their life and viewpoints, but the famous figures also interact, sharing opinions and even arguing.

Jayne Meadows portrays most of the women, from stunning Egyptian Queen Cleopatra to demure British poet Elizabeth Barrett Browning, giving a particularly masterful performance as geriatric Florence Nightingale. But other actresses also take part in the Emmy-winning series, including Salome Jens as Byzantine Empress Theodora, Katherine Helmond as reclusive New England poet Emily Dickinson, and Beulah Quo as Chinese Empress Tz'u-hsi (Cixi). The costumes and makeup are first-rate, as can be seen especially on Ms. Meadows, who looks unrecognizable from one episode to the next, sporting a mammoth wig of curls and an ornate satin dress as Marie Antoinette in one entry, while wearing a severe bun, scrubbed face, and wire-rimmed glasses as Susan B. Anthony in the next.

Allen usually chats with four historical figures per episode, three men and one woman. While that gender distribution is by no means equal, it was reasonably enlightened by 1970s standards. Still, what a powerful statement it would have made in a time of newly resurgent feminism to have afforded women equal representation around the *Meeting of Minds* table.

5. *Hallmark Hall of Fame* (1951– , 260 episodes, USA)

This award-winning anthology series debuted in 1951 as *Hallmark Television Playhouse*, a weekly series with live, half-hour telecasts of operas, dramas, and Shakespearean plays. In 1955, bearing the title *Hallmark Hall of Fame*, the series switched to specials, often aired around the holidays, in 90-minute or 120-minute time slots. Watching some of the early episodes, which were recorded on kinescopes, gives a sense of traveling back in time to the modern viewer, of watching television history being made. They are from a different TV age.

Not only did the *Hallmark Hall of Fame* make history, but it depicted it as well, sometimes presenting programs about well-known historical women, and even revisiting the same women via different stories and actresses. The series devoted three productions to one of history's most famous women, beginning in 1952 with *Joan of Arc*, starring Sarah Churchill, followed by *The Lark* (1957), with Hall of Fame standout Julie Harris as Joan, and finally *Saint Joan* (1967), starring Geneviève Bujold. Once was also not enough for Florence Nightingale, who was profiled in two presentations, *Florence Nightingale* (1952), starring Sarah Churchill, and *The Holy Terror* (1965), with Julie Harris as the nursing pioneer.

The *Hallmark Hall of Fame* is one of the most honored programs in television history, with more than 50 Emmy awards to its credit, including an Outstanding Single Performance Emmy for Julie Harris, who won for her portrayal of the queen in *Victoria Regina* (1961). Preeminent actors from stage, screen, and television were featured in Hall of Fame productions, including Judith Anderson and Charlton Heston in *Elizabeth the Queen* (1968), Basil Rathbone and Boris Karloff, along with Harris, in *The Lark*, and Roddy McDowall and Raymond Massey, along with Bujold, in *Saint Joan*.

Nowadays it's hard to imagine watching stage plays for free in your own living room, plays with a sustained level of quality and talent, but that's what the Hall of Fame brought to the airwaves year after year. While the series is undoubtedly one of the treasures of TV history, it might have accomplished even more had it drawn from a larger list of historical women.

6. *Iron Jawed Angels* (2004, USA)

The passage of the 19th amendment to the U.S. Constitution, which gave American women the right to vote in 1920, had historic impact on the lives of 27 million women at the time, and has ramifications to this day. *Iron Jawed Angels* tells the story of this momentous achievement, focusing on two women, Alice Paul (Hilary Swank) and Lucy Burns (Frances O'Connor), who made harrowing sacrifices for the cause of women's suffrage in America. The film is at its best in depicting those sacrifices, which included imprisonment, hunger strikes, and force-feedings, finding inspiration in the ferocious commitment of these trailblazers to making a better life not just for themselves, but for other women.

The movie uses popular cinematic techniques, including quick cutting and handheld camera work, and modern music by Lauryn Hill and Sarah McLachlan, prompting some reviewers to complain about the jarring effects in a period piece. These stylistic choices, however, make director Katja von Garnier's film crackle with excitement, bringing an old, but little-known story to life for 21st-century viewers.

The fiction half of the historical fiction amalgam was a bigger problem than cinematic style in the movie. Characters who never existed in real life were included, such as Emily Leighton (Molly Parker), a senator's wife who ever so slowly realizes that there might be more to life than doing what your husband tells you. While her journey to awareness resonates, it's a letdown to find out there's not a real woman to match with the satisfying story.

Another issue is the rushed ending of the film, which collapses the more than two-and-a half-years it took to pass and ratify the 19th amendment into a single scene. Here the work of Carrie Chapman Catt (Anjelica Huston), who is portrayed mostly as an antagonist to Paul and Burns, should have been acknowledged, since Chapman Catt was instrumental in winning the fight for ratification of the amendment in the states.

But the whole is greater than the sum of the parts in *Iron Jawed Angels*. The film conveys the powerful message that women weren't given the vote, they fought for it for more than 70 years, as referenced in the touching scene where Alice Paul caresses the desk of suffrage leader Susan B. Anthony. Not only did women fight for the vote, they earned it, enduring insults, ridicule, brutality, and imprisonment, but never putting aside the dream of having a say in the laws that affect them.

7. *Voyagers!* (1982–1983, 20 episodes, USA)

NBC's *Voyagers!* was a rare TV show, especially for one from the big three networks, because it encouraged viewers to study history, both with the historical subjects it portrayed and with a direct message to embrace learning. At the end of each episode, as the credits rolled, young series star Meeno Peluce told the audience how to learn more about the subject(s) of that week's show. "...take a voyage down to your public library. It's all in books!"

As a newly minted professional librarian at the time, those words gave me a thrill, so much so that I listened to them every week, even though I wasn't someone in need of convincing. Although our modern media choices and delivery methods have multiplied since then, and our voyages for information may no longer take us out of our homes, the show's message about the quest for knowledge still resonates.

Phineas Bogg (Jon-Erik Hexum) and Jeffrey Jones (Peluce) travel through time by means of a small device called an "Omni," correcting history, which has a distressing tendency to wander off course in the *Voyagers!* universe. The series has a "boy's adventure" feel to it, with hunky Hexum and tweener Peluce playing their parts with gusto, the man of action and the sincere kid, who actually paid attention during history class. Many of their missions involve important men of history, but they haven't forgotten the ladies, including Nellie Bly, Queen Victoria, Annie Oakley, Molly Brown, Harriet Tubman, and Abiah Folger Franklin.

Some of the characterizations are broad, as when an English-speaking Cleopatra (Andrea Marcovicci) is accidentally transported from ancient Egypt to 1929 New York, and some of the appearances are brief, as when Nurse Clara Barton (Patricia Donahue) receives mouth-to-mouth resuscitation from Jeffrey (who apparently paid attention in EVERY class). But the show's historical heart was always in the right place, even when dramatic license led it in the wrong direction. If only there were an Omni to correct that.

8. *Doctor Who* (1963–1989, 2005– , 850+ episodes, UK)

If there were an award for the most creative TV plots involving historical figures, it would certainly go to the long-running science fiction series *Doctor Who*. Whether it's an encounter between Queen Victoria (Pauline Collins) and a werewolf in "Tooth and Claw" (2006) or contact between Agatha Christie (Fenella Woolgar) and an alien wasp in "The Unicorn and the Wasp" (2008), historical fiction has never been so pliable. Since the main character of the show is a Time Lord who bounces across space and time, the stories have no temporal or spatial limits. One day the (first) Doctor (William Hartnell) is in the 1880s Arizona Territory, where he meets Doc Holliday (Anthony Jacobs) and Kate Fisher (Sheena Marshe) just in time for the gunfight at the O.K. Corral. The next day (so to speak) he is in 1572 France, where he becomes embroiled in a plot by Catherine de' Medici (Joan Young), leading to the St. Bartholomew's Day massacre.

Visits by the Doctor are also possible at different times within the same historical figure's life, and those occurrences always bring complications. The Tenth Doctor (David Tennant) pays a call on the future Madame de Pompadour when she is a seven-year-old girl called Reinette (Jessica Atkins), saving her from an attack by a clockwork android in "The Girl in the Fireplace" (2006). The Doc's quick return through a spaceship's time window into Reinette's 18th-century bedroom finds her now a young woman (Sophia Myles), and later as the king's mistress, but still bedeviled by the androids. Reinette is prepared to throw over the king of France for the lord of time, but, time, a slippery force within the universe, brings the Doctor back seven years too late, because Pompadour has died.

While there are often flights of sf fancy in the series, sometimes the Doctor's missions provide more grounding. In the episode "Rosa" (2018), the historical significance of the life and work of civil rights activist Rosa Parks is center stage. The Thirteenth Doctor (Jodie Whittaker) and her team arrive in 1955 Alabama, and must stop a racist criminal named Krasko (Joshua Bowman) from altering the timeline. The Doctor and her companions succeed in thwarting Krasko's plans, so Rosa Parks (Vinette Robinson) can ride a Montgomery bus to an arrest that will ignite a bus boycott and the civil rights movement. When Doctor Who later explains that Rosa "changed the world," the Doctor, as a Time Lord, would be in the best position to know.

9. *Murdoch Mysteries* (2008–, 200+ episodes, Canada)

Murdoch Mysteries is a long-running Canadian series set in 1895 Toronto, where historical figures occasionally cross the path of police detective William Murdoch (Yannick Bisson). Some of the figures are famous American women, such as sharpshooter Annie Oakley (Sarah Strange) and temperance leader Carrie Nation (Valerie Buhagiar). Helen Keller (Amanda Richer) and her teacher Anne Sullivan Macy (Severn Thompson) also pay a call, participating in a dinner conducted in the dark, so the other guests can experience what it's like to navigate in a world of darkness, as is Keller's challenge all the time. Needless to say, a murder follows.

It is a particular delight of this series that Canadian women are highlighted, women who have not been seen in other scripted shows. Businesswoman and cosmetics pioneer Elizabeth Arden (Kathryn Alexandre), née Florence Nightingale Graham, appears in the 2018 episode "Operation: Murder," where her interest in burn treatments as a Toronto nursing student leads her to experiment with beauty creams, and a new career under a new name is born.

Margaret Haile (Nicole Underhay), the first woman to run for provincial office in Ontario, appears in seven episodes of the series, culminating in "Election Day" (2015), an outing which highlights not just the fight for suffrage, but the struggle women faced in getting their names on the ballot. Lucy Maud Montgomery (Alison Louder), author of *Anne of Green Gables* (1908), visits Toronto in "Unlucky in Love" (2016), and receives an inept lesson in writing from Constable George Crabtree (Jonny Harris), who gives mansplaining new meaning.

Murdoch Mysteries is a fanciful whodunit, so it will come as no surprise that some of these portrayals are creative in their use of historical details. In the case of both Arden and Montgomery, for example, Crabtree becomes a romantic interest for each of them, although a disclaimer at the end of Montgomery's episode reminds us that "he's not real." Flights of fancy notwithstanding, *Murdoch Mysteries* brings stories of female pioneers, such as Margaret Haile, to a larger audience, and does so while leaving significant details of the historical record intact, educating viewers along the way.

10. *Betty and Coretta* (2013, USA)

Betty and Coretta, a movie produced for the Lifetime television network, tells the story of Betty Shabazz (Mary J. Blige) and Coretta Scott King (Angela Bassett), two legends of the civil rights movement, who bonded after the assassinations of their husbands, Malcolm X (Lindsay Owen Pierre) and Dr. Martin Luther King, Jr., (Malik Yoba). Iconic actress Ruby Dee serves as on-screen narrator and witness, movingly describing her memories of the women and their times. "…they were a sisterhood born of sorrow, yes, but they became a sisterhood of greatness."

Their greatness is amply displayed in the film, as both women raise their children and find ways to serve their communities and the world. Shabazz cares for her six daughters as a single mother, while volunteering for educational causes, and eventually earns her PhD, taking a teaching position at Medgar Evers College in Brooklyn. King leads a peace march in Memphis, the city where her husband was assassinated, just four days after his death, and works to establish a national holiday in honor of MLK, presenting a petition to Congress and leading a demonstration in Washington, D.C.

The film is by no means perfect, with a sometimes disjointed feel, as it jumps back and forth between the stories of the two women, and compresses a long history into its 90-minute running time. The perennial problem of historical accuracy also rears its head, an even thornier issue in a film where some of the principals portrayed are still alive. Ilyasah Shabazz, for example, one of the six Shabazz daughters, noted inaccuracies in her mother's story, such as her depiction as weak and insecure, not the strong, regal woman her daughter knew. Such objections are understandable from those close to the subject, and especially from those depicted in the production itself. On the other hand, Coretta Scott King once noted that historical fiction is just that, fiction. When she addressed complaints about the inaccuracy of the miniseries *King* (1978), she said, "*King* is a drama and not a documentary; therefore it should be judged as such."

So, how are *we* to judge? In the case of *Betty and Coretta*, two remarkable women, who, to this day, are described first and foremost as "the widow of…," are depicted as the formidable people they actually were. The film shows them surmounting the most tragic circumstances imaginable, and moving forward, never forgetting their obligations to their families or to society. That's an important story with an uplifting message, a story that had never been told on television before. We judge, or at least I judge, by taking the whole picture into account, balancing the positives against the negatives. On that score, *Betty and Coretta* is a Hall of Fame program, at least in my book.

Appendix B: Historical Women Hall of Fame—Actresses

In the same way that some programs stood out for their usefulness and inspirational value during the writing of this book, some actresses rose above the rest in their depictions of historical women on television. Each of the actresses listed below distinguished themselves, showing range, dedication, or a certain *je ne sais quoi* in bringing notable females to life on the small screen, comprising my Historical Women Hall of Fame—Actresses.

1. Julie Harris (1925–2013)

Julie Harris was one of the most acclaimed actresses of her generation, known particularly for her work on stage, where she won five Tony Awards among 10 nominations over 45 years. Those who couldn't travel to see Harris on Broadway, however, still had the opportunity to see her work on the small screen, as she carried some of her Tony-winning roles over into television productions. Her first Tony-to-TV transition in portraying a historical figure occurred in *The Lark*, a 1957 presentation for the *Hallmark Hall of Fame*, where she reprised her 1956 Tony Award-winning role as Joan of Arc, the French warrior and national hero.

Almost 20 years later, she accomplished a similar feat, winning a Tony Award for her portrayal of First Lady Mary Todd Lincoln in the Broadway play *The Last of Mrs. Lincoln*, and performing the role again in a 1976 production of the same title for PBS's Hollywood Television Theatre. Harris won yet another Tony for her portrayal of poet Emily Dickinson in *The Belle of Amherst*, a one-woman play in which Harris played 15 different characters. A taped version of Harris's live performance of the play in 1976 was aired by PBS, and within a few moments of watching today, the viewer is aware that they are in the presence of greatness.

Harris, of course, was no stranger to television accolades either, earning three Emmy Awards, including one for her performance as Queen Victoria in *Victoria Regina* (1961), another Hallmark production. She played the queen from her accession to the throne at age 18 through Victoria's diamond jubilee 60 years later. Harris showed her acting range again with a similar age progression as nursing pioneer Florence Nightingale in *The Holy Terror* (1965), also for Hallmark. She begins the production as a young girl, who insists she has spoken to the angel of God, and ends as an aging victim of Crimean fever, who fights for reform from her bed.

Joan of Arc, Mary Todd Lincoln, Emily Dickinson, Queen Victoria, and Florence Nightingale. How lucky viewers are that Julie Harris devoted her rare talent to the televised depiction of some of history's most remarkable women.

2. Jayne Meadows (1919–2015)

Jayne Meadows holds the record for the most historical portrayals included in this volume, at six. She played all six notable women on the award-winning series *Meeting of Minds* (1977–1981), which used a talk show format to "interview" guests from world history. Probably best known as the sister of *Honeymooners*' actress Audrey Meadows and as the wife of Steve Allen, who created and hosted the series, Meadows steals the show whenever she is on it, proving that she wasn't just a spousal tagalong.

Despite the limitations of the show's format and the use of the historical figure's actual words, wherever possible, Meadows brings each of the six women to life with impressive intelligence. Given that talk and not action is the name of the game on this innovative show, she recites pages of dialogue with authority. As Egyptian Queen Cleopatra, for example, she reels off fact after fact, describing her role in the life of the people. But she also digs below the historical facts to reveal the emotional essence of the characters, such as Elizabeth Barrett Browning, whose personal life, with its tale of forbidden romance, tended to overshadow her literary contributions, especially in popular culture.

Although the set for the series is always the same, talk-show drab, Meadows herself looks unrecognizable from one episode to the next, switching from the regal grandeur of Marie Antoinette or Catherine the Great to the plain sincerity of Susan B. Anthony. And Meadows doesn't always play the women in their prime, portraying nursing pioneer Florence Nightingale in her geriatric years.

All in all, her work on *Meeting of Minds* was a tour de force, and it broke new ground as well. For her portrayal of Susan B. Anthony, Jayne

Meadows received the first Women's Equality Day Award from the Los Angeles Chapter of the National Organization for Women in 1979.

3. Jane Alexander (1939–)

Jane Alexander has appeared in productions about historical women throughout her career, playing First Lady Eleanor Roosevelt not once, but twice, first in *Eleanor and Franklin*, a 1976 miniseries, and later in its sequel *Eleanor and Franklin: The White House Years* (TV movie, 1977). Alexander ages from 18 to 60 in the role, portraying both the public Eleanor, who travels the world to advance the interests of her husband, and the private woman, who must deal with FDR's affair and paralytic illness. Alexander's acting connection to the Roosevelts took an ironic turn years later, when she played Eleanor's mother-in-law, Sara Delano Roosevelt, in *Warm Springs* (TV movie, 2005), with Cynthia Nixon as Eleanor.

But Alexander didn't get stuck in a Roosevelt rut, portraying historical women with less privileged backgrounds as well. Alexander traded ball gowns for buckskins in *Calamity Jane*, a 1984 TV movie about the legendary frontierswoman, which highlighted elements of Calamity's story, such as a secret marriage to Wild Bill Hickock (Frederic Forrest), that are disputed by historians. The next year she went from buckskins to big hats in *Malice in Wonderland* (TV movie, 1985), about Hollywood gossip columnist Hedda Hopper and her relationship with rival rumor merchant Louella Parsons (Elizabeth Taylor).

Jane Alexander received Emmy nominations for all five of the above roles, winning the statuette in the supporting actress category for her performance in *Warm Springs*. Whomever she is portraying, Jane Alexander's name is synonymous with quality work. She has also demonstrated her commitment to artistic excellence by serving for four years as chairwoman of the National Endowment for the Arts.

4. Elizabeth Montgomery (1933–1995)

Elizabeth Montgomery portrayed a witch on the successful sitcom *Bewitched* (1964 to 1972), but Samantha Stephens was a good witch, whose trouble arrived mostly in the form of interloping relatives. After the show ended, bad girls became more Montgomery's style, and she played several of history's famous troublemakers in TV movies over the next decade.

Montgomery's trail of historical bad girls began with Etta Place in *Mrs. Sundance* (TV movie, 1974). Etta was married to one of the Old West's most famous outlaws, the Sundance Kid, and Montgomery is affecting in the role of a woman who loved her late husband and is lured out of her quiet life by a rumor that he might still be alive. The actress covers similar territory in *Belle Starr*, a 1980 TV movie, playing a legendary "queen of the outlaws," while dressed in frontier chic.

But the role that took her furthest from good Mrs. Stephens on *Bewitched* didn't find her in the Old West, but in 19th-century Fall River, Massachusetts. There, in 1892, two of the world's most famous murders occurred, perpetrated by Lizzie Borden. Or were they? Lizzie, as portrayed by Montgomery in *The Legend of Lizzie Borden* (TV movie, 1975), was a woman strongly suspected of brutally murdering her father and stepmother, but was ultimately acquitted of the crimes. Montgomery plays Lizzie, at least in her public persona, as eerily detached, behavior which is consistent with the historical record. The film speculates that Borden committed the murders in the nude and then bathed, a theory which provides an explanation for why no blood was found on her clothing. This daring, especially for '70s TV, plot development and the complexity of her role took Montgomery a long way from her sitcom work on *Bewitched* and made her the queen of television's historical bad girls during the '70s.

5. Christina Ricci (1980–)

At the tender age of 10 years old, Christina Ricci took the world by storm in *The Addams Family*, a feature film from 1991. Ricci imbued the character of Wednesday Addams with a morbid, sardonic wit, and reprised the role in *Addams Family Values* (1993). Her flair for playing dark, unusual characters continued into adulthood, especially when she tackled the roles of some of history's famously troubled women.

Ricci began her history tour by confronting one of the great crime puzzles of all time in *Lizzie Borden Took an Ax* (TV movie, 2014). While the murders of Lizzie Borden's parents in 1892 are still unsolved, Ricci's portrayal of Borden is unambiguous. Lizzie did it, and she isn't above torturing her sister Emma (Clea DuVall) by whispering details of the crime into her ear. Ricci continued to portray Lizzie in a follow-up, limited series, *The Lizzie Borden Chronicles* (2015), which picks up Lizzie's story four months after her acquittal for the infamous murders.

Ricci's next historical figure had more nuance in *Z: The Beginning of Everything* (2015–2017), an Amazon Studio series. The Z of the title is Zelda Fitzgerald, wife of renowned Jazz Age writer F. Scott Fitzgerald, and Ricci does double duty as the title character and executive producer here. The first and only season covers the early relationship of Zelda and Scott (David Hoflin), including some of the tensions between them, such as Scott's use of Zelda's diaries for his stories. While *Z* got off to a promising start, especially with Ricci's sympathetic portrayal of Zelda, the series

Appendix B: Historical Women Hall of Fame—Actresses

wasn't renewed, leaving us to wonder how she might have handled Zelda's later struggles with mental illness.

Ricci then went on to portray groundbreaking 19th-century journalist Nellie Bly, but only sort of, in *Escaping the Madhouse: The Nellie Bly Story* (TV movie, 2019). The real Nellie Bly took on an undercover assignment as a patient at an asylum to expose the deplorable conditions there for Joseph Pulitzer's *New York World*. The film's Nellie, however, has amnesia, so she's not historical Nellie nor is she quite herself, because she doesn't remember who she is. The film is less historical fiction than a horror tale, with lots of grisly doings, though perfectly within Ricci's gothic wheelhouse, which had grown to accommodate the lead roles of adulthood.

6. Jane Lapotaire (1944–)

British actress Jane Lapotaire has made a specialty of portraying historical women during her long acting career. In 1977, she starred in the five-part miniseries *Marie Curie*, portraying the famous physicist, chemist, and two-time Nobel Prize winner. Produced by the BBC, the program won the BAFTA TV award for Best Drama Series/Serial in 1978. Her breakout performance as Curie led to further starring roles and eventually to Broadway, where she won the 1981 Tony Award for her work as French singer Edith Piaf in the play *Piaf*. After that triumph, British TV found another historical role for her to play, Cleopatra, in Shakespeare's *Antony and Cleopatra*, a 1981 production from the BBC. During taping of the production, Lapotaire should have won an award for bravery, as her fear of snakes and the need to handle one during a scene did not detract from her powerful performance.

More historical roles beckoned, including the part of reclusive Victorian poet Elizabeth Barrett Browning in *The Barretts of Wimpole Street*, a 1982 TV movie. Lapotaire continued to play real women on TV, such as Letizia Bonaparte, mother of Napoleon I of France, in *Napoleon and Josephine: A Love Story* (1987) and Princess Alice of Battenberg, mother-in-law of Queen Elizabeth II, in *The Crown* (2019). She found similar roles on the big screen, such as Queen Mary I of England in *Lady Jane* (1986). Lapotaire has portrayed so many notable females that it seems like she has her own Accelerator à la *Quantum Leap*, jumping into historical life after historical life.

7. Susan Clark (1943–)

Canadian actress Susan Clark appeared in feature films during the late '60s, such as *Tell Them Willie Boy Is Here* (1969), with Robert Redford, but found her niche on mid-'70s television portraying trailblazing historical women. In 1976, she starred in the television biopic *Amelia Earhart*, based on the life of the pioneering aviator. Earhart broke records set by both female and male pilots, but she is best known for the flight she did not complete, her attempted 1937 circumnavigation of the globe, during which she disappeared. Clark's delicate features are a counterpoint to her character's strength and resolve. After her first attempt at circling the world ends in a harrowing escape from a crash in Hawaii, Clark's Amelia says, "We've spent four months planning this adventure, and I'm going regardless." Clark is riveting in her portrayal of this formidable woman, whose courage and tenacity showed what a woman could do in "a man's world."

A year earlier, Clark had portrayed another formidable woman in the television movie *Babe*, based on the life of Babe Didrikson Zaharias, one of the greatest athletes, male or female, of the 20th century. Babe was as natural an athlete as they come, playing basketball, track and field, for which she won two gold medals at the 1932 Olympics, golf, earning 10 LPGA titles, and even some Major League baseball, pitching in exhibition games. Susan Clark is thoroughly convincing in her athletic scenes as Babe, looking taut and strong, a natural in her own right. But she also transforms from a powerful, young athlete to a middle-aged cancer patient in the film, and Clark never hits a false note there either.

Susan Clark went on to win a 1976 Emmy Award for her portrayal of Babe. Her intelligent and energetic performances as both Babe and Earhart brought stories of women's achievements to a popular audience at a time of renewed interest in feminism.

8. Jaclyn Smith (1945–)

One of television's most beautiful women, as seen for five seasons on *Charlie's Angels* (1976–1981), Jaclyn Smith brought glamour to her historical roles, a quality that worked particularly well in her depiction of Jackie Kennedy in *Jacqueline Bouvier Kennedy* (TV movie, 1981). Jackie K. brought her iconic fashion sense into the White House as wife of President John F. Kennedy (James Franciscus). Smith shows how Jackie found her mission as first lady in renovating and restoring the deteriorating White House, later charming the nation and the world with a televised tour of the first family's home.

But Smith moves beyond style to substance in the film, especially after the assassination of JFK. In an interview only a week after the Dallas tragedy, the first lady tells reporter Theodore H. White (Will Hunt) about her late husband's favorite musical, *Camelot*, and the "one brief shining moment" that was King Arthur's reign. She says, "There'll never be another Camelot again," and we are right back there with Mrs. Kennedy in 1963.

A few years later, Smith portrayed another title character in *Florence Nightingale* (TV movie, 1985) about the famed nursing pioneer and social reformer. Here the glamourous approach is misplaced, especially when Nightingale makes the rounds in a wartime military hospital, one that is understaffed and unsanitary, where you hear the words "better maggots than gangrene." You'd think that she might look a little less perfect under those harrowing conditions, if not bedraggled, at least smudged. The production even feels the need to remind us how beautiful its protagonist is, as when a burn victim says to Nightingale, "Pretty eyes like yours should never have to see such things." Smith, however, takes the portrayal of such an important and worthy historical figure seriously, and the film does serve as a people-pleasing introduction to the life and work of Florence Nightingale.

9. Halle Berry (1966–)

Halle Berry is well known for her roles in theatrical films, such as *Monster's Ball* (2001), for which she won the Academy Award for Best Actress, the only black woman to have received that honor in the leading role category. Berry's award-winning work also extends to television, where she picked up practically every acting award there is for her portrayal of the title character in *Introducing Dorothy Dandridge* (TV movie, 1999). Her awards for that performance include a Golden Globe Award, an Emmy Award, an NAACP Image Award, and a Screen Actors Guild Award. Berry also served as an executive producer on the film, fighting to bring the project to the screen again and again after multiple rejections, and finally achieving her goal with a production for the small screen from HBO.

As a teen, Berry became fascinated with Dorothy Dandridge after seeing her performance in the film *Carmen Jones* (1954), and continued to make a study of Dandridge's life and work. Given Berry's knowledge of the subject, her own renowned beauty, and acting talent, she is perfectly cast as Dandridge, the first black woman to be nominated for an Academy Award for best actress. Dandridge's professional life was full of such firsts and successes, but as a black woman, she also found many doors closed to her career advancement during a time of legalized discrimination and segregation. Dandridge also faced personal sorrows, including an abusive childhood, and died from a prescription overdose, whether accidental or otherwise. Halle Berry is mesmerizing in this performance, and receives additional kudos here for fighting to bring the story of groundbreaking actress Dorothy Dandridge to a wider audience.

10. Alia Shawkat (1989–)

Alia Shawkat has specialized in comedy roles during her career, known especially for her work as Maeby Fünke in the long-running TV series *Arrested Development* (2003–2006, 2013, 2018–2019). It's not surprising, then, that she showed up as a guest star several times on one of TV's craziest comedies, *Drunk History*, putting a comic spin on some of history's notables.

Her first stop was "First Ladies" (2014), portraying Frances Cleveland, wife of President Grover Cleveland. The country becomes enthralled with Frances, who prefers to be called "Frank," the youngest first lady in U.S. history. Frank becomes an "it girl," whose image appears on all types of products and advertisements without her permission. The first lady chooses to ignore this exploitation, preferring to use her fame to help working women and impoverished black women. She says, "Like, if everyone's gonna be paying attention to me, let's make sure they're paying attention to me for the right reasons."

Drunk History is a unique acting gig, because when an actor, like Shawkat, appears as a character in a historical vignette, the inebriated narrator's voice is heard as though it were the actor's own voice, so everything must be synchronized perfectly. Here the partnership is between Shawkat and narrator Molly McAleer, and Alia's facial expressions match Molly's tone, and the lip-synching is seamless.

Shawkat next appeared as World War II secret agent and hero Virginia Hall in "Spies" (2015). Hall's most famous exploit was climbing over a pass in the Pyrenees Mountains to escape pursuing Germans, who were onto her spy games. She accomplished that while wearing a prosthetic leg she called "Cuthbert." Shawkat portrays "the limping lady" with spirit, moving quickly through the phases of her life, as British spy, American spy, Distinguished Service Cross recipient, and CIA officer, while Claudia O'Doherty narrates. O'Doherty is one of the less animated *Drunk History* narrators, and an exciting real-life story becomes a little blander than it might have been. But the message comes through that Virginia Hall was an amazing woman, who never let disability or danger stand in the way of what she wanted.

Although the focus of this book is historical women, Shawkat receives extra credit in the Hall of Fame for portraying a historical man, Alexander Hamilton, in the *Drunk History* episode "Hamilton" (2016). Much of women's history is the story of restrictions placed upon them, such as not being allowed to act on stage, which meant that men had to play the female roles. Shawkat's taking a man's role is a rich irony in this light, and I mention it here in tribute to all those women who were kept from doing things that "women aren't supposed to do."

A Note on Sources

Researching this book presented a big initial question. Should I start with a list of historical TV programs, following them to notable females? Or should I start with the women, tracing them to their televised representations? As I quickly learned, the research moved in both directions, where the TV series and movies led to more notable females, and the women led to more TV presentations, a kind of cross-pollination, but for historical television.

Many of the TV titles came from my memory, based upon decades of viewing, such as the western series *Death Valley Days* (1952–1970), the miniseries *The Adams Chronicles* (1976), and the TV movie *The Legend of Lizzie Borden* (1975). The initial roster was fleshed out with additions from lists at *IMDb* (imdb.com), based on keyword searches such as "TV Movie, Biography" and "Historical Fiction." My own book *Women of Science Fiction and Fantasy Television* (McFarland, 2019) reminded me of sf/fantasy series with time-travel themes or historical flashbacks, such as *Bewitched* (1964–1972), *Forever Knight* (1992–1996), and *Doctor Who* (1963–1989, 2005–).

Additional titles arrived by the cross-pollination route mentioned above, where a notable female led to a TV program, which led to more notable females and more TV programs. *Wikipedia* (en.wikipedia.org) was a valuable resource here, as its "In popular culture" sections of biographical articles often mentioned televised depictions of subjects. New-to-me TV shows found this way included the anthology series *Telephone Time* (1956–1958) and the western series *Stories of the Century* (1954–1955).

For the list of historical women, I also searched my memory, based on a background in history from undergraduate and graduate studies. A book on my shelf, *Women in Modern America: A Brief History* by Lois W. Banner (Harcourt Brace Jovanovich, 1974), added more American women to my list. A surprising source of suggestions was *A Mighty Girl* (facebook.com/amightygirl), especially its "Born on this day" posts, celebrating the birthdays of important women in recent history. On the cross pollination side, wikis for individual TV shows at *Fandom* (fandom.com), such as the one for *Sleepy Hollow* (2013–2017), led to more notable females of history.

Each entry in this book was a research project in itself, and enumerating the sources consulted for all 120 entries might be another book on its own. The most important sources, of course, were the TV presentations themselves, viewed from DVDs, satellite TV, and streaming services. My own DVD collection provided some assistance, with series such as *Timeless* (2016–2018), *Voyagers!* (1982–1983), and *Jack of All Trades* (2000). Satellite TV also helped, with *Murdoch Mysteries* (2008–) from Ovation TV, *Drunk History* (2013–) from Comedy Central and MTV Classic, *Death Valley Days* from STARZ Encore Westerns, and more.

Video sharing service *YouTube* (youtube.com) was a valuable resource, with full programs, especially for older presentations, such as *The Great Adventure* (1963–1964), and even (relatively) recent fare like *Let Them Eat Cake* (1999). *YouTube* also offered clips and trailers, which stood in when full programs were not available. *Dailymotion* (dailymotion.com), another video sharing service, contributed a few full programs, as did the *Internet Archive* (archive.org) and *Alexander Street Video* (video.alexanderstreet.com), a subscription educational service. Streaming services *Tubi* (free) and *Prime Video* (subscription) filled in some of the blanks, with programs such as *Sleepy Hollow* and *The Californians* (1957–1959) respectively. Even *Audible* (audible.com) helped, with audio versions of *Meeting of Minds* (1977–1981), when some video versions of the series were not available on *YouTube*.

Information about the TV programs came from a large variety of sources. *Wikipedia*, *IMDb*, *Fandom*, and the *Paley Center for Media* (paleycenter.org) provided program summaries and cast lists. Other sites, such as the *Classic TV Archive* (ctva.biz), *TV Tropes* (tvtropes.org), and *Inner Toob* (toobworld.blogspot.com) offered special nuggets tailored to their own audiences in addition to the usual program info. Reviews, especially for TV movies and miniseries, came from newspapers, the *New York Times* (nytimes.com), *Los Angeles Times* (latimes.com), *Variety* (variety.com), and many others.

Wikipedia and *Britannica* (britannica.com) were good starting points for biographies of the women featured. Other useful general biographical sources included *Biography* (biography.com), *Encyclopedia.com*, *History* (history.com), *History Extra* (historyextra.com), and *History Daily* (historydaily.org). Sites such as *National First Ladies' Library* (firstladies.org) and *True West* (truewestmagazine.com) were helpful for biographies in their specialty areas. *TimesMachine* (timesmachine.nytimes.com), a digital archive of the *New York Times* as it originally appeared, was a good

A Note on Sources   209

resource for tracking down news stories about late-19th-century women, including Pearl Hart and Carrie Nation.

The *New York Times* was an information star again with its "Overlooked" obituaries series, providing retrospective death notices for Mary Ellen Pleasant, Emily Warren Roebling, and others. Websites dedicated to individual notable women, such as Agatha Christie (agathachristie.com), Margaret "Molly" Brown (mollybrown.org), and Elizabeth Arden (elizabetharden.com/about-us.html), were also consulted, where available.

Many of the resources I used were one-offs for individual entries, and are too numerous to mention. Examples in that category include "Mother of California Civil Rights Movement" at *Gold Chains: The Hidden History of Slavery in California* (aclunc.org) for Mary Ellen Pleasant and "Unsung Heroes: First Female Detective Kate Warne" at *Pinkerton* (pinkerton.com) for Kate Warne.

Inconsistencies between sources were par for the course, and I did my best to resolve them wherever possible.

Index

Ahern, Casey 169–170
Alexander, Jane 43, 45, 117, 153–154, 201
Alexandre, Kathryn 19
Allan, Patti 176–177
Allen, Steve 9, 41, 58–59, 72, 123, 136, 191, 200
Alstrup, Amalie 163
Anderson, Judith 77–78
Andrews, Stanley 21, 26, 64, 85
Annis, Francesca 104–105, 109–110
Appleby, Elizabeth 180–181
Atkins, Finn 36, 38
Atkins, Jessica 150
Aykroyd, Dan 55

Baird, Sharon 64
Bari, Lynn 164–165, 167
Barrett, Malcolm 92, 100, 137, 175, 189
Bassett, Angela 106, 108, 144–145, 159
Bayer, Vanessa 133–134
Beard, Sugar Lyn 185
Bergman, Ingrid 125–126
Berrington, Elizabeth 122
Berry, Halle 68–69, 205
Bevan, Michelle 182, 184
Bingham, Alandra 182, 184
Birdsell, Lilli 180, 182
Bisset, Jacqueline 104, 106
Black, Dorothy 77
Blige, Mary J. 108, 158–159
Bobulov, Barbora 54–55
Boles, Karen 111, 114
Bonazzi, Elaine 111–112
Bonet, Lisa 144–145, 149
Bradley, Ruth 56–57
Brown, Blair 104–105
Bubbs, Kim 65–66
Buhagiar, Valerie 133
Bujold, Genevieve 98–99
Burnett, Carol 43, 45–46

Butler, Yancy 98–99
Byers, Jacqueline 143–144

Campbell, Sheila E. 164, 166
Candy, John 55
Carter, Dixie 109, 111
Carter, Helena Bonham 32–33, 169–170
Chapman, Graham 77–78
Chavarria, Kyle 182, 184
Churchill, Sarah 98–99, 135–136
Civita, Diane 138, 140
Clark, Susan 75–77, 187–188, 203–204
Clayton, Melissa 164, 166
Coates, Phyllis 90
Coleman, Jenna 176–177
Collins, Pauline 176–177
Connell, Jane 176, 180–181
Cooper, Jeanne 164–165
Cormack, Danielle 49, 51
Cornell, Katharine 40–41
Cox, Christina 98–99
Cox, Courteney 185
Crane, Norma 43, 45
Crosbie, Annette 47–49
Crosby, Denise 116–117
Cross, Yvonne 64, 129–130
Cunningham, Katherine 92
Curtin, Jane 153, 155
Curtis, Jamie Lee 138–139

Dana, Leora 13–14
Daniels, Tiffany 22
Danner, Blythe 82
Dasher, Erica 98, 146
Davis, Gail 138–139
Davis, Josephine 58–59
Davis, Judy 93, 125–126
Davis, Phyllis 124
De Carlo, Yvonne 64
Dee, Ruby 172–174

Dern, Laura 30-31
Deschanel, Emily 187-188
DeYoung, Gypsi 23
Diamond, Kim 75, 77
Dillman, Pamela 65-66
Donahue, Patricia 26-27
Dorian, Angela 156-157
Dormer, Natalie 32-33
Duffy, Julia 30-31
Duke, Patty 180-181
Dunst, Kirsten 56-57

Edwards, Penny 20
Eisenberg, Hallie 101-102
Ejogo, Carmen 106-107
Ellis, Mary Elizabeth 86
Ellis, Nadine 99-100, 190

Fenn, Sherilyn 169-170
Fennell, Emerald 118
Fischer, Jenna 186
Fisher, Frances 23
Flanagan, Fionnula 39
Foch, Nina 87-88
Follows, Megan 69-70
Ford, Julia 114
Foy, Claire 32-33
Francis, Anne 91
Fraser, Laura 135, 137

Garland, Beverly 91
Garner, Kelli 127-128
Garver, Kathy 63, 73-74
Gaye, Lisa 70-71
Geer, Ellen 153, 155
Gilbert, Melissa 101, 182-183
Giordano, Domiziana 124
Gish, Lillian 111, 114
Gless, Sharon 116-117
Gold, Tracey 127
Goodwin, Ginnifer 104-105
Grainger, Holliday 143
Gray, Vanessa 116-117
Griffiths, Susan 127-128
Guilbert, Ann Morgan 58, 61

Hamilton, Victoria 176-177
Harper, Tess 182, 184
Harris, Julie 71-72, 98-99, 111, 135-136, 176-177, 192, 199-200
Hart, Emily Anne 170
Hauser, Fay 172, 174
Hayes, Margaret 90
Heath, Dody 43, 45
Heckart, Eileen 153, 155
Helm, Anne 115-116
Helmond, Katherine 71-72

Henderson, Florence 164, 166
Henner, Marilu 39
Hennessy, Jill 104, 106
Hexum, Jon-Erik 6, 27, 39, 84, 194
Hicks, Catherine 127
Holmes, Jennifer 84
Hope, Charlotte 47, 49
Horn, Christine 172, 175
Hudgens, Vanessa 98-99, 124
Hunnicutt, Gayle 16-17
Huston, Anjelica 42-43, 46, 51-52, 140, 147
Hyde, Jacquelyn 176

Ingram, Karen 104, 106
Issová, Klára 65-66

Jackson, Glenda 77-78
Jacques, Hattie 77-78
Jean, Gloria 64
Jens, Salome 171-172
Jones, Suranne 114, 115
Judd, Ashley 127
Jurado, Katy 25-26

Kash, Linda 39
Keating, Tracy 160
Keaton, Diane 75, 77
Kellerman, Sally 64
Kelly, Moira 101-102
Kemper, Ellie 30-31
Kennedy, Maria Doyle 47-49
Krige, Alice 85-86

Ladd, Cheryl 103
Lanter, Matt 92, 98, 137, 189
Lapotaire, Jane 40-41, 58, 60, 65-66, 203
LaRusch, Suzanne 23
Lawrence, Sharon 75-76
Leachman, Cloris 39
LeMaire, Monique 122
Leslie, Bethel 132
Lesser, Lily 118
Lewis, Daisy 13, 15
Linney, Laura 13-14
Lockhart, June 63, 73
Lohan, Lindsay 169
Lombard, Karina 137
Louder, Alison 131
Lyons, Collette 28-29

MacIsaac, Martha 179
MacLaine, Shirley 54-55
Madonna 127-128
Manzy, Charde 144-145
Marcovicci, Andrea 58-59
Marsh, Linda 121

Marshe, Sheena 28, 30
Martin, Anna Maxwell 160–161
Martin, Mary 138–139
Maslany, Tatiana 141
Massey, Anna 56–57
Massingham, Celia 108–109
Mathews, Carmen 34
Mathews, Carole 164–165
May, Jodhi 32–33
Mays, Jayma 13, 15, 72–73
McClurg, Edie 65–66
McCormack, Patty 101
McDonald, Audra 94–95
McEntire, Reba 138, 140
Meadows, Jayne 9, 18, 40–41, 49, 51, 58–60, 122–123, 135–136, 191, 200–201
Medina, Patricia 129–130
Merchant, Tamzin 96–97
Merman, Ethel 138–139
Mirren, Helen 77, 79
Monroe, Meredith 182, 184
Montgomery, Elizabeth 34–35, 147–148, 164, 166, 201–202
Montgomery, Flora 161–162
Montgomery, Poppy 127–128
Moore, Mandy 26–27
Moore, Mary Tyler 111–113
Moreno, Rita 129–130
Morgan, Paula 129
Murphy, Donna 111, 114
Myles, Sophia 150

Natwick, Mildred 77–78
Needham, Tracey 143–144
Nicholas, Danielle 58–59
Nixon, Cynthia 153, 155

O'Brien, Erin 134
O'Connor, Frances 42, 52
Ormond, Julia 49–50
Orr, Ashley Rose 170
Osborne, Madolyn Smith 87–88

Page, Joanna 77, 80
Palicki, Adrianne 179
Palin, Michael 176, 178
Parker, Jean 53
Parker, Paula Jai 94–95
Payton-Wright, Pamela 15–16
Peake, Maxine 114, 115
Peluce, Meeno 5–6, 27, 39, 84, 193–194
Philipps, Busy 153, 155, 175–176
Phillips, Mackenzie 153–154
Phillips, Siân 141–142
Pickles, Vivian 73, 75
Pirrie, Chloe 37–38
Plaza, Aubrey 156–157

Pleasence, Angela 77, 80, 96–97
Portail, Romane 54
Powers, Stefanie 43, 45
Purl, Linda 30–31

Quo, Beulah 57

Rare, Vanessa 156–157
Raymond, Paula 67–68
Redgrave, Lynn 58, 60
Redman, Joyce 176–177
Retta 151
Ricci, Christina 30–31, 34, 36, 82–83, 202–203
Richardson, Miranda 77–78
Richardson, Natasha 82–83
Riley, Chantel 28, 30
Rincon, Dayana 156–157
Robinson, Vinette 144–145
Ross, Katharine 147, 149
Routledge, Patricia 176–177
Ryder, Winona 161–162

Scacchi, Greta 16–17
Schilling, Taylor 152
Seagrove, Jenny 109, 111
Serna, Assumpta 47, 49
Shawkat, Alia 61, 89, 206
Sidibe, Gabourey 81–82
Simpson, Jeanne 98–99
Smith, Jaclyn 104, 135, 137, 204–205
Sobieski, Leelee 98–99
Sokolovic, Sarah 97
Solo, Ksenia 161–162
Sorvino, Mira 127
Spain, Fay 43, 45
Spencer, Abigail 5, 22, 66, 85, 97, 100, 137, 146, 189
Spencer, Octavia 172, 175
Stapleton, Jean 153, 156
Stone, Carol 28–29
Strange, Sarah 138, 140
Stuart, Randy 47
Sutherland, Alyssa 108–109
Suzman, Janet 58, 60, 135–136
Swank, Hilary 42, 52, 146–147

Taylor-Isherwood, Sally 104, 106
Temple, Juno 82, 119, 127–128
Tennant, David 56, 80, 151, 195
Thaxter, Phyllis 67
Thayer, Lorna 85
Thompson, Elizabeth 58–59
Thompson, Emma 77, 80
Thompson, Sada 111–113
Toksvig, Sandi 141–142
Torres, Gina 58–59

Index

Trachtenberg, Michelle 13, 15
Trotter, Kate 65–66
Tucker, Brooke 164–165
Tutin, Dorothy 27–28, 32, 48
Tuttle, Lurene 140, 176
Tyson, Cicely 106–107, 172–173

Underhay, Nicole 88

VanCamp, Emily 104, 106
Varela, Leonor 58, 60
Vassilieva, Sofia 84
Visnjic, Goran 100, 189

Walker, Kathryn 13–14
Waters, Derek 134, 168, 176, 185–186
Watkins, Michaela 55–56
Weigert, Robin 43, 46
Whalley, Joanne 47, 49, 104, 106
Whitfield, Lynn 22
Whitney, Grace Lee 28–29, 47

Wiley, Samira 62
Willes, Jean 164–166
Williams, Olivia 21–22, 56–57
Wilson, Casey 120
Windsor, Marie 164
Winningham, Mare 101–102
Winters, Gloria 115–116
Wood, Evan Rachel 158, 160
Woodward, Shannon 168
Woolgar, Fenella 56–57
Wright, Bonnie 56–57

Yeager, Caroline 16–17
York, Francine 109–110
York, Rachel 23–24, 117
Young, Annie 161–162
Young, Joan 69–70

Zeta-Jones, Catherine 49–51
Zima, Madeline 23–24, 117

www.ingramcontent.com/pod-product-compliance
Lightning Source LLC
Chambersburg PA
CBHW032042300426
44117CB00009B/1163